I0473482

THE WALL OF FAME

OTHER BOOKS BY RICHARD B. RESSMAN

Lines & Curves

Lines & Curves 2

Godiva: A Modern Pictorial Adventure

THE WALL OF FAME

RICHARD B. RESSMAN, M.D.

COYOTE CREEK BOOKS | SAN JOSÉ | CALIFORNIA

Copyright © 2015 by Richard B. Ressman. All rights reserved.

No part of this book may be reproduced or transmitted in any form by any means, electronic or mechanical, including photocopying, recording, or by any information storage and retrieval system, without written permission from the author, except for the inclusion of brief quotations in a review.
http://photosurgeon.net/contact

Printed in the United States of America.

Front cover photograph © Tony Berardi, Chicago Tribune Magazine

Published by Coyote Creek Books
www.coyotecreekbooks.com

25 24 23 22 21 20 19 18 17 16   2 3 4 5 6

ISBN: 978-0-9961824-5-4

DEDICATION

This book is dedicated to the three Davids:
Ressman, Miller and Ressman, my father, my best man,
and my son.

CONTENTS

ABOUT THE AUTHOR

Dr. Richard Ressman practiced orthopaedic surgery for thirty years before becoming a full-time photographer in 2002. He bought his first Nikon camera in 1969 as a surgical intern in Chicago and has been taking photographs since. He calls himself a PHOTOSURGEON, a term he made up; that's an orthopaedic surgeon who aspires to do photography on the Cutting Edge. His exhibits include three photos in the 2001 eMotion Pictures Exhibit sponsored by the American Academy of Orthopaedic Surgeons that traveled from San Francisco to Chicago, Washington D.C., New York, and Madrid, Spain. The 2008 eMotion Pictures Exhibit in San Francisco also included one of his photos. More recent exhibits include photos displayed at the Triton Museum of Art in Santa Clara, California both in 2012 and 2013, and a 2013 solo exhibit at the Martin Luther King, Jr. Library at San José State University, San José, California.

In 2005 Dr. Ressman donated all his unused surgical equipment. He convinced two orthopaedic equipment companies to donate thousands of dollars of equipment, and as a volunteer he taught surgical techniques to surgeons in Ho Chi Minh City, Viet Nam. His reason: The Vietnamese people suffered enough during the Viet Nam-American war and he wanted to give something back to the Vietnamese people. It was a very rewarding experience for everyone involved.

Dr. Ressman continues to shoot with Nikon professional equipment using the latest single lens reflex digital cameras as well as PhaseOne medium format digital equipment. He lives in the San Francisco South Bay area. His wife of nearly sixteen years, Gabriele Rico, passed away in March 2013. She was a professor of Humanities and Creative Arts at San Jose State University and author of books, chief among them *Writing the Natural Way*, which has been in bookstores for more than thirty years.

FOREWORD

Richard Ressman is either a lunatic or a genius. He allows no middle ground. He is unapologetically and uniquely himself. This photographic collection, which I have taken the liberty to subtitle: Portraits with a Punch Line, serves well to introduce his personality and artistry.

What can be said about a grown man who insists on carrying a backpack containing fifty pounds of camera gear everywhere he goes, and I do mean everywhere. But it is precisely that kind of behavior that lies at the heart of, "how in the world could one man take so many photographs?" It is remarkable, as you will see. He has been "camera ready" for nearly fifty years. This collection, it must be noted, is but a sample of his magnum opus: wall of fame. His home, previously in Colorado, Indiana, Chicago and now in Northern California, contains a wall of confluent portraits stretching floor-to-ceiling, thirty feet wide (and there are stacks of unused gems in closets).

Over the past three decades, I have been the recipient of these unsolicited 8x10" photographic gifts. The breath and depth of these photographic representations are the result of Richard's confident mastery of his own eye, camera (always the gigantic Nikon), lens (the more glass the better), light and dark (he always looked for both), subject (preferred locating notables), and software (a minimalist when it came to Photoshop). Which brings up an interesting fact. He was a very early adapter of digital technology. I believe he bought a new camera about every six months for ten years in order to keep current as the technology evolved. His obsession did not end with camera bodies though. He has cases of lenses, a room of Apple computers, five back-ups, and printers (one the size of a Subaru). Madness can be expensive.

Behind every artist is a persona trying to appear "normal". Richard did this by appropriating the education and training necessary to become a board certified orthopaedic surgeon. He even operated on me several times; unfortunately for me he stopped practicing orthopaedics too early and I kept reinjuring my knee. My theory about artists is simple: normal people see the world, well, normally, like a bell-shaped curve in statistics class—most see things the same way, smack in the middle, or within two standard deviations of the mean. Artists do not fall into the normal zone, they reside in the "tails" and by nature, they do not see things the way normal people see them. Normal people delight in the way artists see things because their work exposes a part of life that is otherwise unseen to them. Richard appears to have the super intelligence necessary to see things both ways, so-to-speak. If you did not know him, personally, you might think he was normal. He is not. He is an artist.

Disciplined photographers are like NBA jump shooters. They analyze every component and rehearse their form a million times in practice: their foot stance, elbow position, eyes locked on the front of the rim, the ball just so on the finger tips, the wrist flexion, the smooth upward arch, and the follow-through. Richard has mastered RAW, light, contrast, shape and pattern, composition, exposure, depth of field, focus and so on. When he shoots, his muscle memory activates all that experience. The results are nothing but net.

Portrait photos are different from landscapes. A good portrait is a moment. It is a pause looking into something intimate and personal. Even a casual examination of Richard's collection will summon comparisons from the great photo portrait artists of the twentieth century: Annie Leibovitz' lush look at stardom's toll, Yousuf Karsh's representation of life forces etched upon a face, the unexpected of Diane Arbus, Dorthea Lange's bleak nobility, or the iconic looks of Steve McCurry. Mostly, I would hope that these remarkable photos do not end-up like Vivian Maier's lost photos. This work deserves to be seen.

As I mentioned, perhaps only a crazy person would spend so much time and energy working on a project that may never be appreciated by anyone except himself. I admit that this view lacks a sense of what defines human beauty. In photography, beauty is not in the eye of the beholder, it's in the eye of the man holding the camera. But, then again, what do I know—I use a pocket point-and-shoot.

David C. Miller, M.D.

PREFACE

For more than forty years I have been taking photos of celebrities, movie stars, musicians, athletes, and politicians. After capturing the images, I would then process the photos, mount them on matte board and place them on my "Wall of Fame," a big wall in my home containing nearly four hundred eight by ten inch photos of recognizable people from Presidents Barack Obama, George W. Bush and Jimmy Carter; athletes from Jack Nicklaus, Michael Jordan, LeBron James and Mohammad Ali; musicians from Paul McCartney, Bo Diddley, Mick Jagger and Dave Brubeck; and actors from Michael Douglas, Jane Fonda and Paul Newman. There are obviously too many to name here. Most are featured on my website www.photosurgeon.net. Whenever I put a new photo on my Wall, I need to take another down.

Dr. David Miller is an anesthesiologist and pain specialist whom I worked with in Northern Indiana and who became a close friend; he also became a patient of mine on several occasions. In addition to the first print going on the Wall, I frequently printed and mailed a second copy to David Miller; however, I would always sign his print with the name of the subject and a "personal" message. David just happened to save all these images and when I told him I was going to write this book about the photos, he let me borrow all the images I had sent him. Because some of the messages have faded a bit over time, I am re-printing each message on the pages opposite the photos. Photos taken before 2002 were taken with film; photos afterwards were taken with my professional digital cameras. Again, I signed all the subjects' names. It is easy to see that David Miller has a lot of friends.

ACTORS

Alan Alda
Actor

David,
I want you to be my anesthesiologist
in my upcoming Mash movie sequel.
Your friend,
Alan

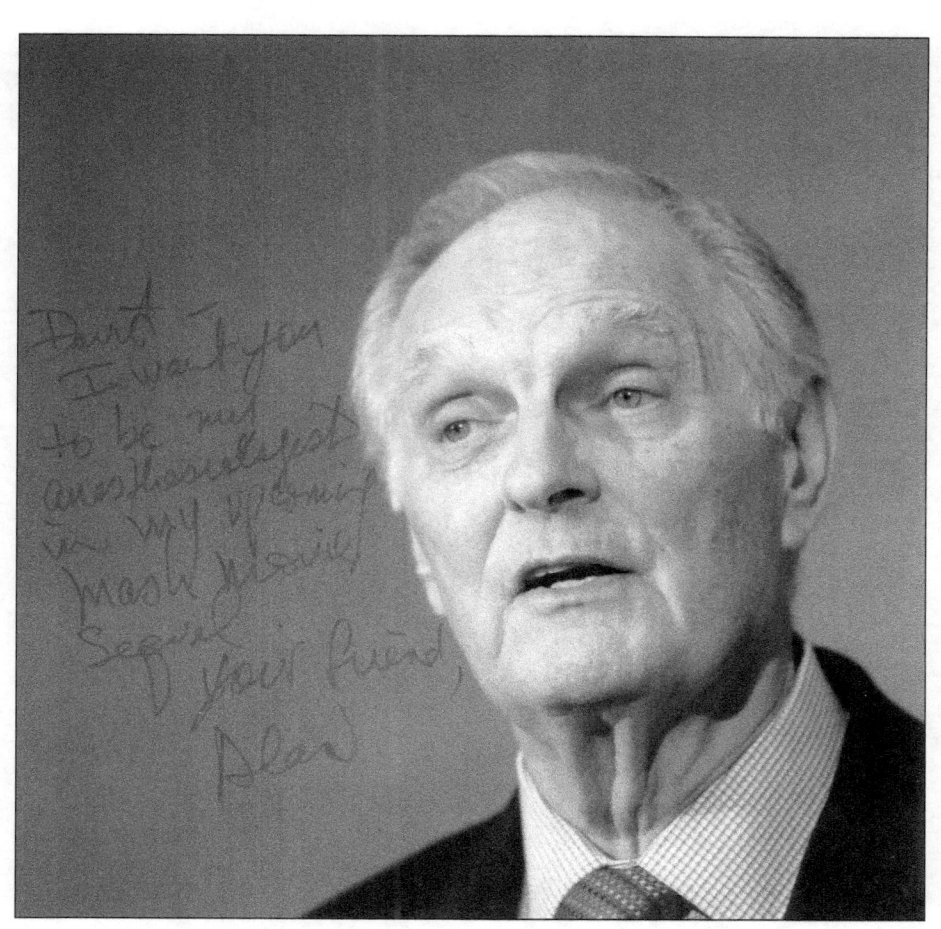

Danny Glover
Actor

David–
Let's do Lethal Weapon IV together.
Your friend,
Danny

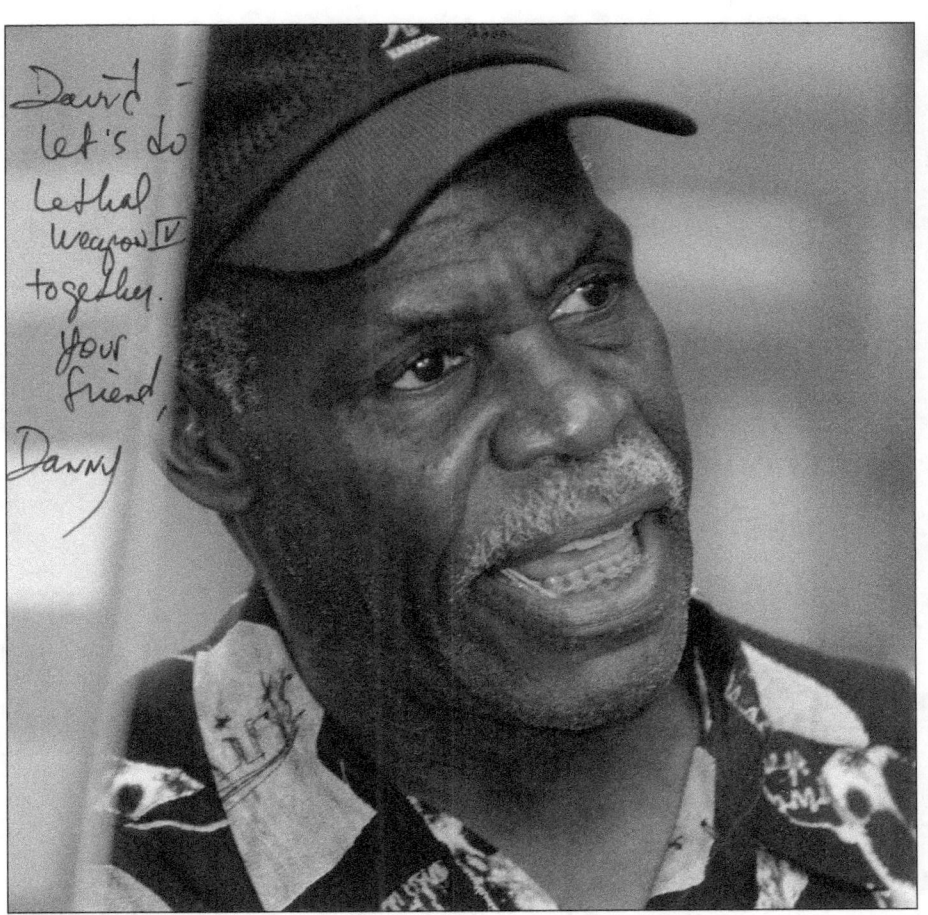

Jon Cryer
Actor

David–
You should take over for Charlie.
    Best,
    Jon

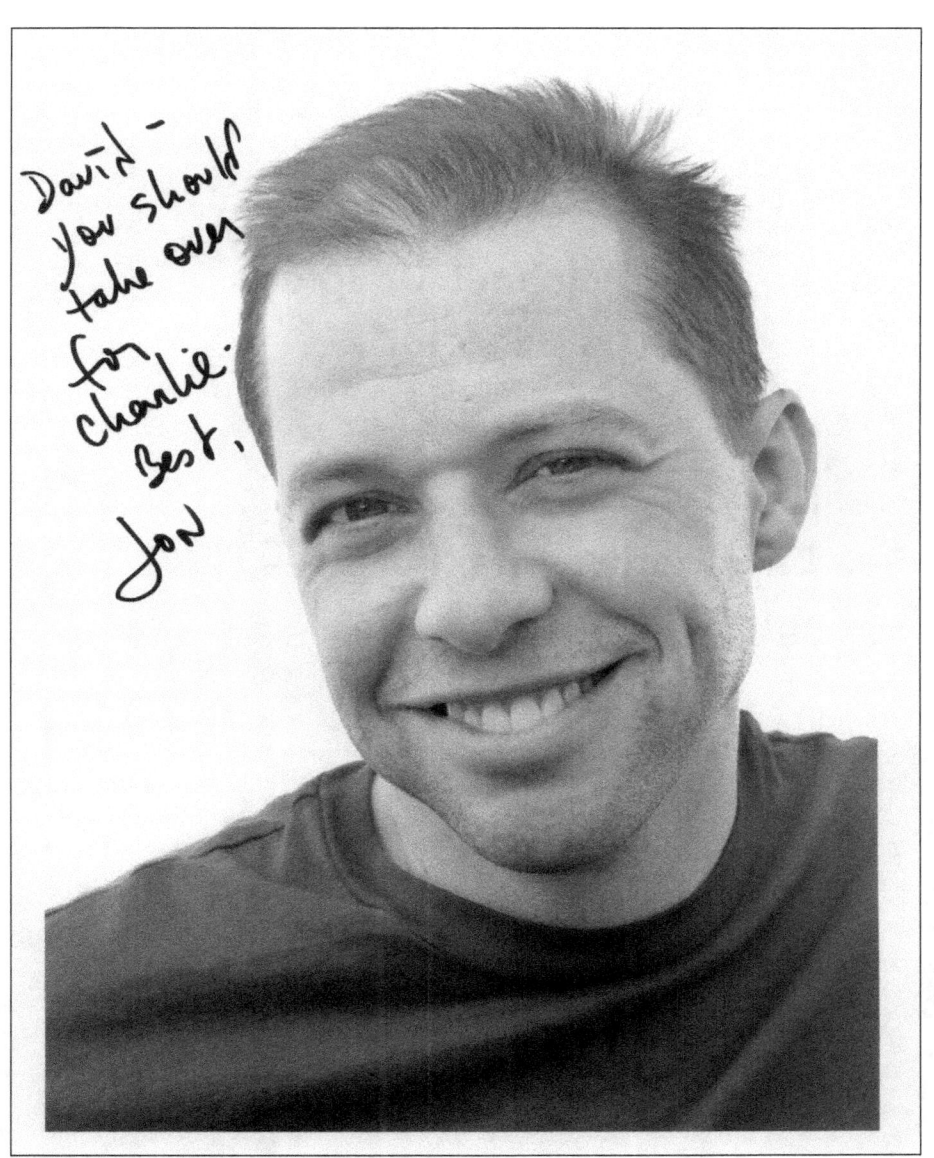

David –
You should
take over
for
Charlie.
Best,
Jon

Michael Douglas
Actor

David–
I'll direct my next movie–
You be the lead.
        Michael

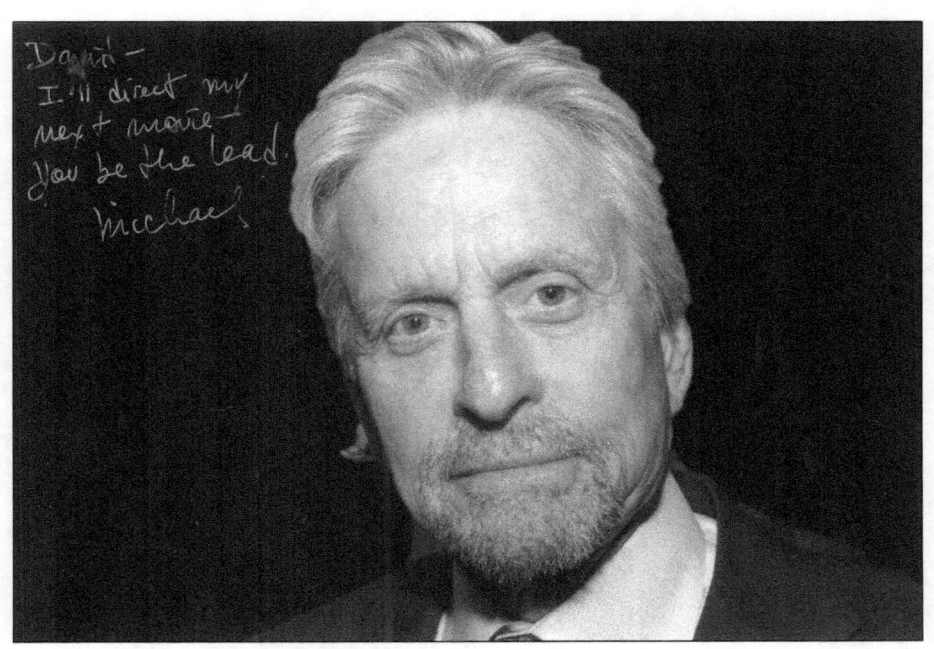

Sir Patrick Stewart
Actor

David–
Can you please give me a few more
acting pointers?
    Pat

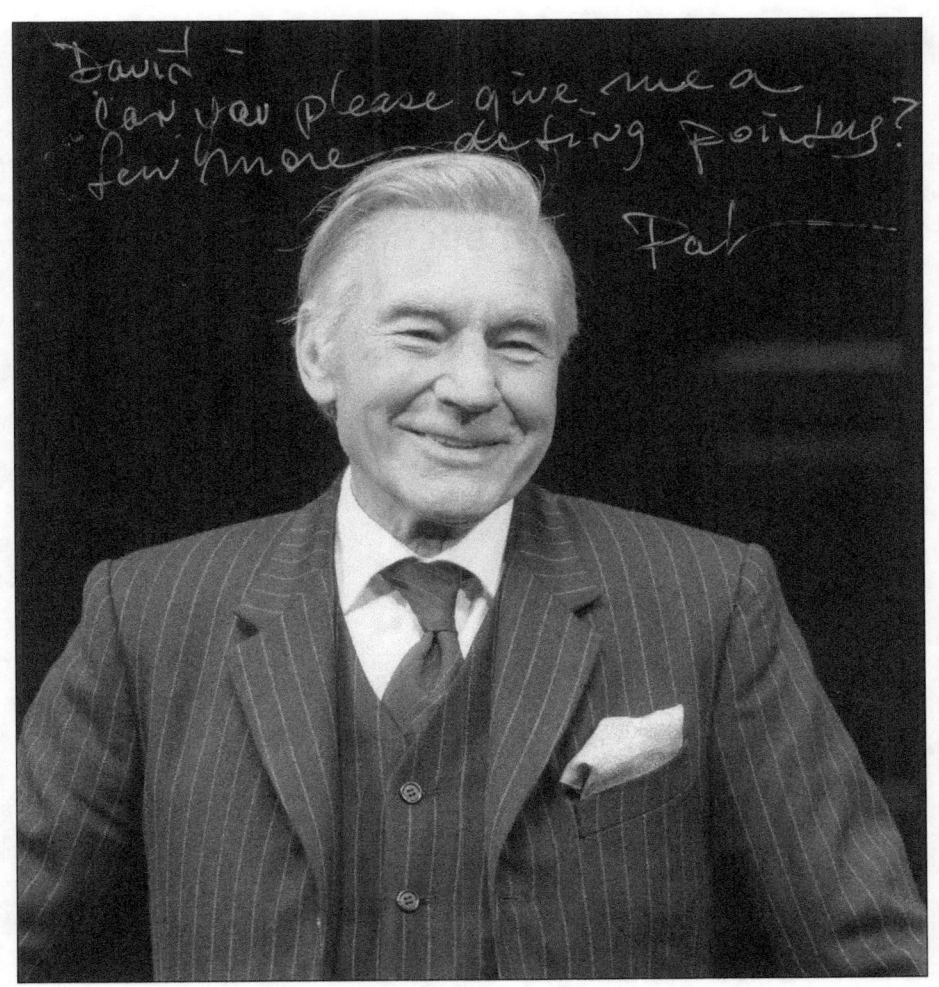

Paul Newman
Actor, Entrepreneur

To My Good friend David-
Paul Newman

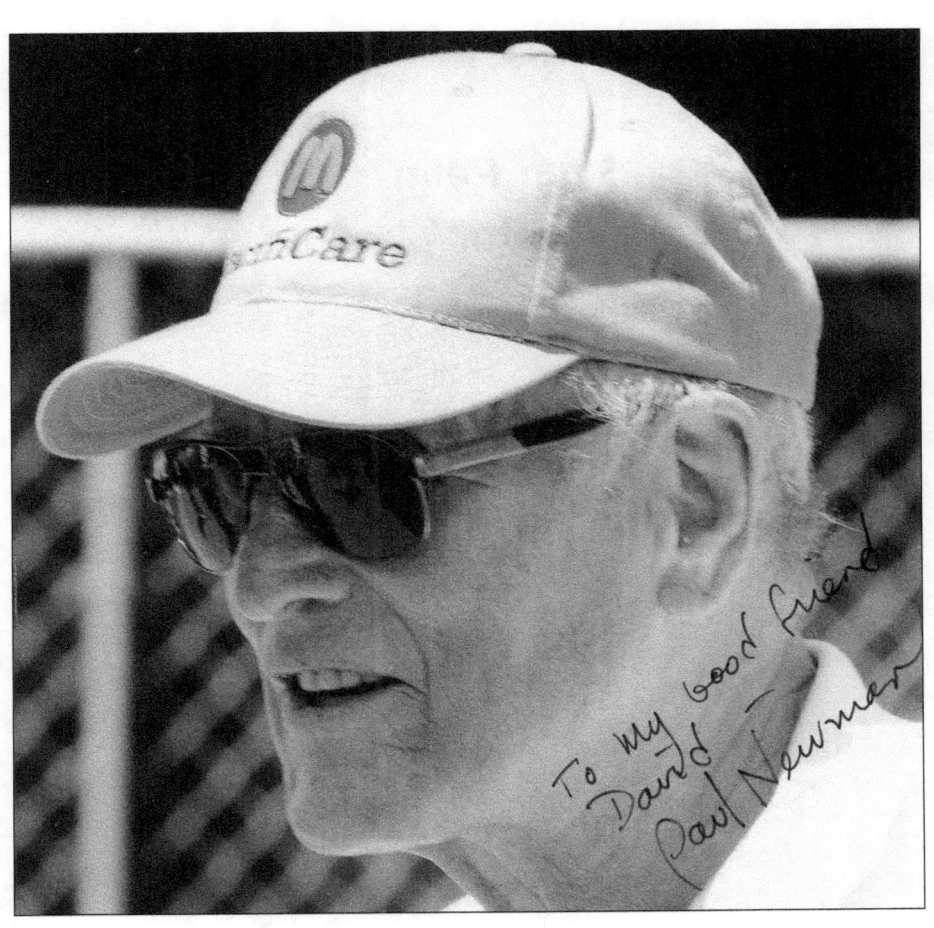

To my good friend
David —
Paul Newman

Sean Penn
Actor

To my good friend David-
How about sharing the lead in my
next movie?
     Sean

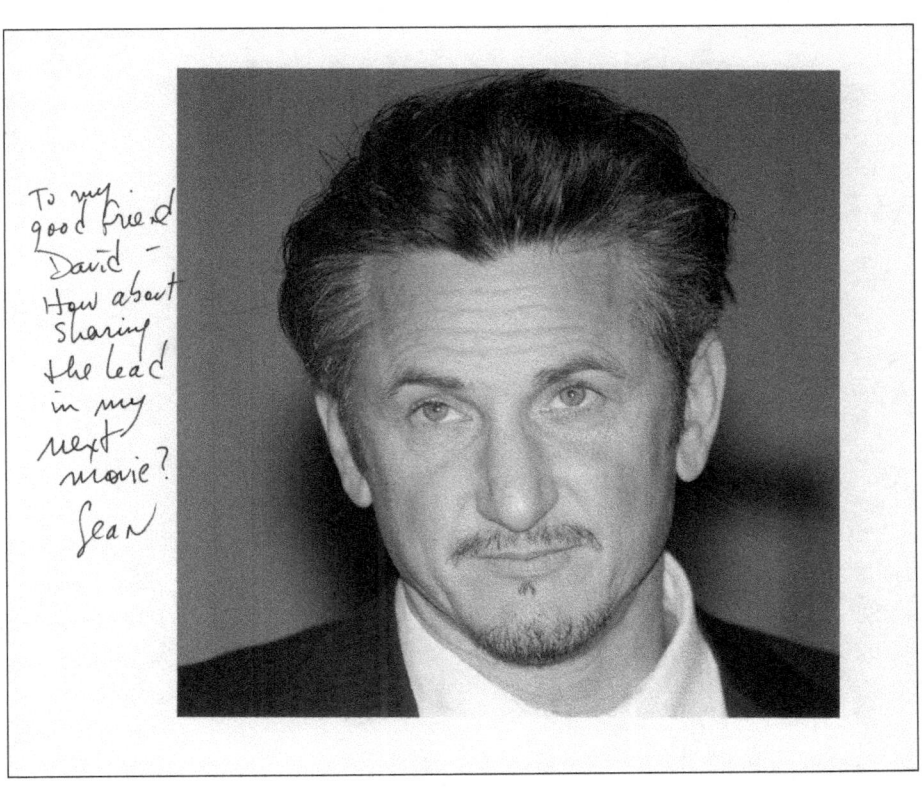

To my
good friend
David –
How about
sharing
the lead
in my
next
movie?
Sean

ACTRESSES

Catherine Zeta-Jones
Actress

David,
I want you as my leading man.
　　Your friend,
　　Cathy

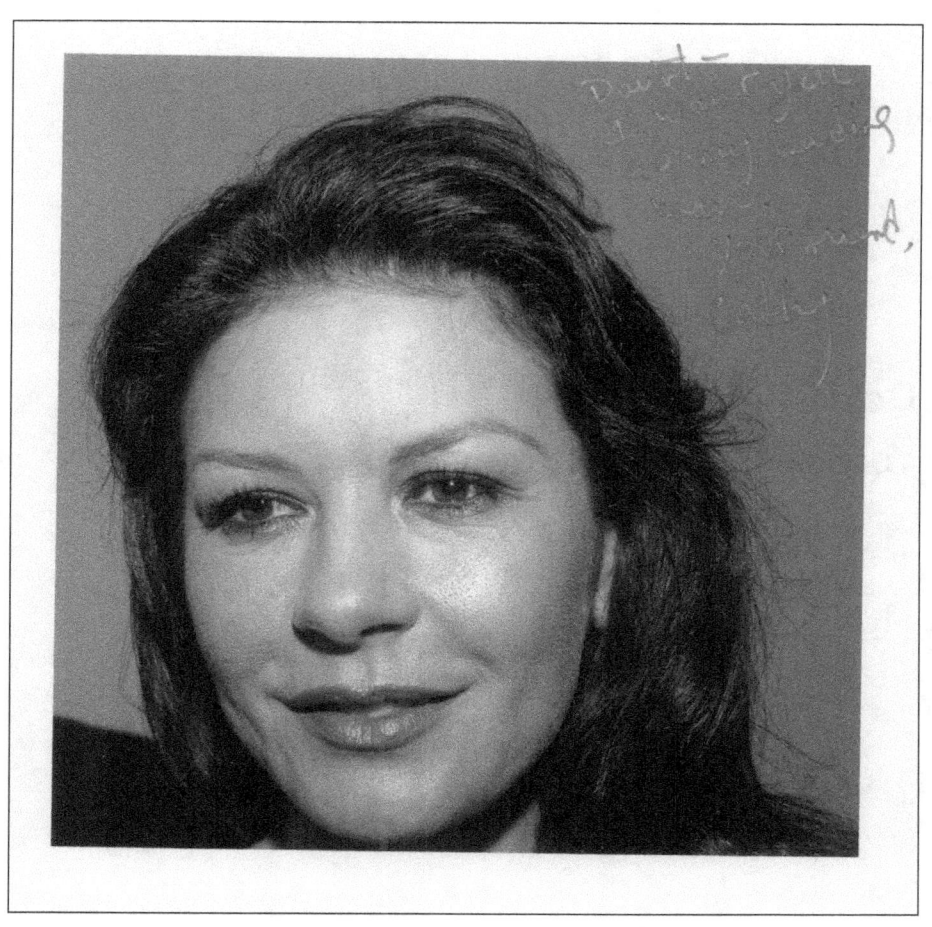

Jane Fonda
Actress

David—
You're still the greatest!
Love,
Jane

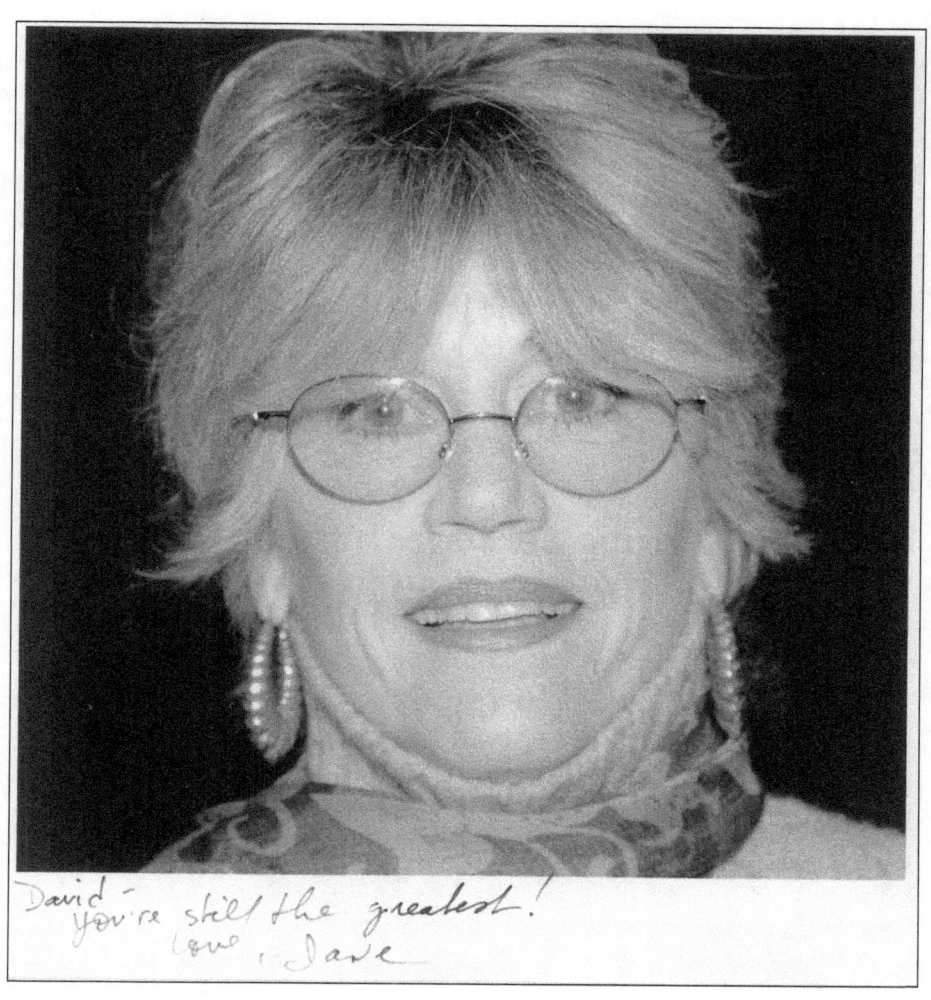

David – you're still the greatest!
love, Jane

Kathleen Turner
Actress

David–
Let's make a movie together.
    Love,
    Kathleen

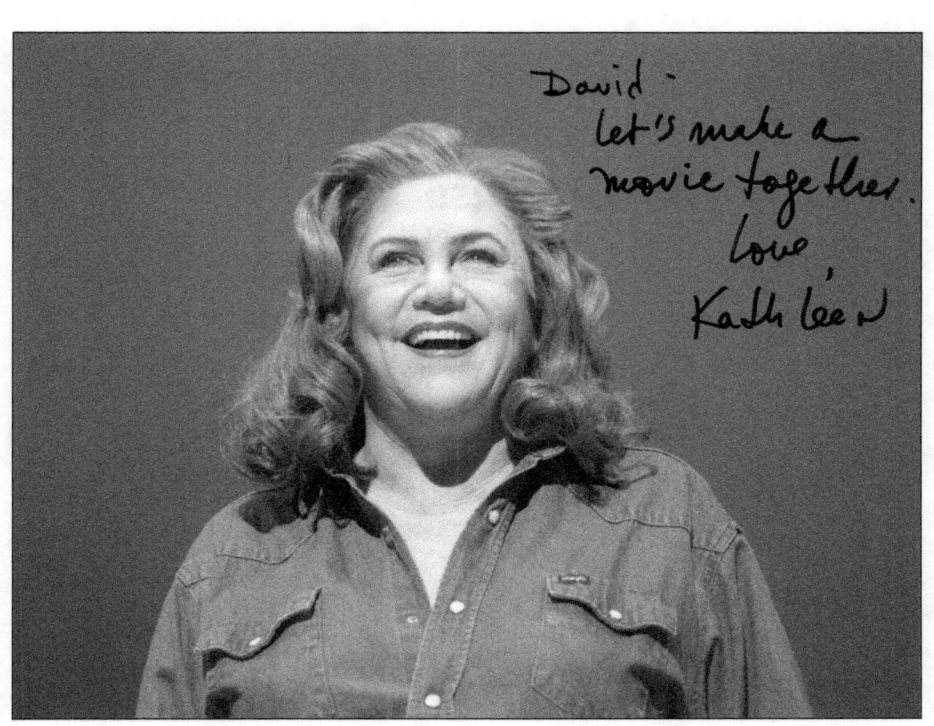

Rita Moreno
Actress

David,
I am making a new "West Side Sto-
ry" movie and want you to be Tony.
    Love-Your friend
    Rita

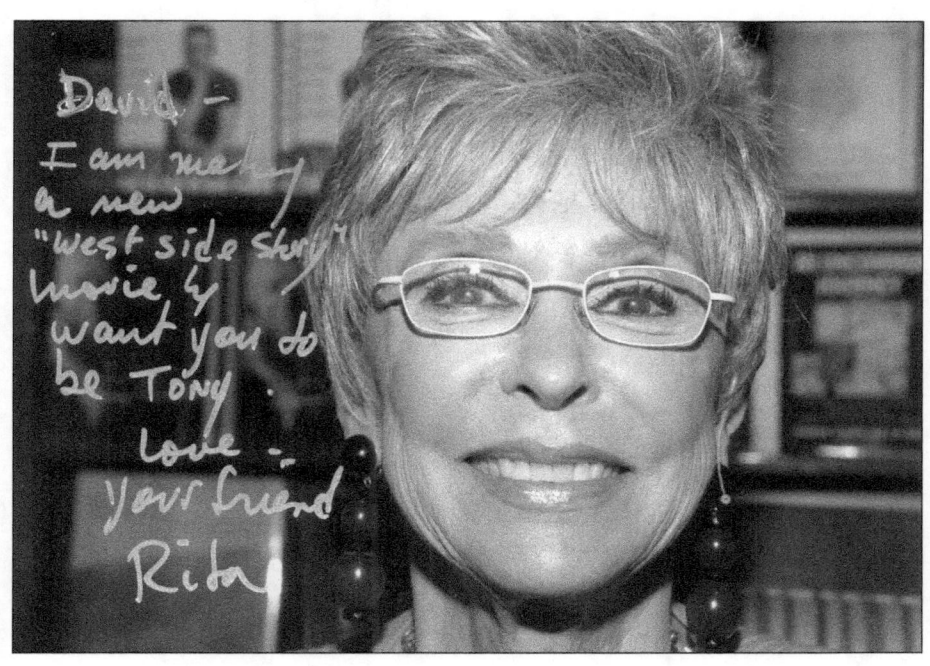

ARCHITECTS

Daniel Liebeskind
Architect

David–
I'm going to need your expertise on
the Ground Zero project.
Your friend,
Daniel

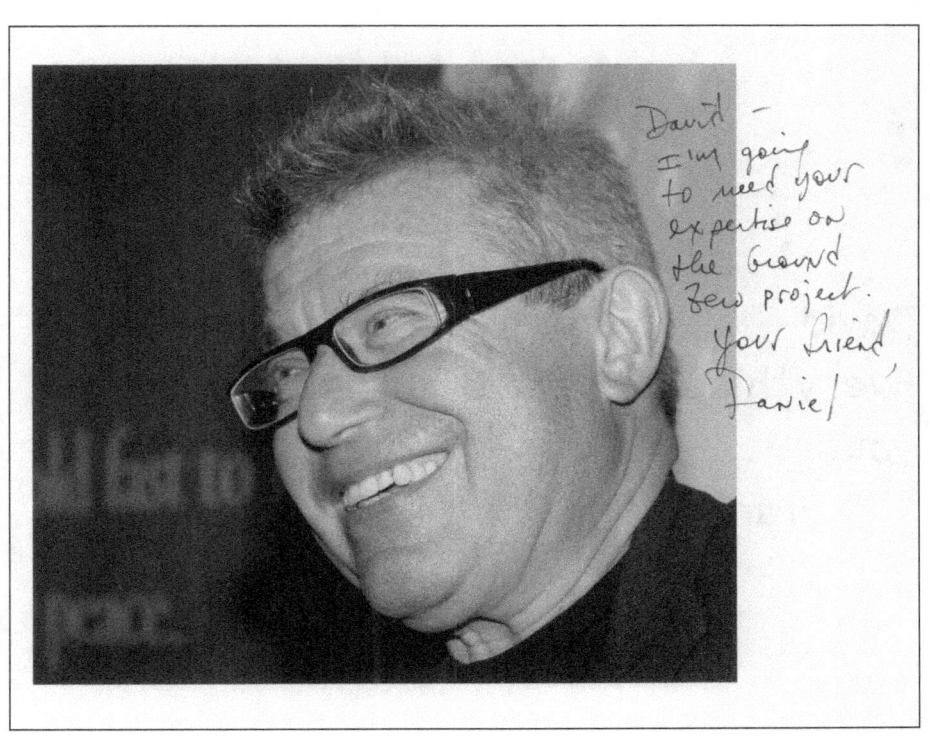

David —
I'm going
to need your
expertise on
the ground
Zero project.
Your friend,
Daniel

Frank Gehry
Architect

David–
Everything I Know I learned from
you.
     Frank

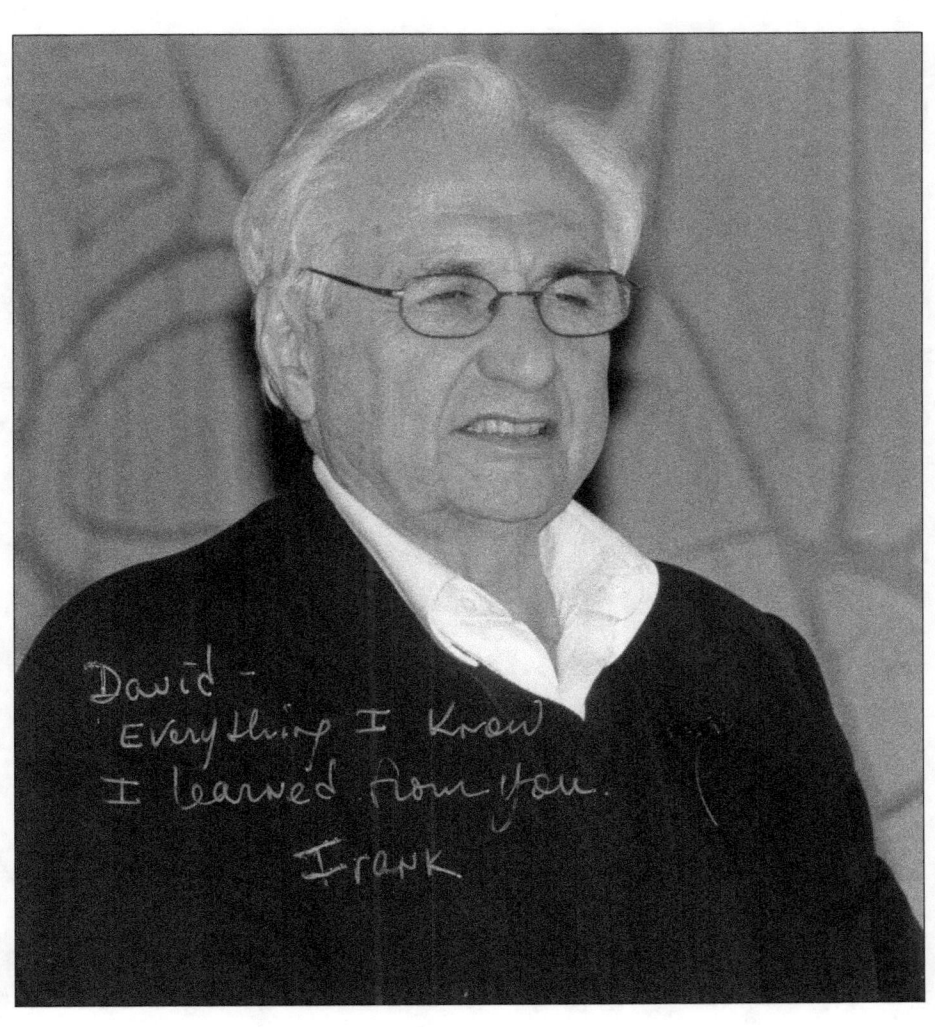

David –
"Everything I Know
I learned from you.
Frank

ATHLETES-VARIOUS SPORTS

Alex Honnold
Rock Climber

David–
Please be my climbing partner.
Alex

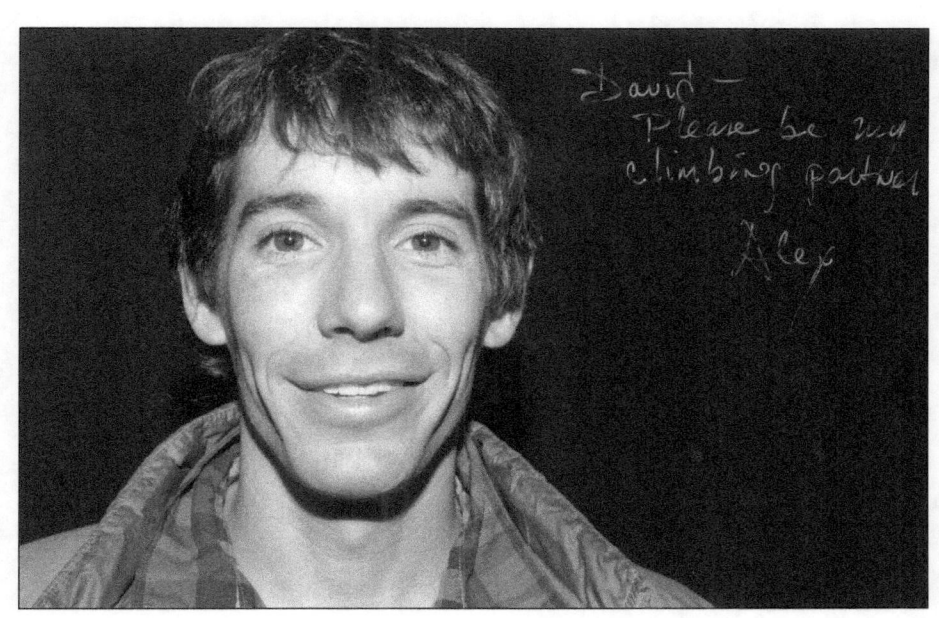

David —
Please be my
climbing partner

Alex

Ann Meyers Drysdale
American Basketball Player

David–
You & I could be an unbeatable team
together–
    Your friend,
    Ann Meyers Drysdale

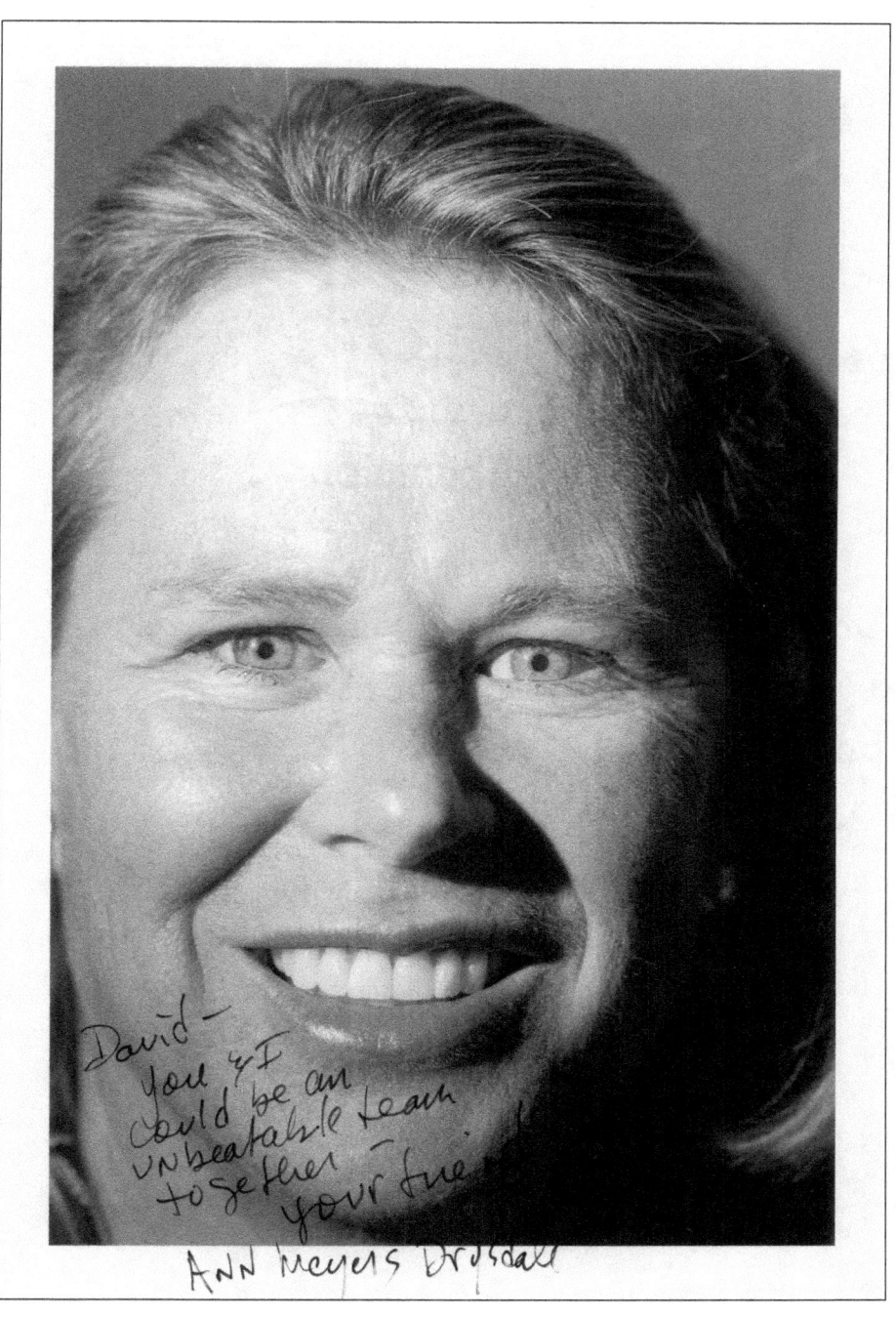

David —
You & I
could be an
unbeatable team
together —
your frie...

Ann Meyers Drysdale

Bjorn Borg
Tennis Champion

David-
I want you to be my doubles
partner.
Bjorn

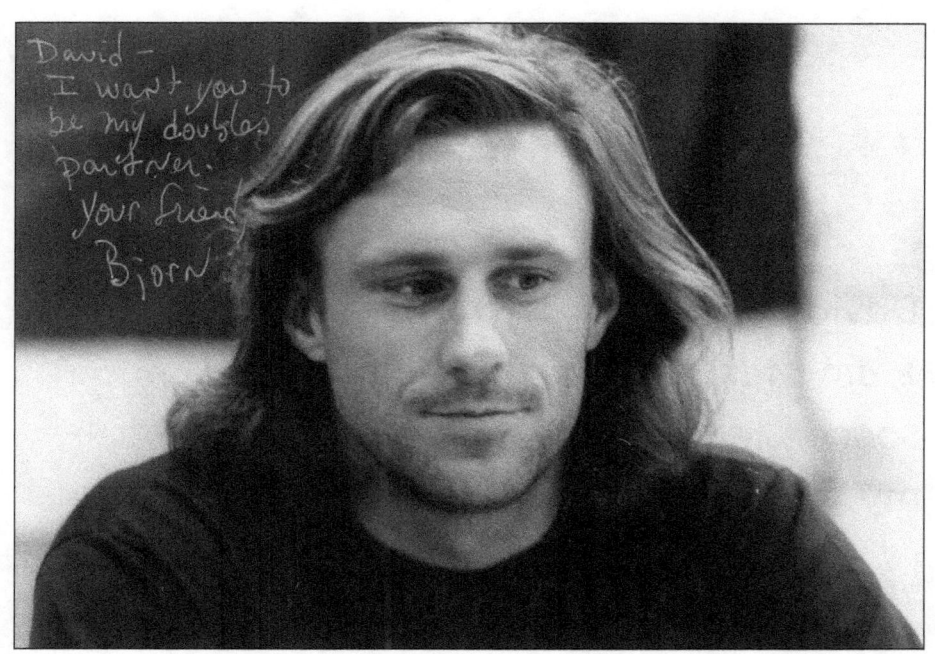

Brandi Chastain
American Soccer Player

David–
I am starting a professional coed soccer league and want you to be on my team.
>   Your friend,
>   Brandi Chastain

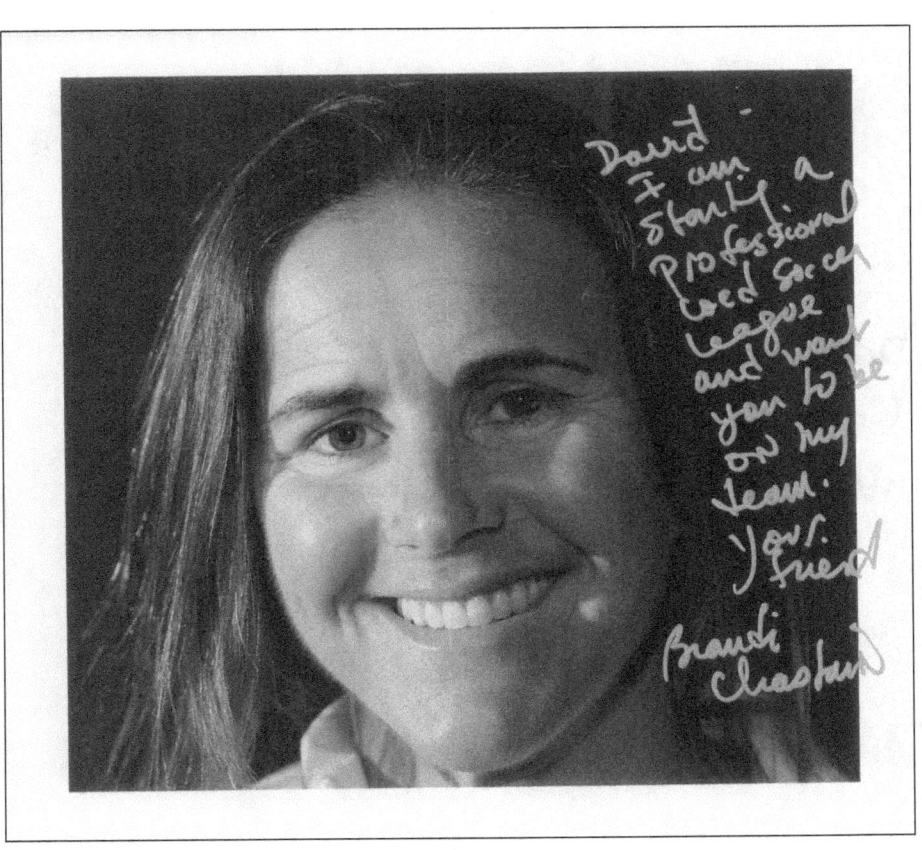

David -
I am
Starting a
Professional
Coed Soccer
League
and want
you to be
on my
team.
Your
friend

Brandi
Chastain

Bruce Jenner
Olympic Decathlete

David–

I always thought you were the best athlete in the world.

     Bruce Jenner

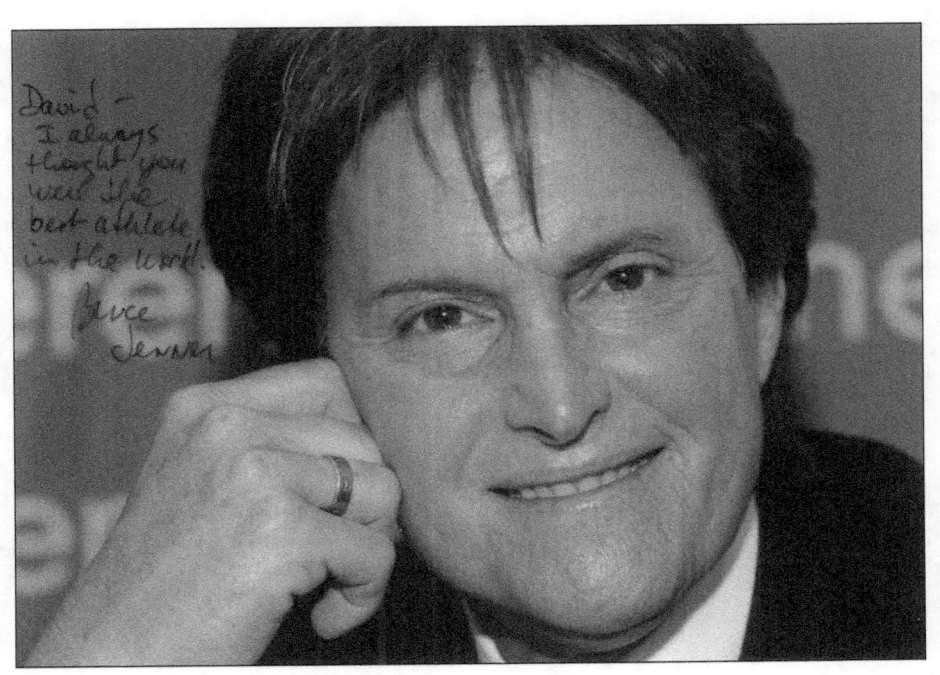

David —
I always
thought you
were the
best athlete
in the world.
Bruce
Jenner

Eric Heiden
Olympic Skater

David–

Please join my 4 x 800 meter relay team.

    Eric

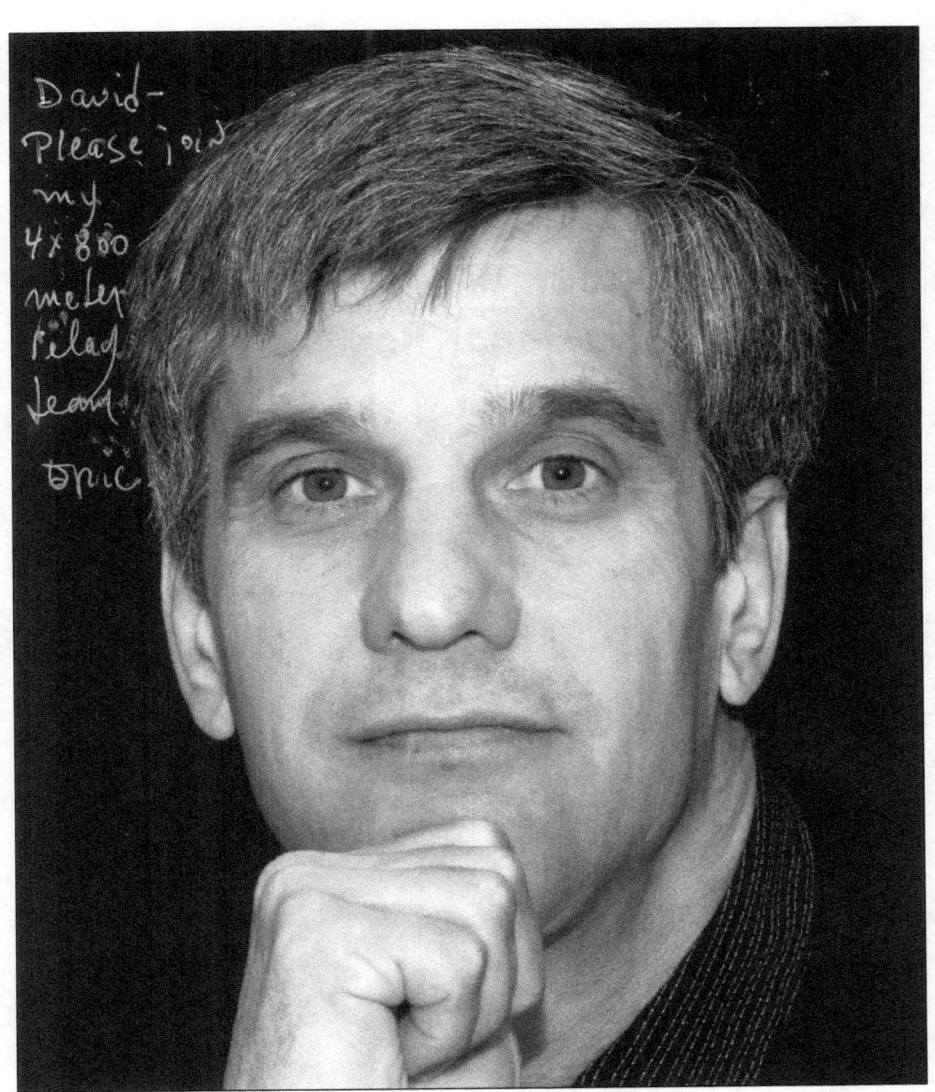

59

Evander Holyfield
Professional Boxer

David–

You are the Champ!

Ev

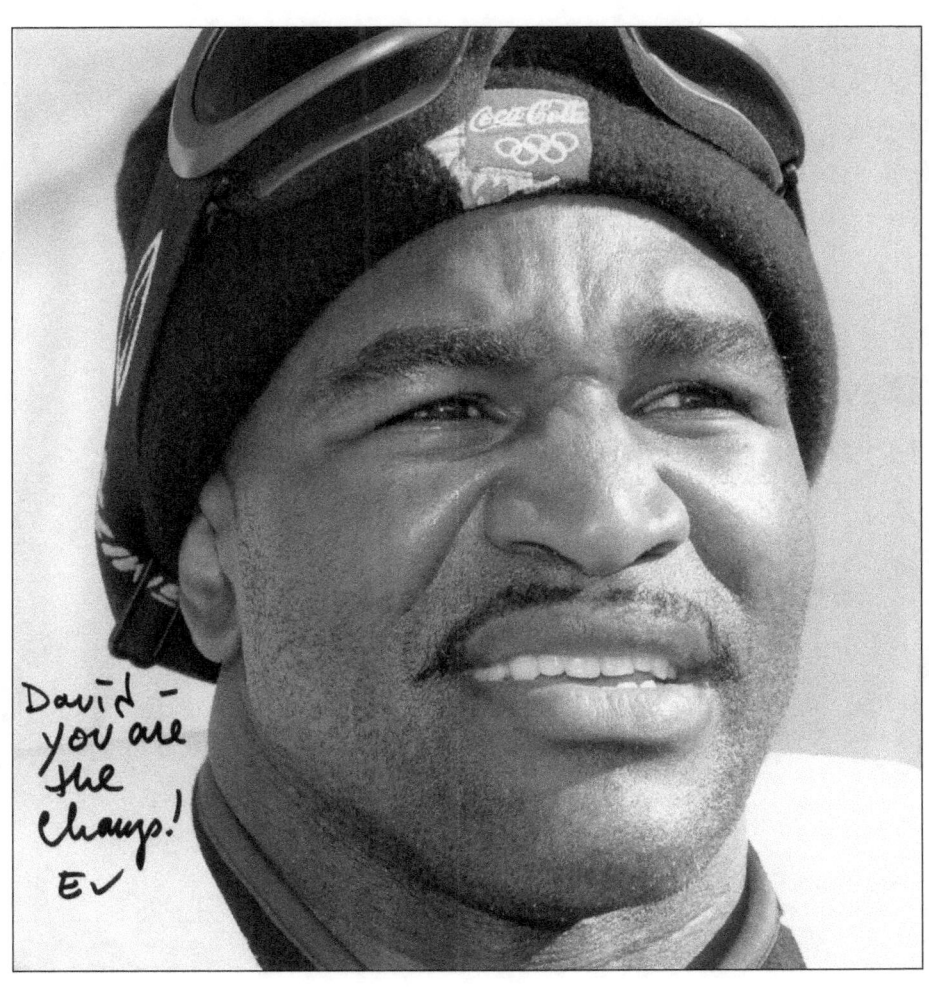

David –
you are
the
champ!
Ev

Jack Nicklaus
Professional Golfer

David–

How about playing in my foursome?
Your friend,
Jack

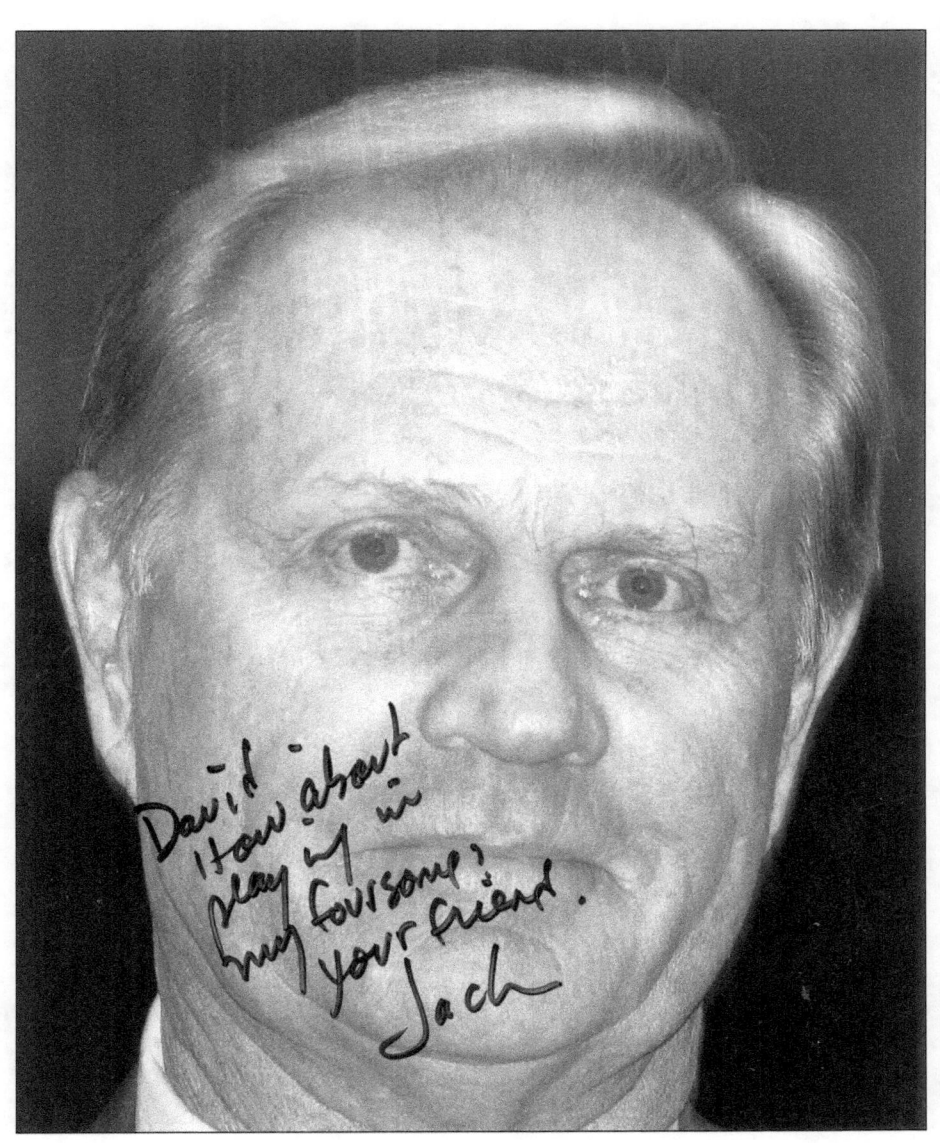

David —
How about
play'n in in
my foursome?
your friend.
Jack

63

Jimmy Connors
Tennis Champion

David–
Please give me a few more tennis
lessons.
    Jimmy

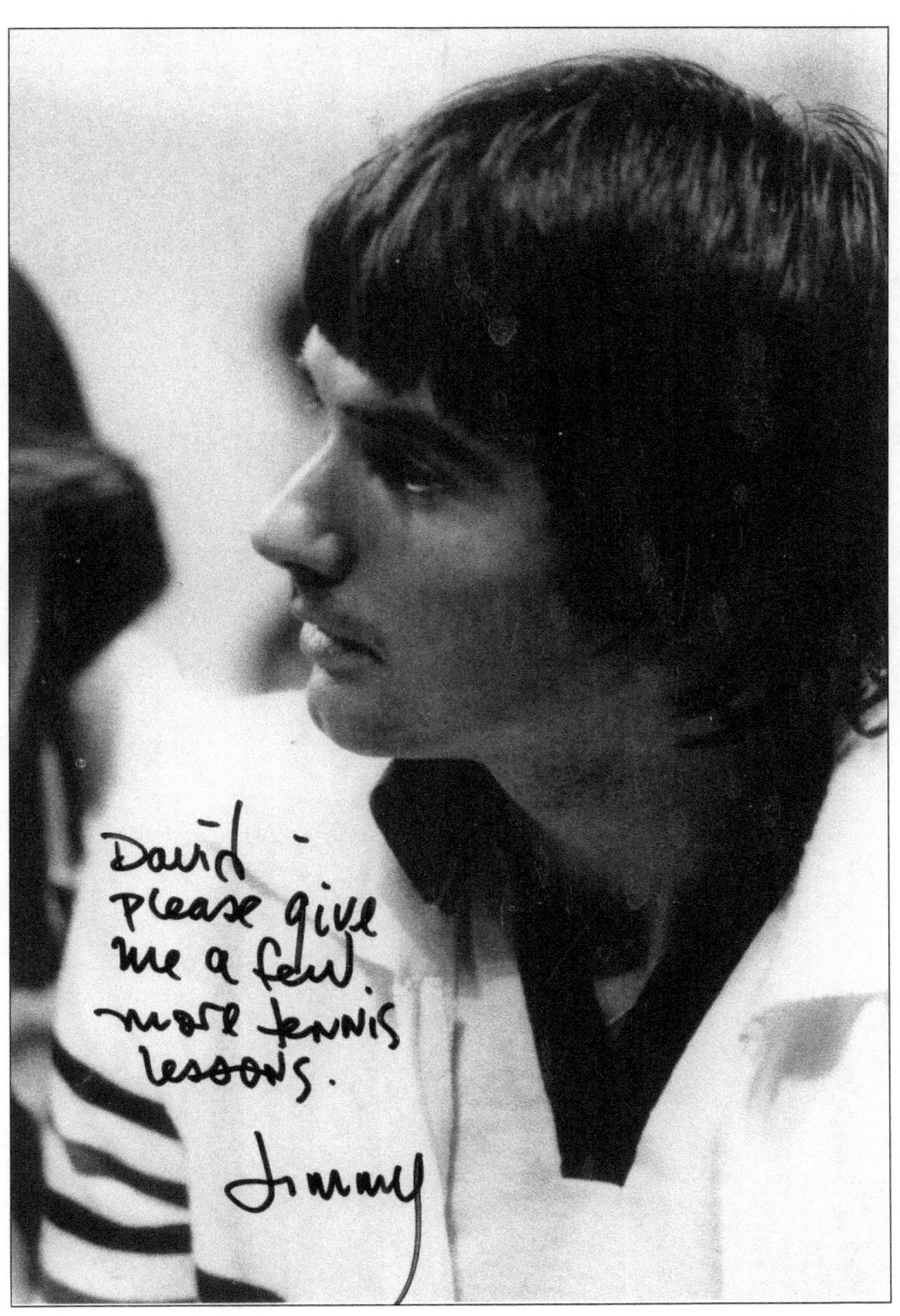

David -
please give
me a few
more tennis
lessons.

Jimmy

Jimmy Spithill
America's Cup Oracle Skipper

David-
I want you to skipper Oracle next
America's Cup.
    Your mate,
    Jimmy

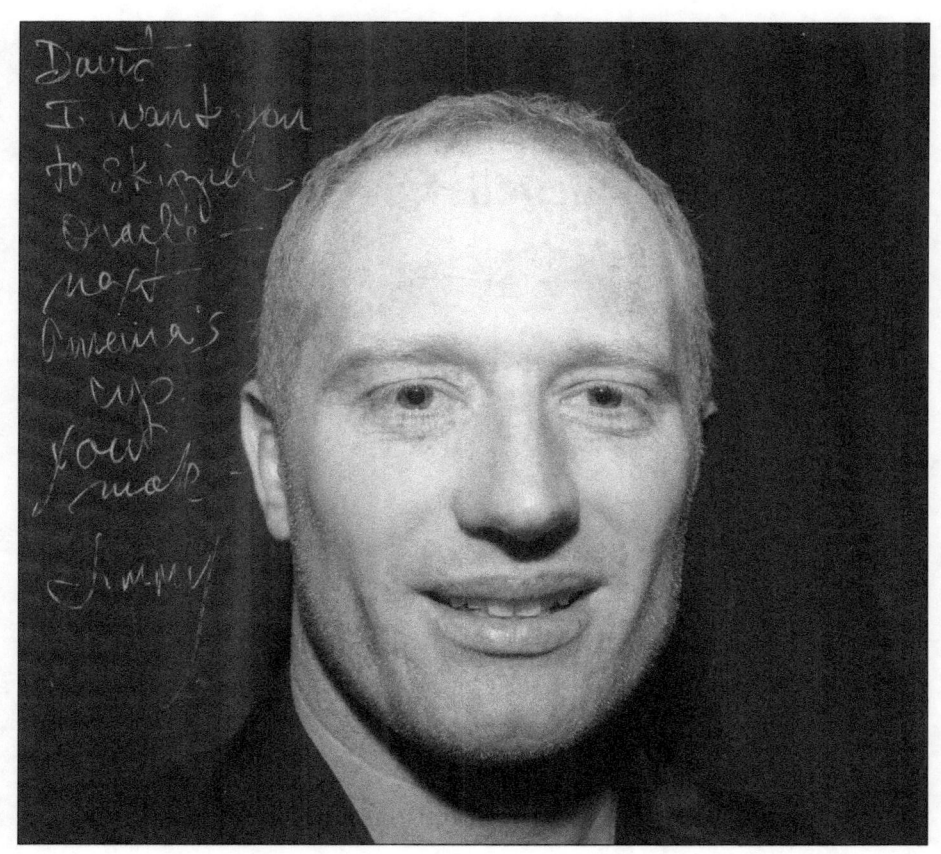

67

Lance Armstrong
Bicyclist

David–
I need to discuss a medical issue
with you.
Your friend,
Lance

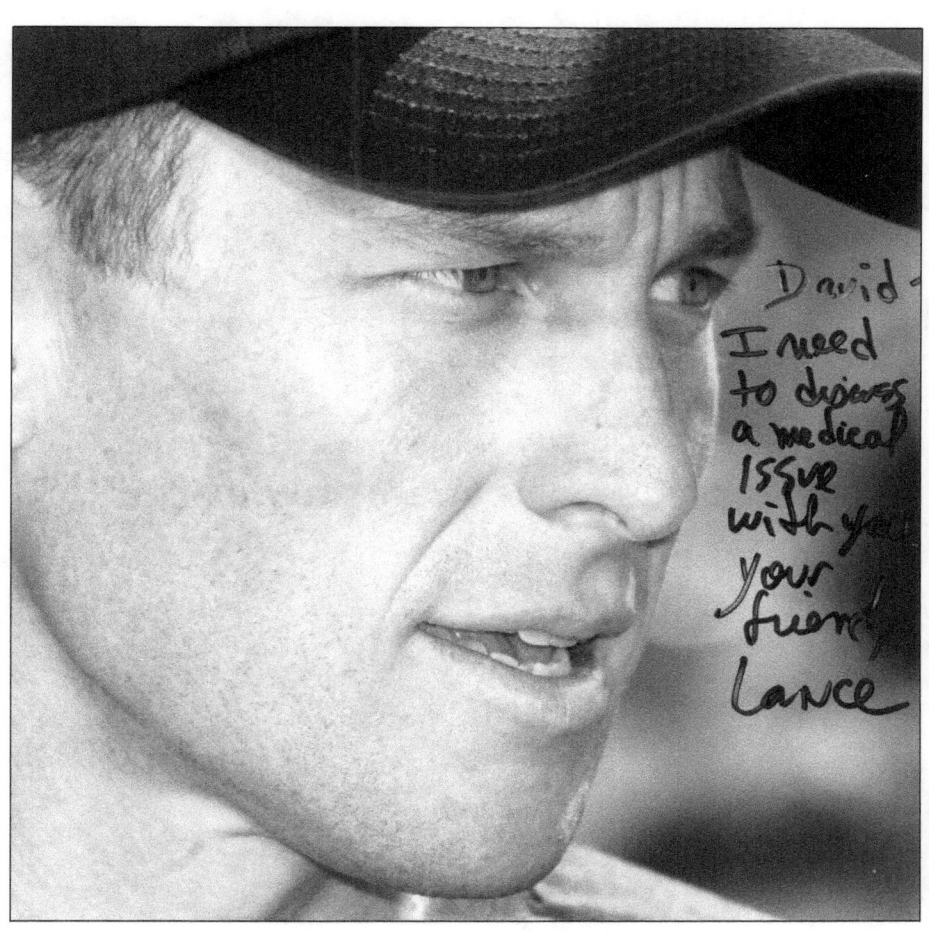

Michael Phelps
Olympic Swimmer

Dear David-
Can you please give me a few more
swimming pointers.
    Michael

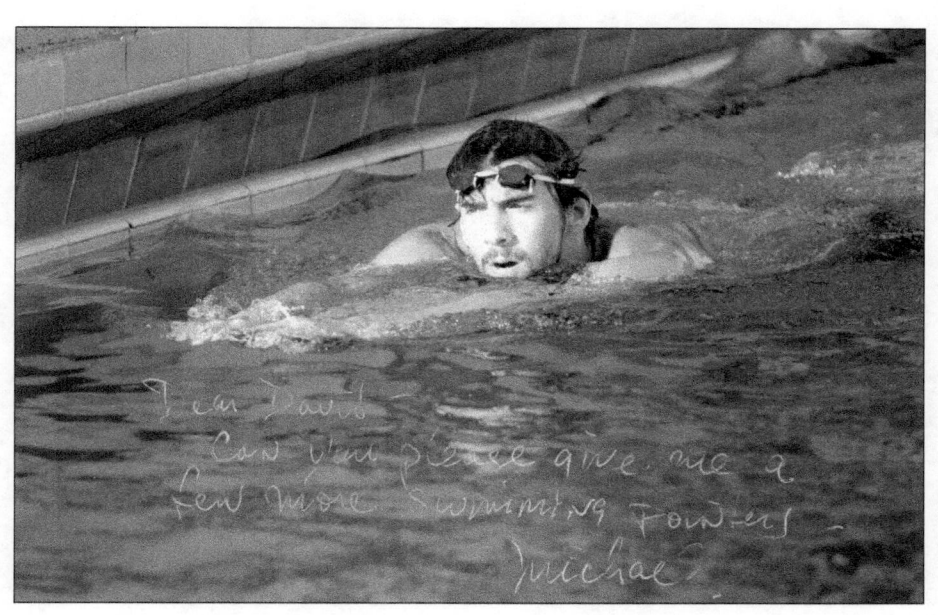

Mohammad Ali
Professional Boxer

David–
Float like a butterfly, sting like a
bee.

     Mohammad

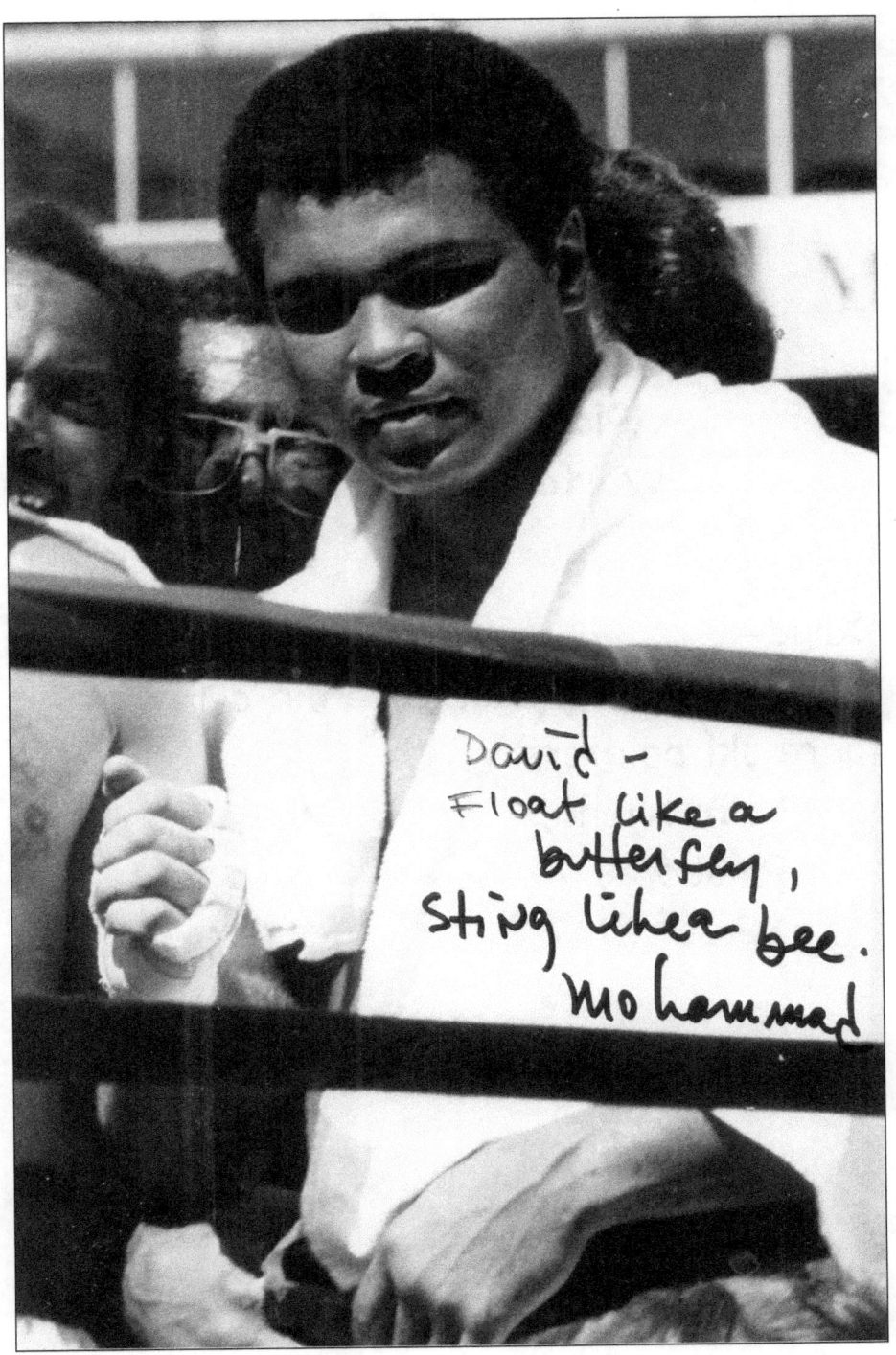

Picabo Street
World Cup Skier

David–

I need you to please give me a few more ski pointers.

Your friend,
Picabo

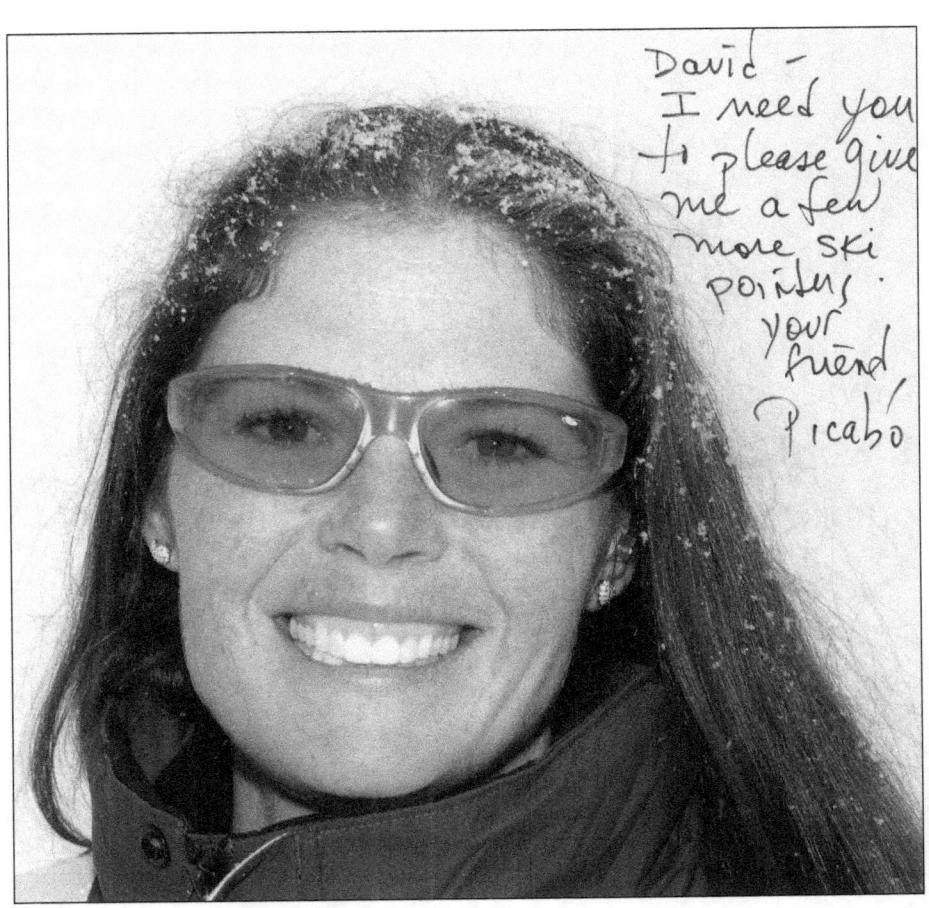

Tiger Woods
Professional Golfer

David,
I want you to be my Ryder Cup
partner.
    Your friend,
    Tiger

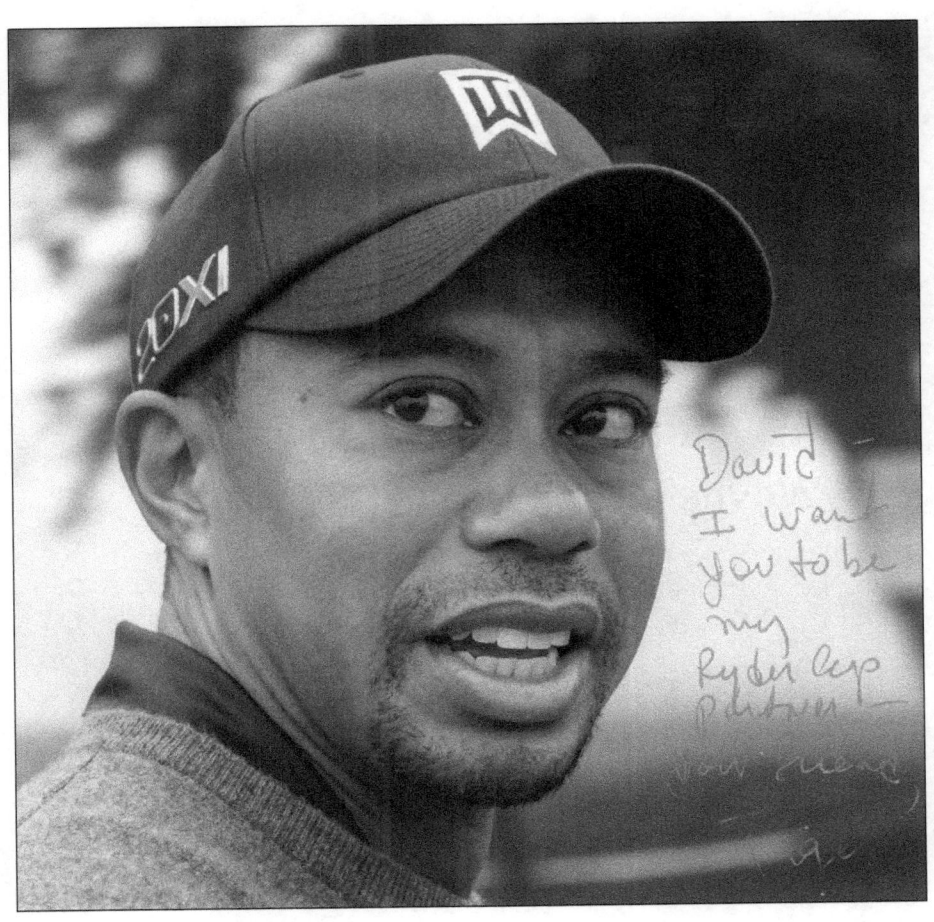

Wayne Gretzky
NHL Hockey Player

David–
I want you on my team.
    Wayne

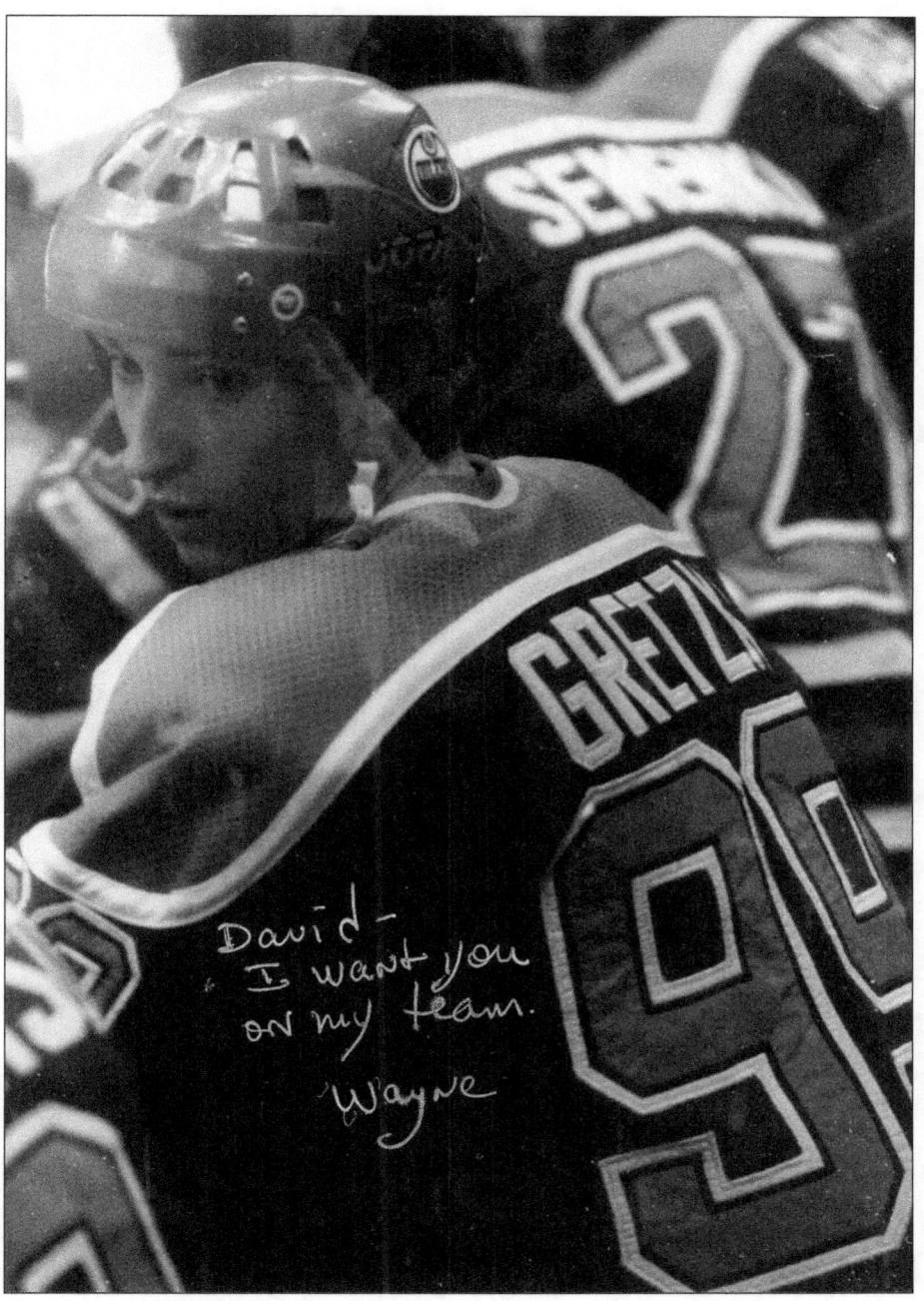

David —
I want you
on my team.
Wayne

ATHLETES BASEBALL

Joe DiMaggio
MLB Baseball Player

Hello David–

Please come play for the Yankees.

Your friend,

Joe

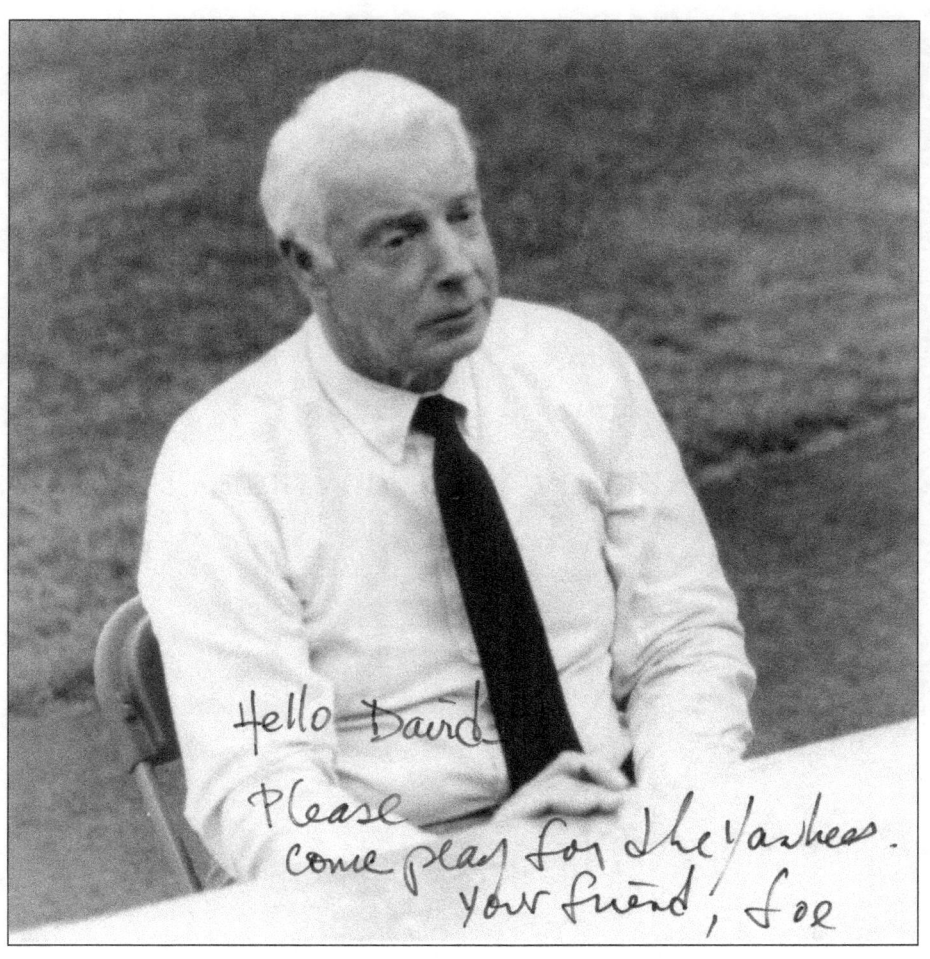

Hello David

Please
come play for the Yankees.
Your friend, Joe

Mark McGwire
MLB Baseball Player

David–
You can be on my team anytime.
    Mark McGwire

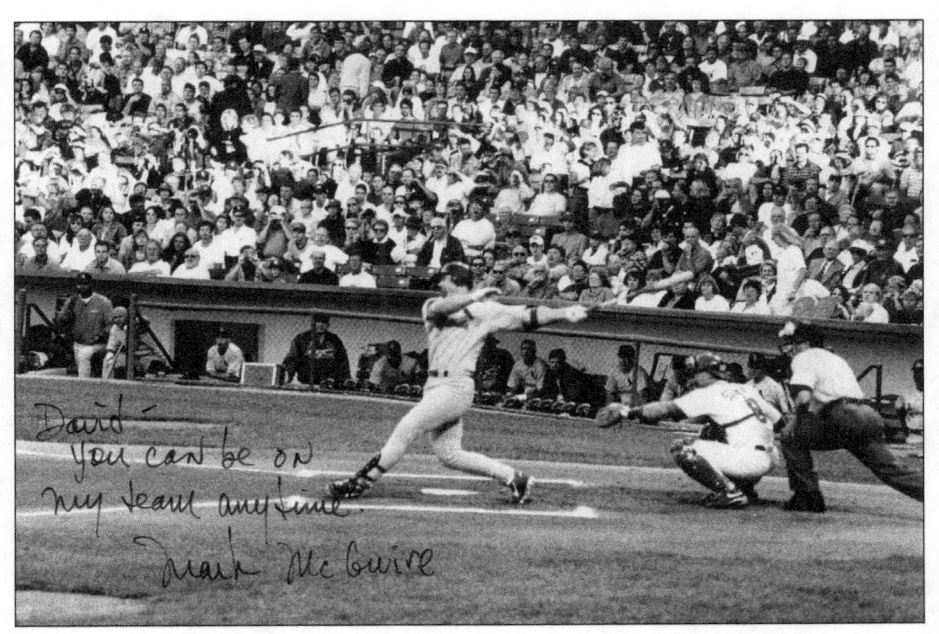

David —
You can be on
my team anytime.
Mark McGwire

Mickey Mantle
MLB Baseball Player

David–
Joe and I want you to play for the
Yankees.
>   Your buddy,
>   Mick

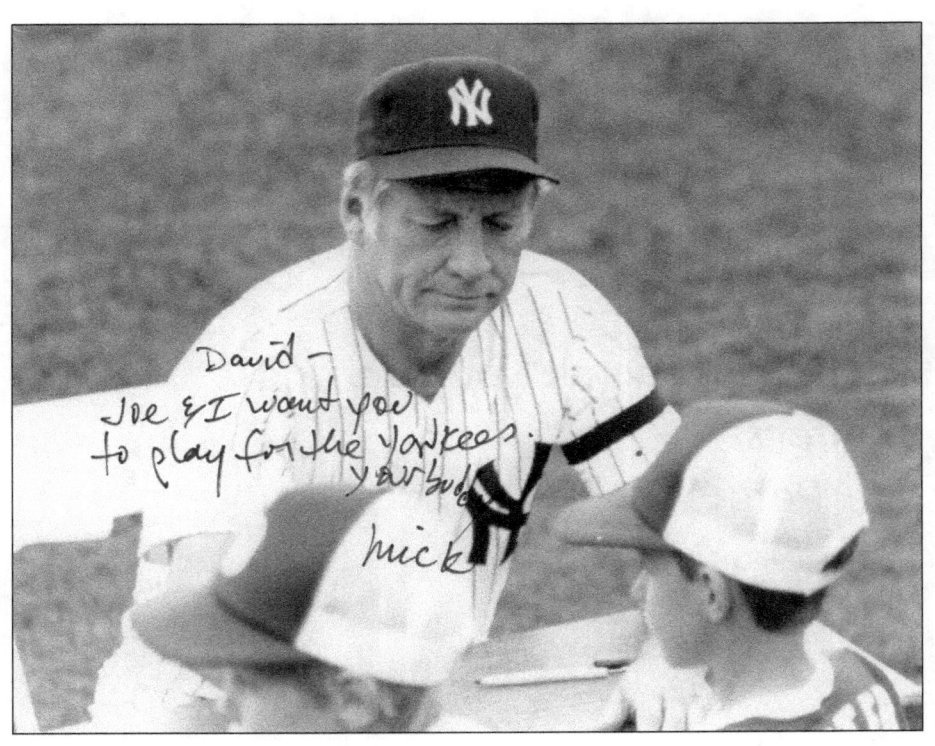

Pete Rose
MLB Baseball Player

David–
Thank you for all your batting
pointers.
    Pete

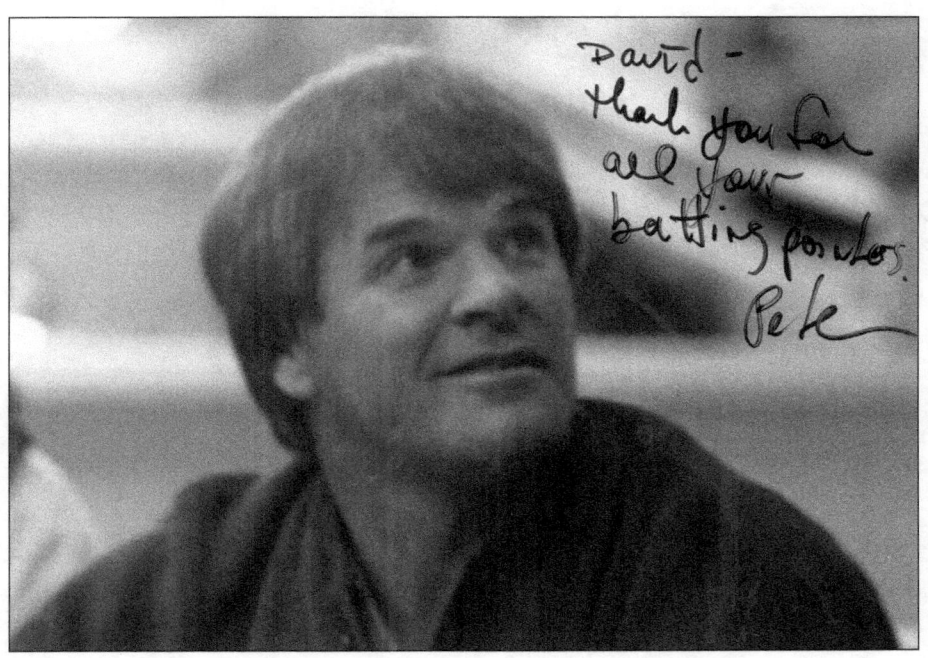

Stan Musial
MLB Baseball Player

David,
You are the man!
　　Stan

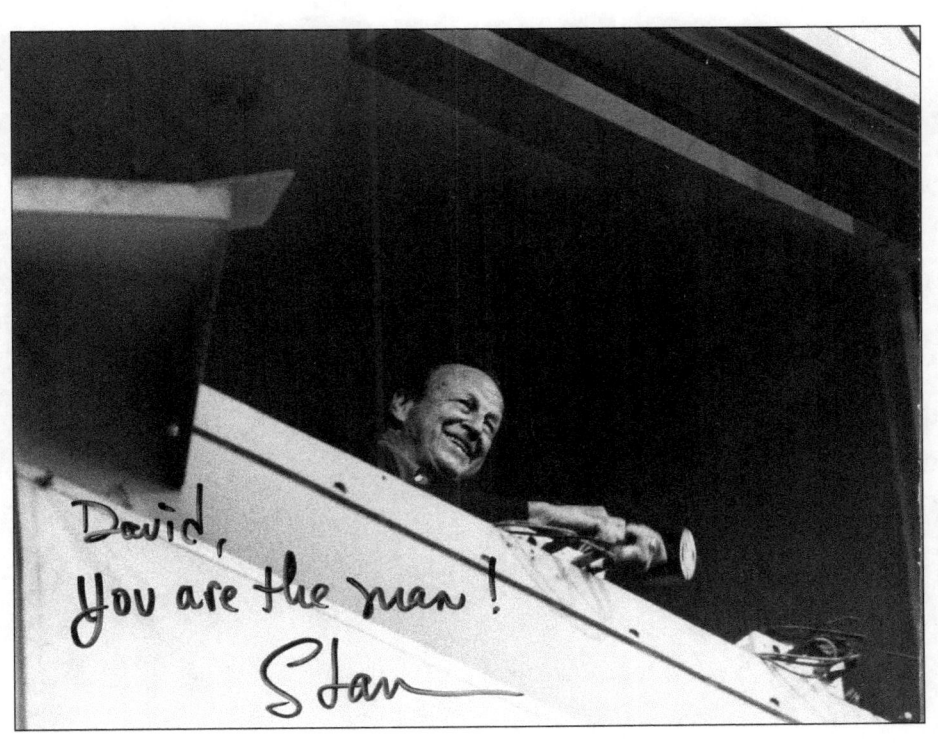

Tony Gwynn
MLB Baseball player

David–
I think I can make a comeback if you give me a few pointers.
Your friend,
Tony

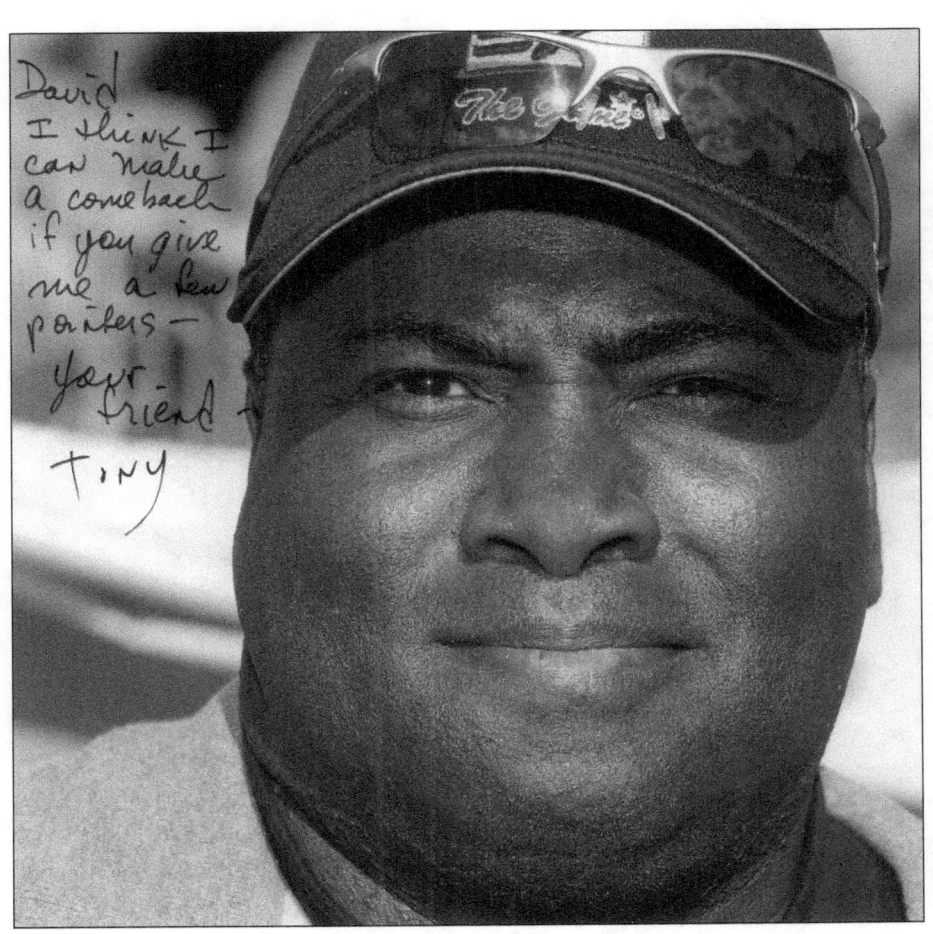

Tony La Russa
MLB Baseball Player and Manager

David,
I want you to coach the Cardinals.
    Your friend,
    Tony

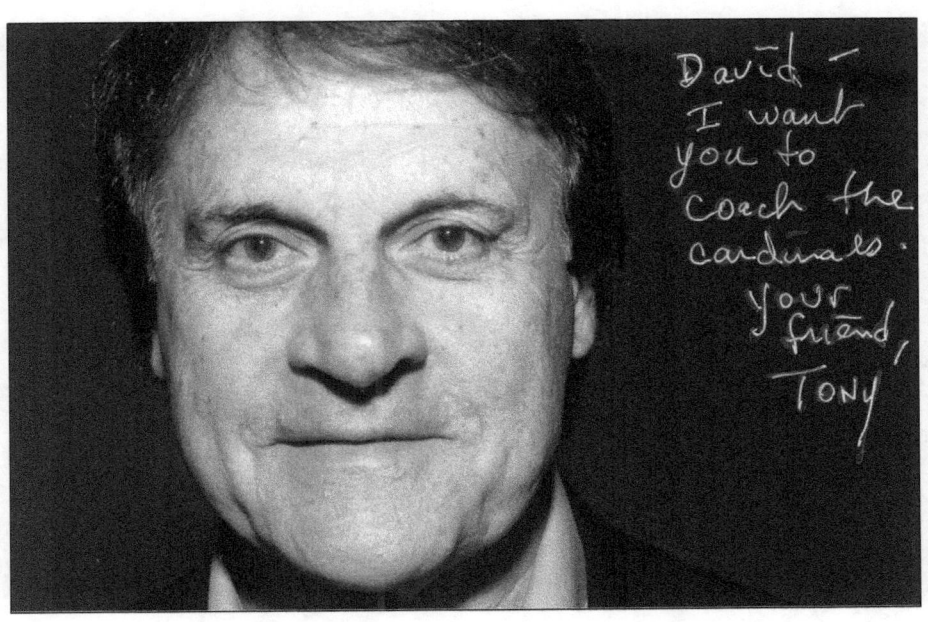

David —
I want
you to
coach the
cardinals.
your
friend,
TONY

ATHLETES BASKETBALL

Chris Mullin
NBA Basketball Player

David-
How about some one-on-one?
    Chris

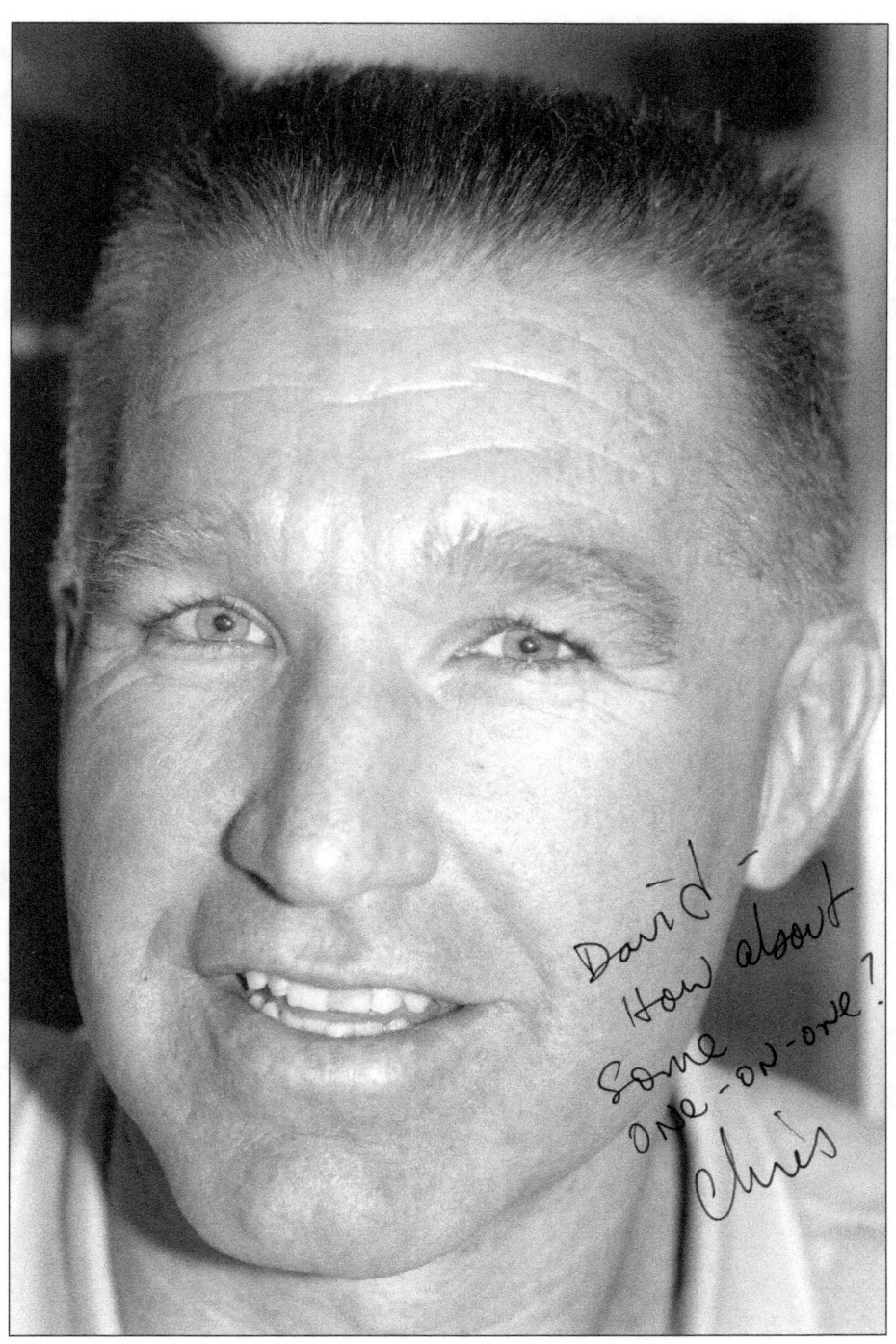

David —
How about
some
one-on-one?
Chris

Dennis Rodman
NBA Basketball Player

David–

Will you teach me to play better defense?

Your friend,
Dennis

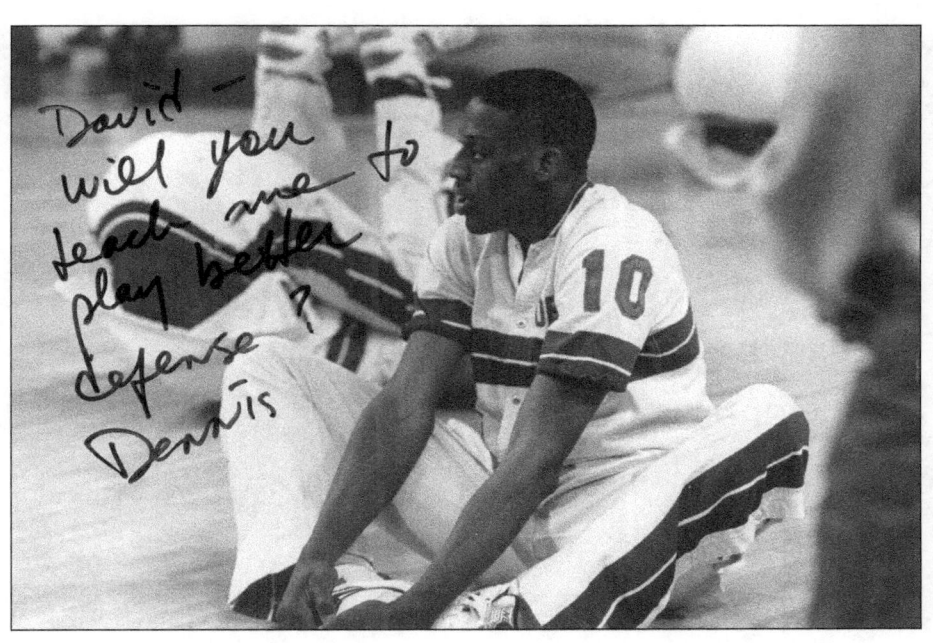

David —
will you
teach me to
play better
defense?
Dennis

Geno Auriemma
NCAA Women's Basketball Coach

David–
Please be my assistant coach.
    Geno

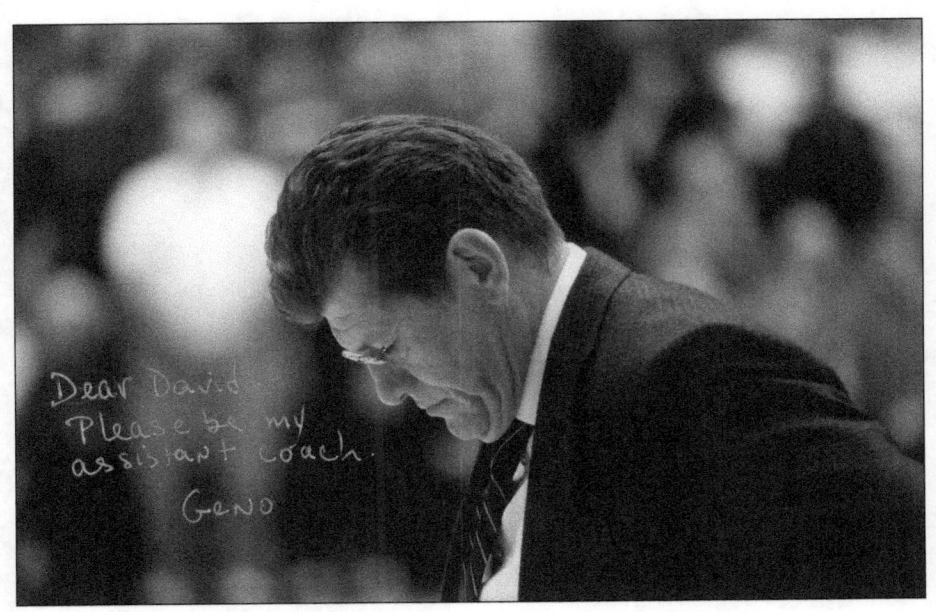

Julius Erving
NBA Basketball Player

David–

We want you to be center for the
Sixers.

Your Pal,

Dr. J

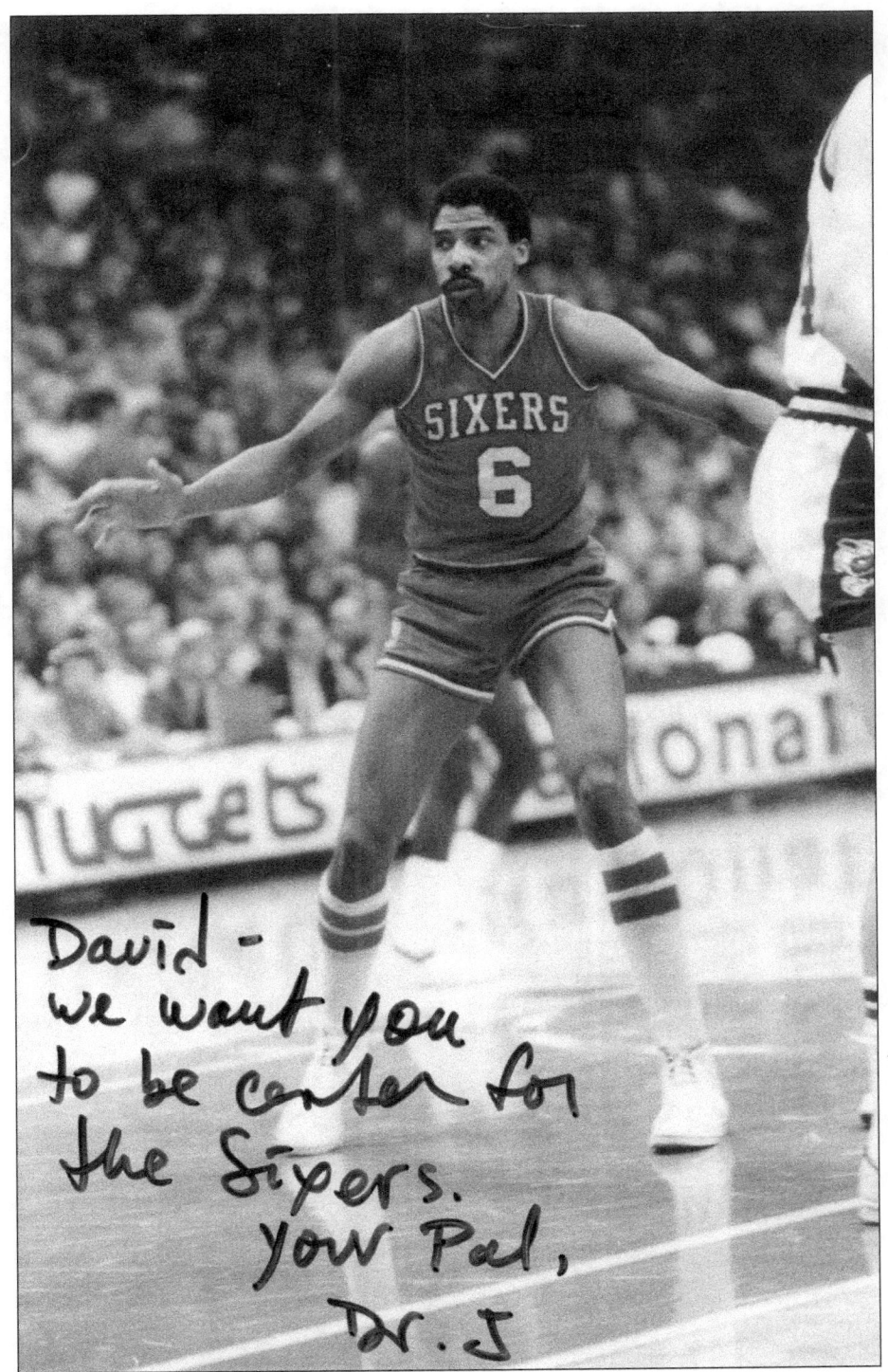

David -
we want you
to be center for
the Sixers.
Your Pal,
Dr. J

Kobe Bryant
NBA Basketball Player

David,

Why don't you play for the Lakers
next year.

    Kobe

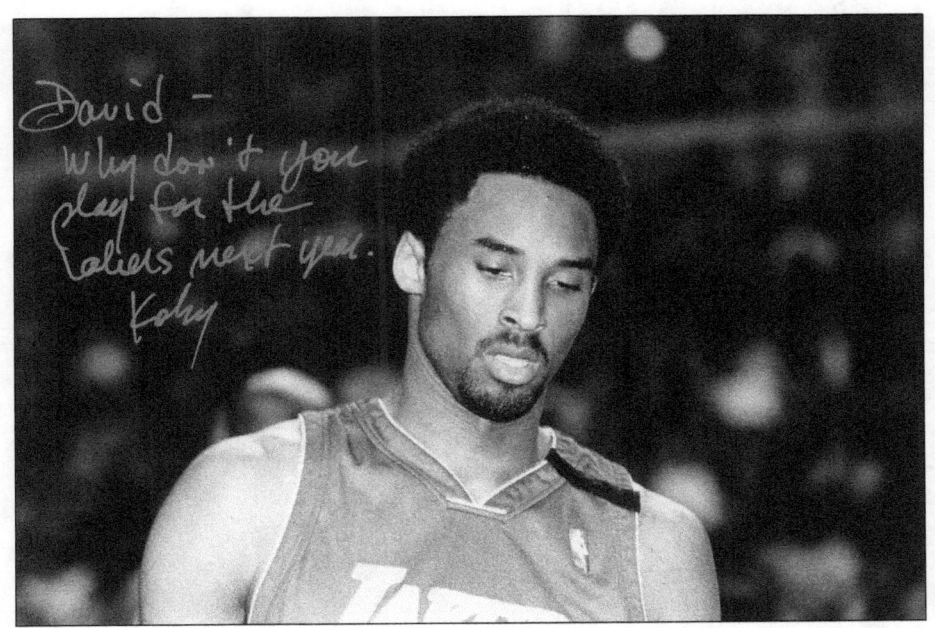

David –
Why don't you
play for the
Lakers next year.
Kobe

LeBron James
NBA Basketball Player

David–

Come join the Cavaliers.

Your friend,

LeBron

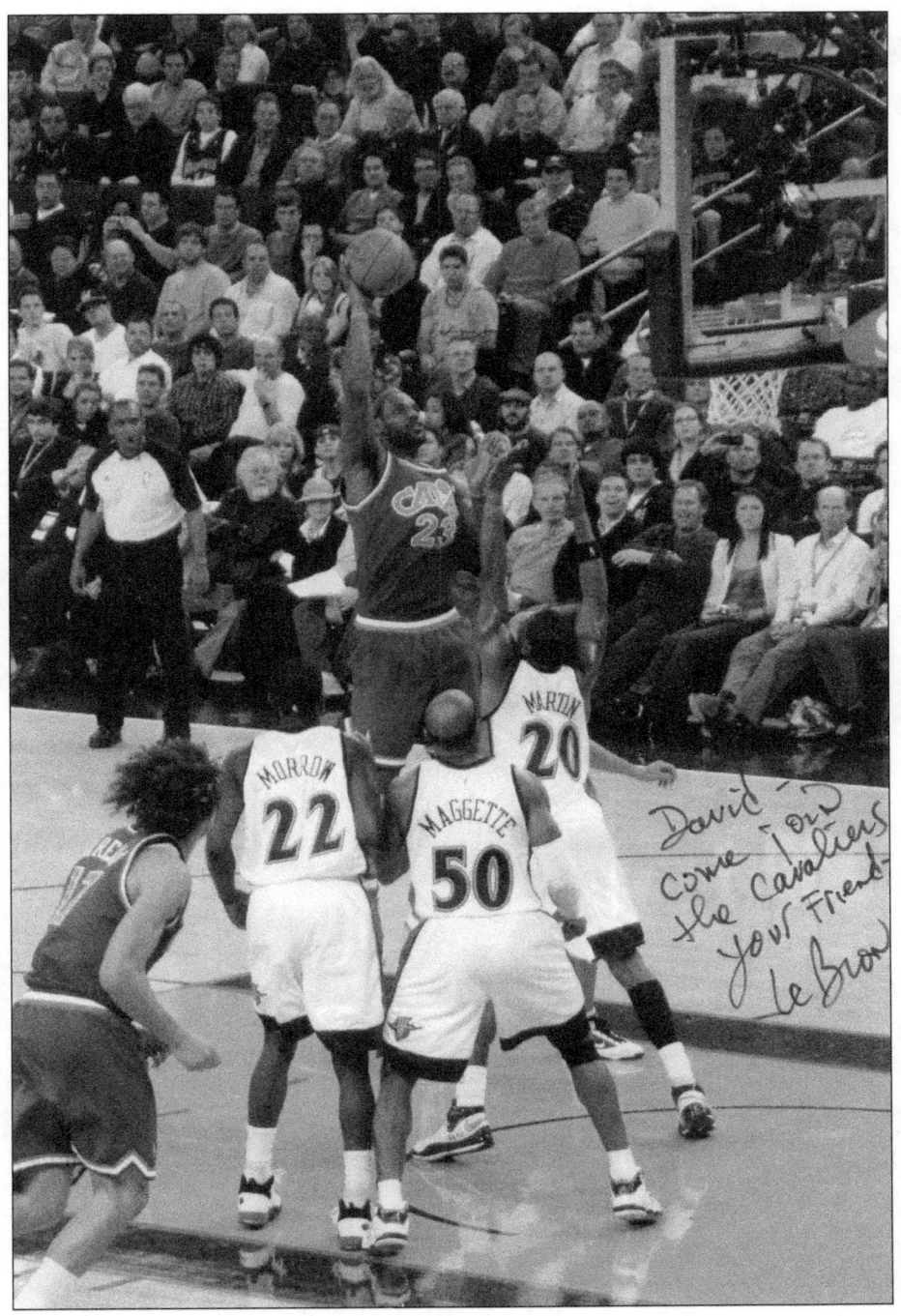

Michael Jordan
NBA Basketball Player

David-

I want you to play power forward
for the Chicago Bulls.

    Mike

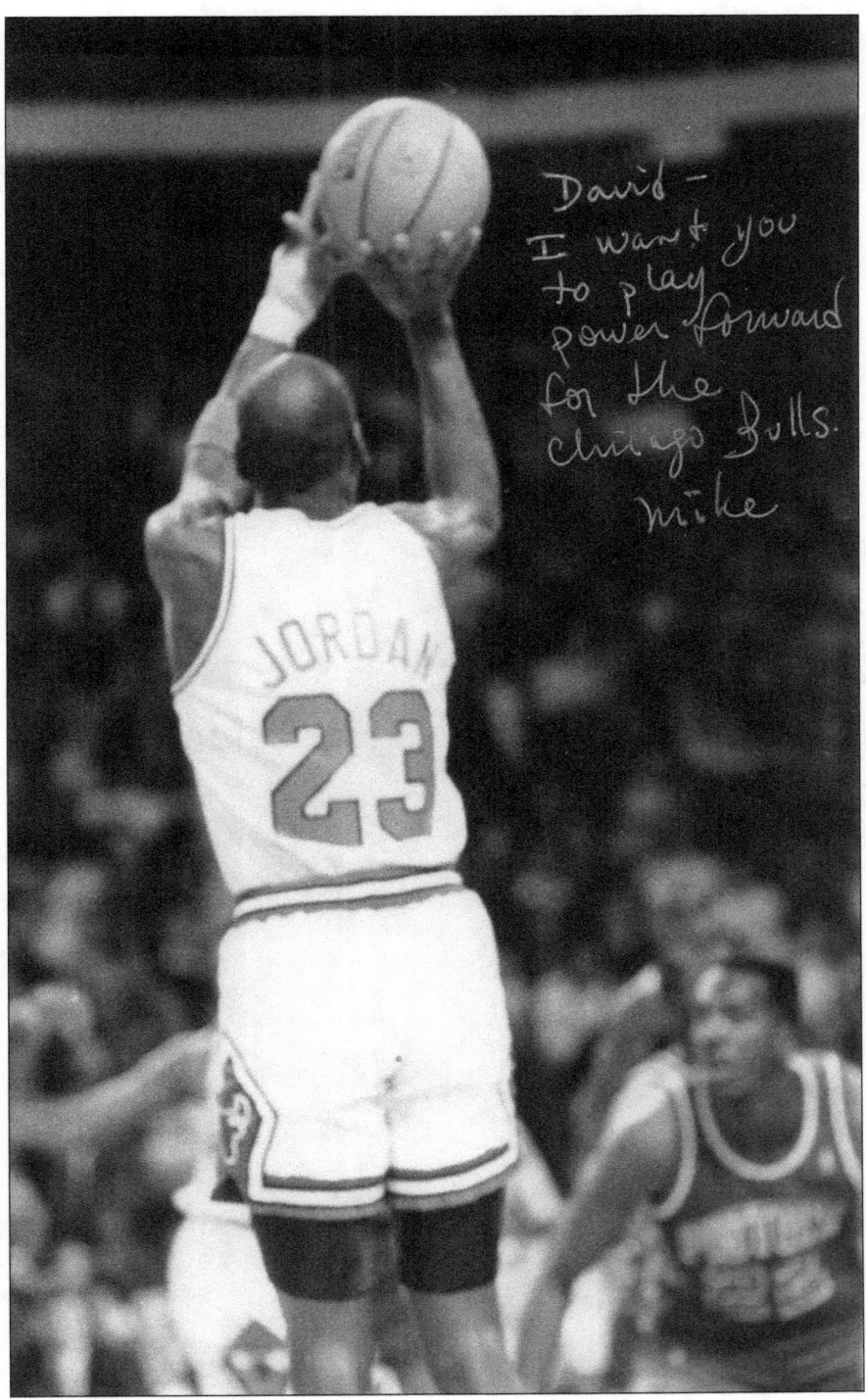

Pat Summitt
NCAA Women's Basketball Coach

David–
I'd like you to be my 1st assistant coach.

    Your friend,
    Pat Summitt

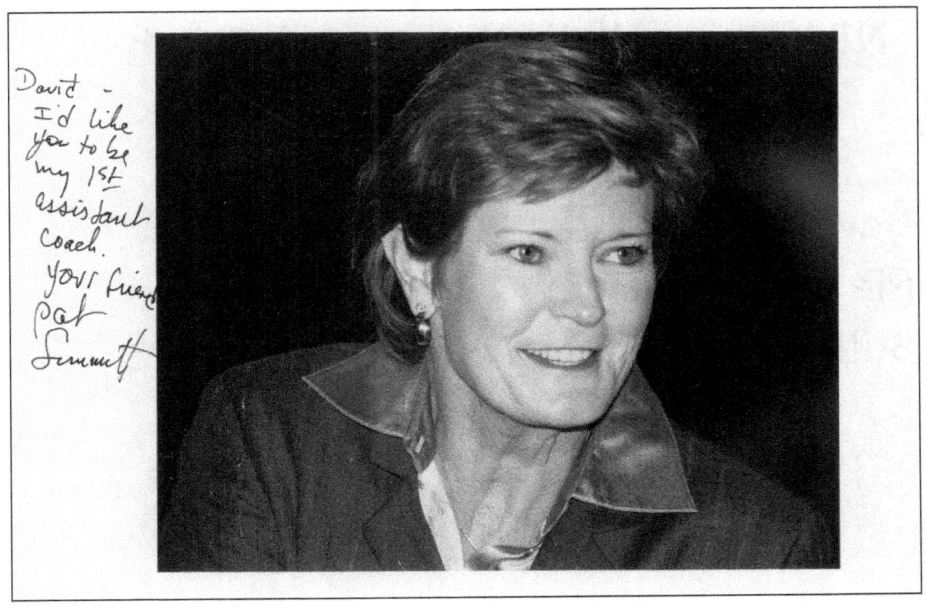

Dan't -
I'd like
you to be
my 1st
assistant
coach.
your friend
Pat
Summitt

113

Phil Jackson
NBA Basketball Player and Coach

David–
Please reconsider & play for the
Bulls
 Your friend,
 Phil

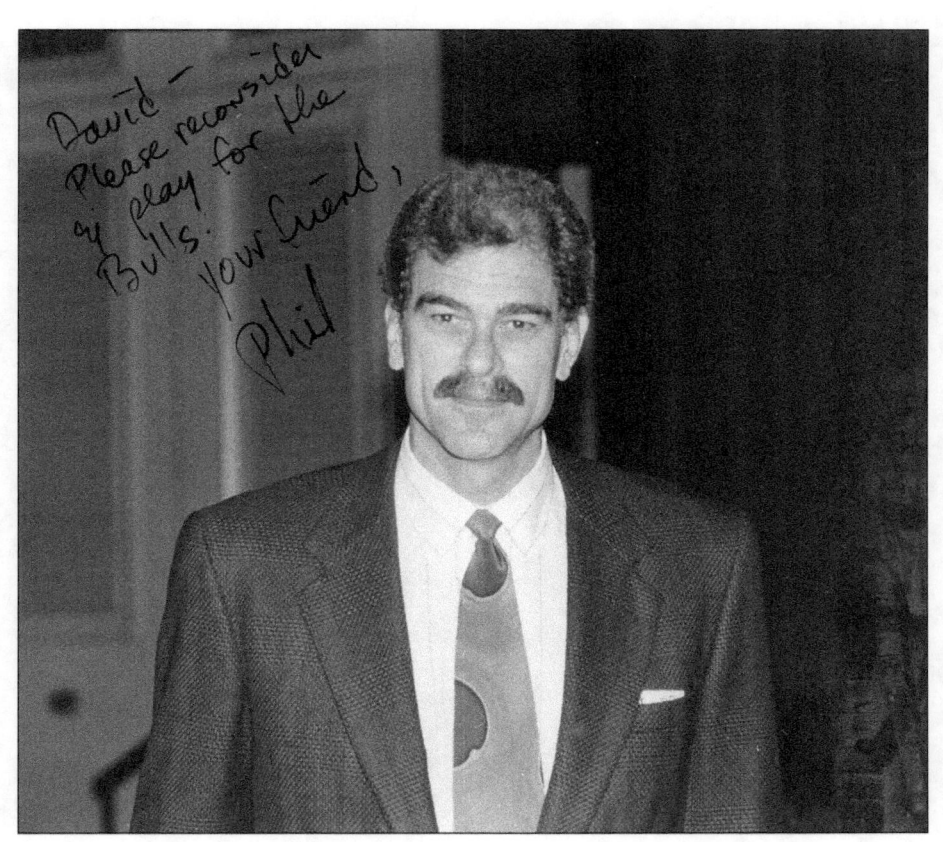

Scottie Pippin
NBA Basketball Player

David–
Please play for the Bulls
     Your buddy,
     Scottie

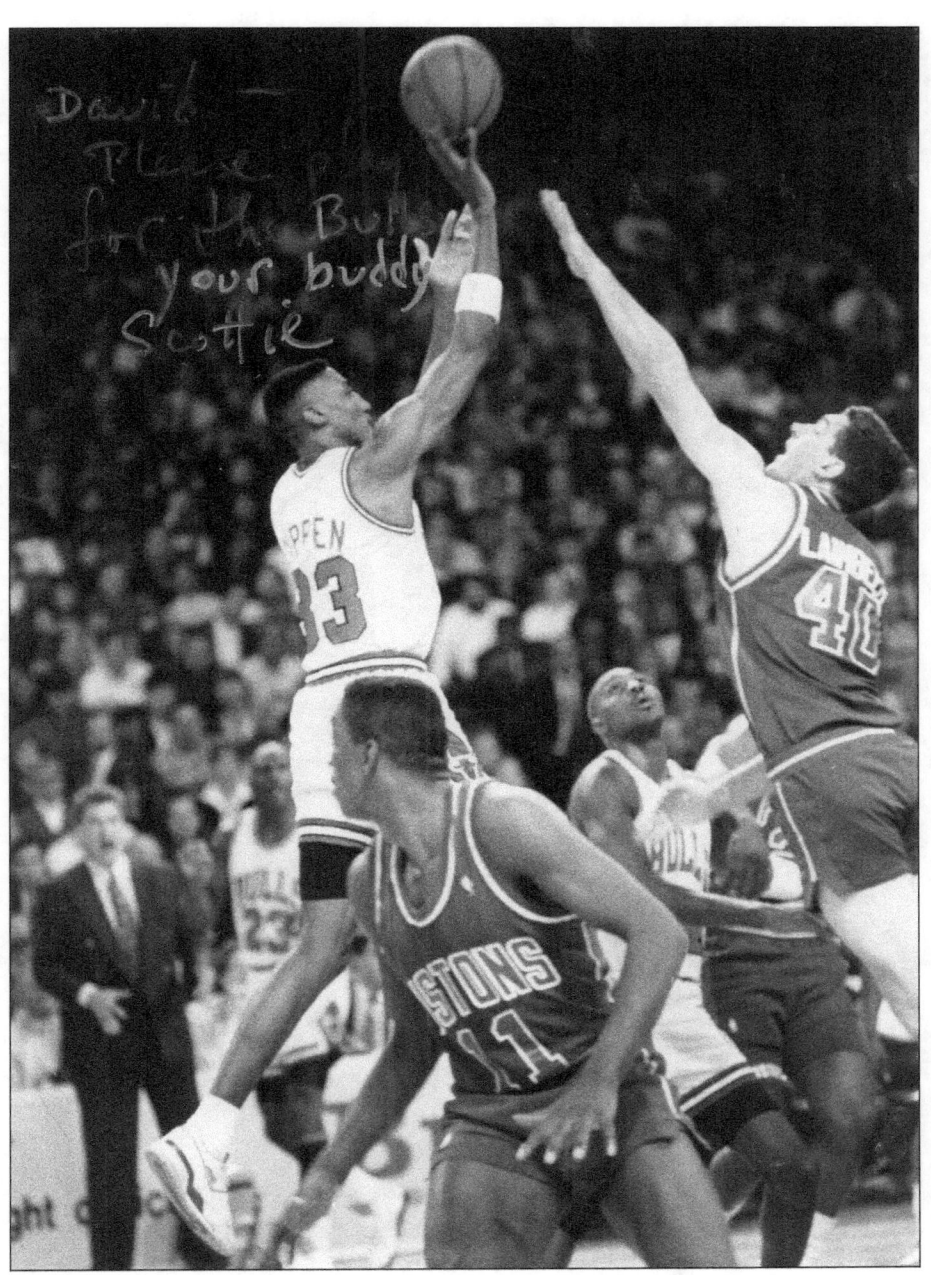

Shaquille O'Neal
NBA Basketball Player

David,
You're my MVP!
    Shaq

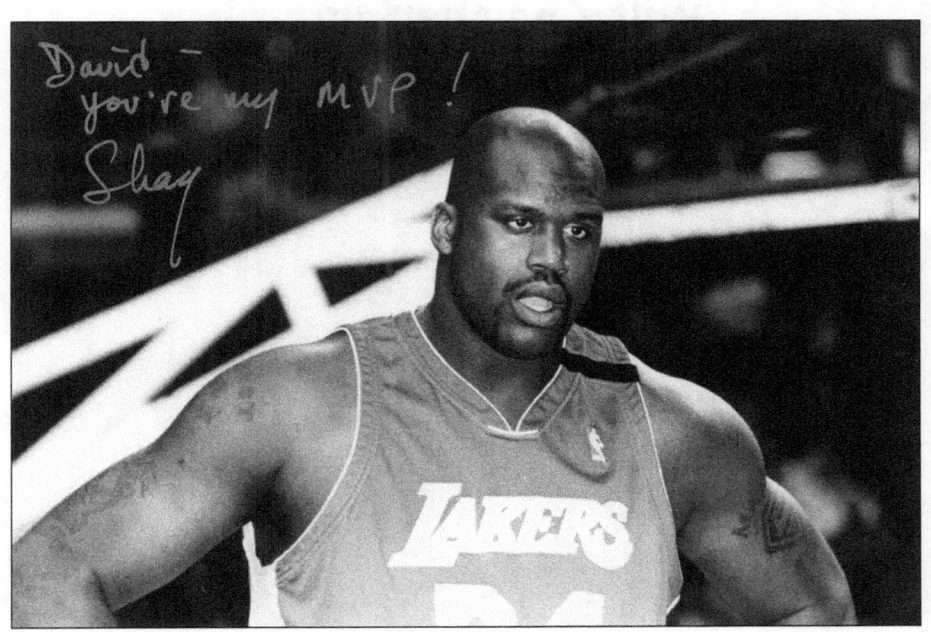

Wilt Chamberlain
NBA Basketball and Professional
Volleyball Player

David–
Be my volleyball partner.
    Wilt

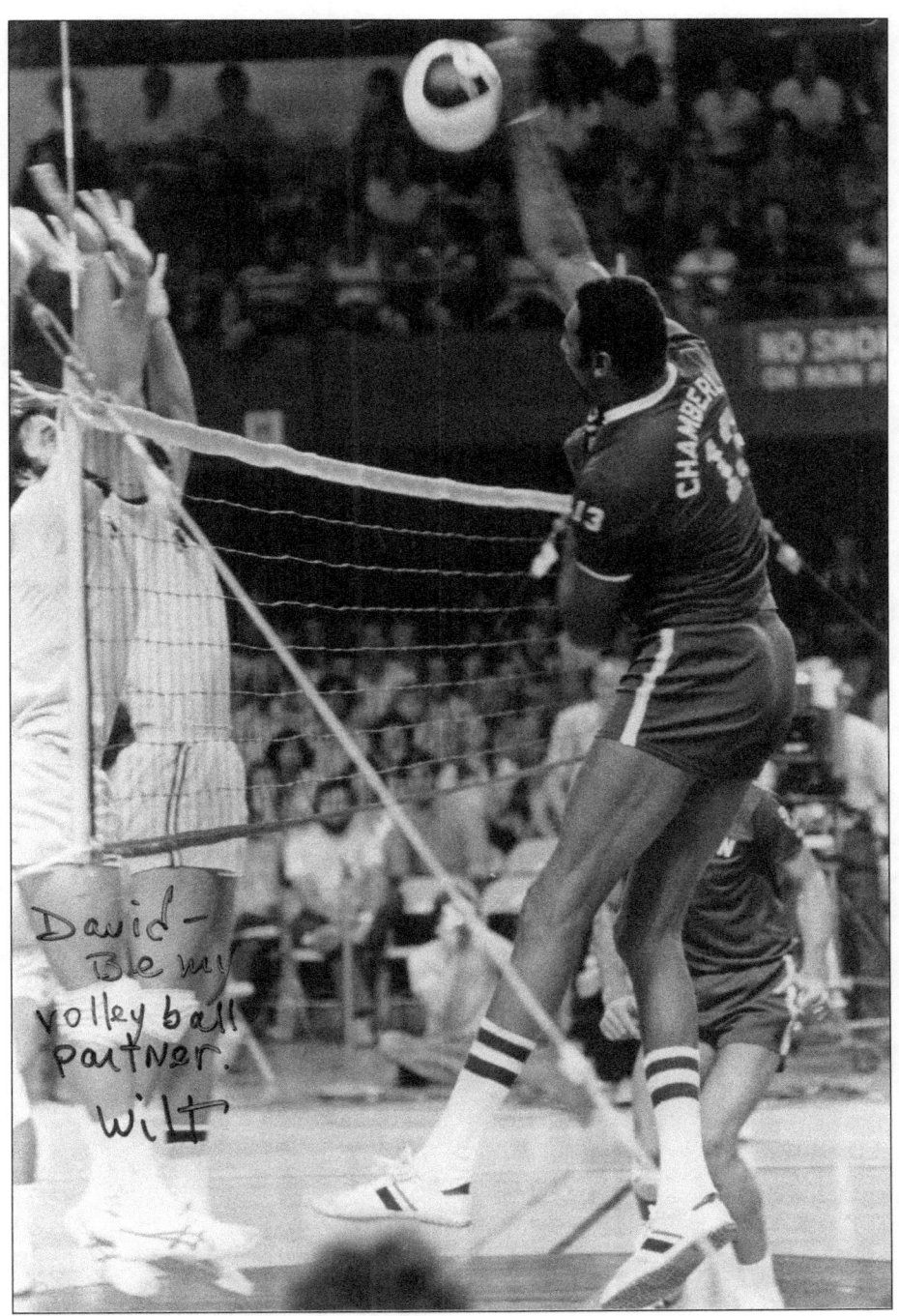

David—
Be my
volley ball
partner.
Wilt

ATHLETES FOOTBALL

Brian Urlacher
NFL Football Player

For David-
    Brian Urlacher

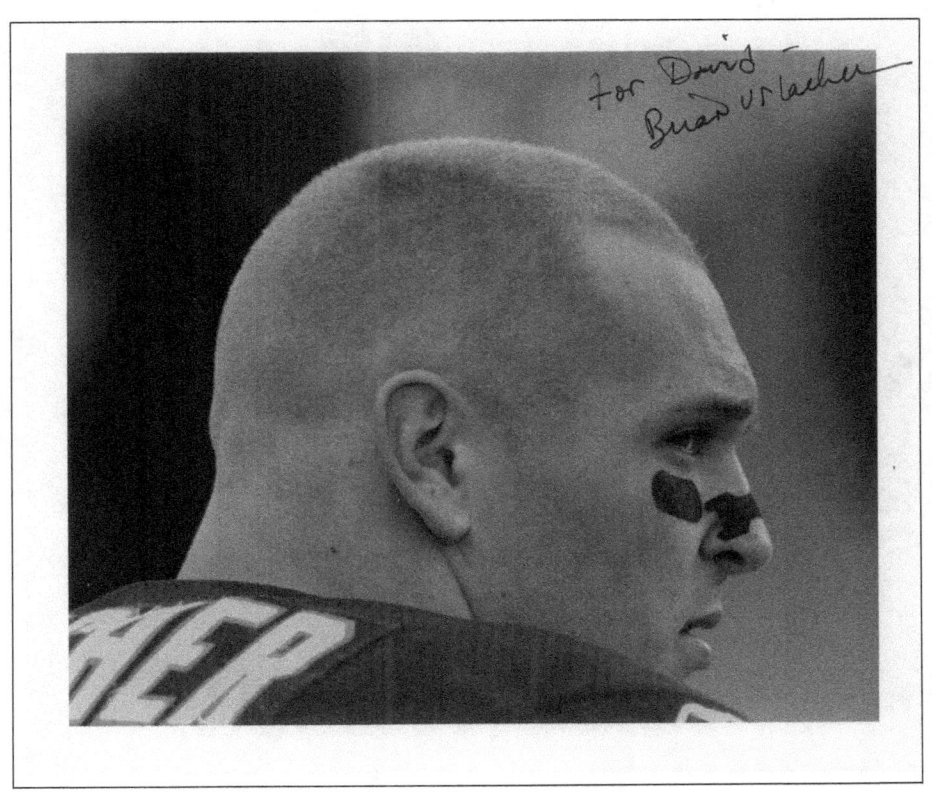

125

Dave Wannstedt
NFL Football Coach

David,
I still wish you would play fullback
for the Bears.
    Your friend,
    Dave

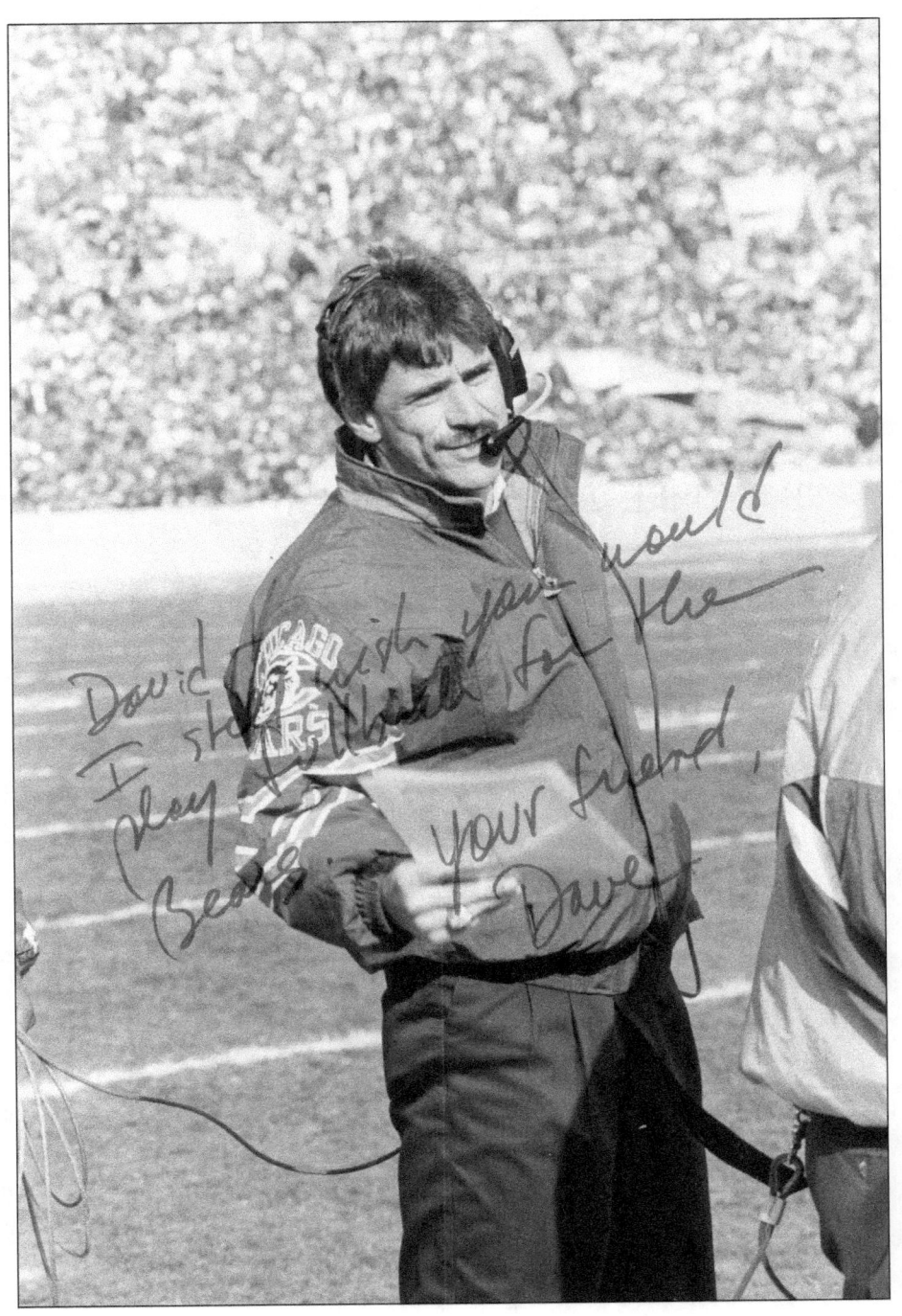

Gale Sayers
NFL Football Player

David–
You are the best halfback I've ever
seen.
Best,
Gale

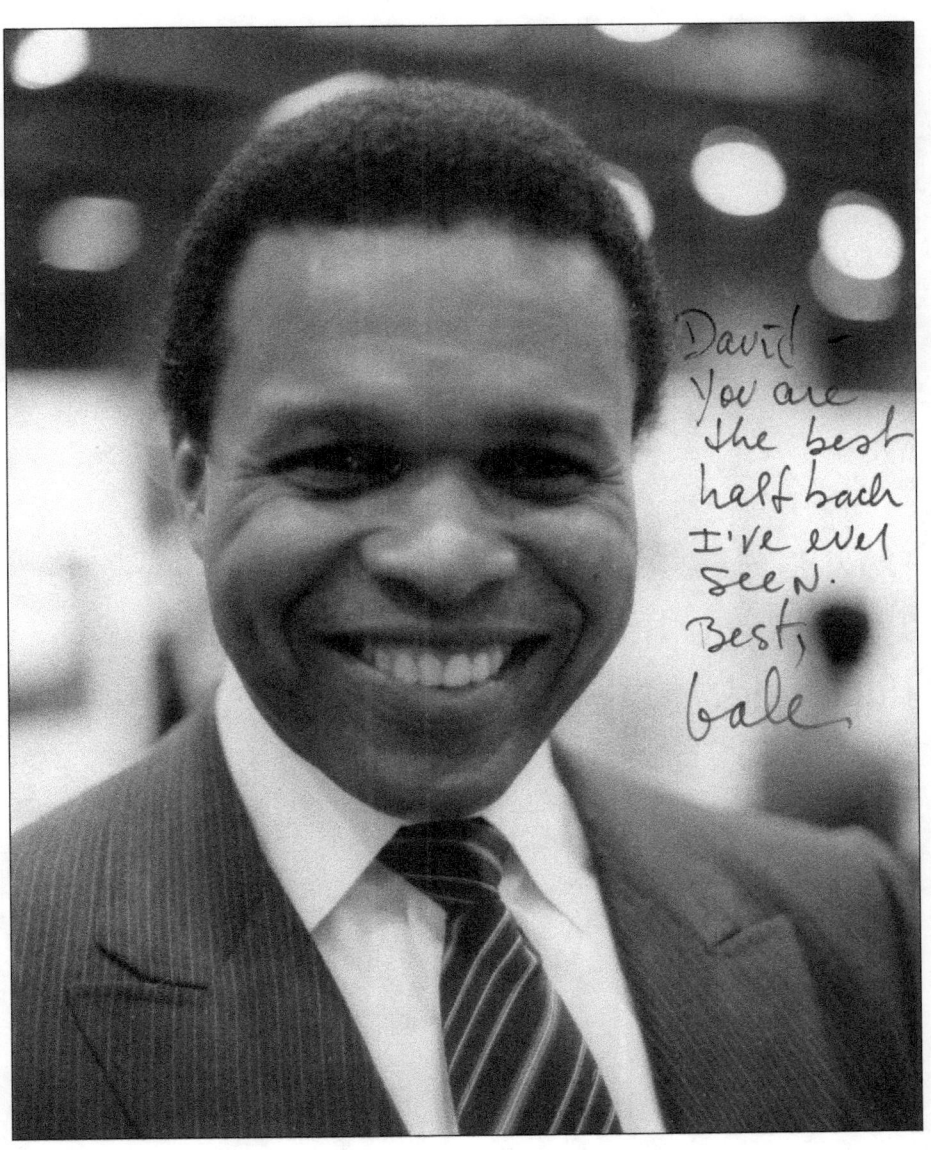

David –
You are
the best
half back
I've ever
seen.
Best,
Gale

Garo Yepremian
NFL Football Player

David–

I wish you had been in our Miami backfield.

Your friend,
Garo

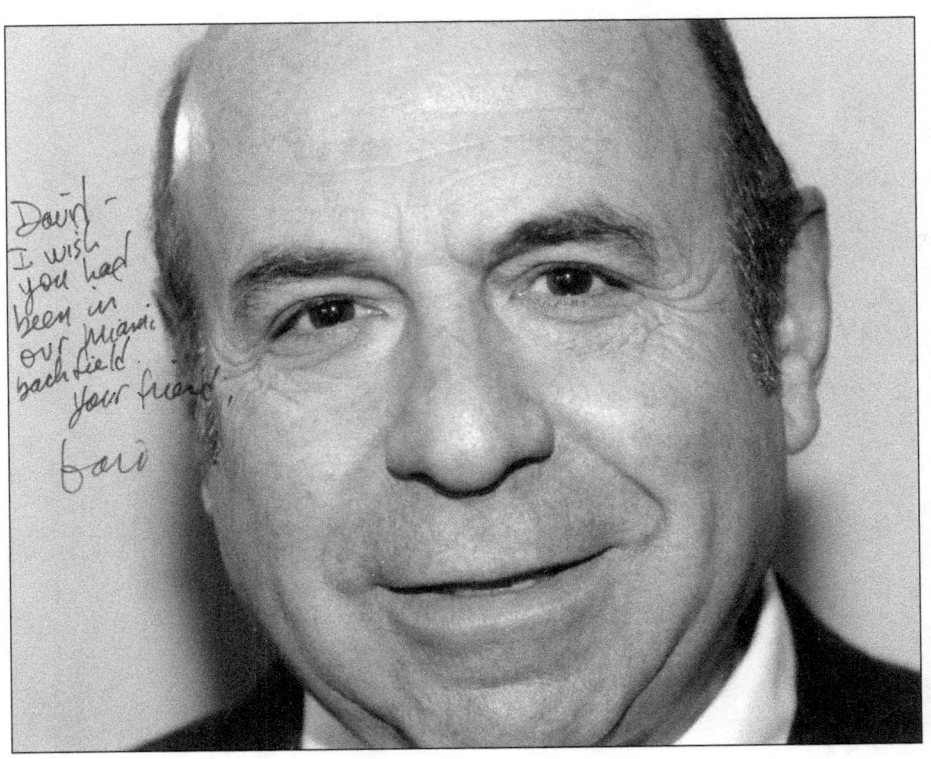

David —
I wish
you had
been in
our Miami
backfield.
Your friend,
Dan

Jerry Rice
NFL Football Player

David,
I want you on my team!
    Your friend,
    Jerry

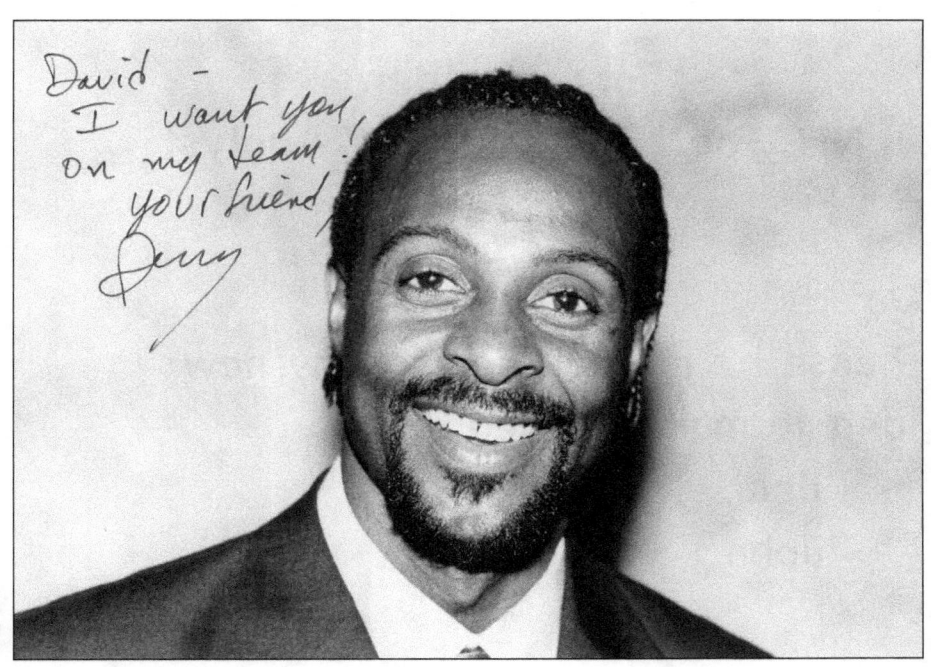

David –
I want you,
on my team!
your friend,
Jerry

John Madden
NFL Football Coach, TV Analyst

David–
Please be my partner for my new
idea to make a video game.
    Best,
    John

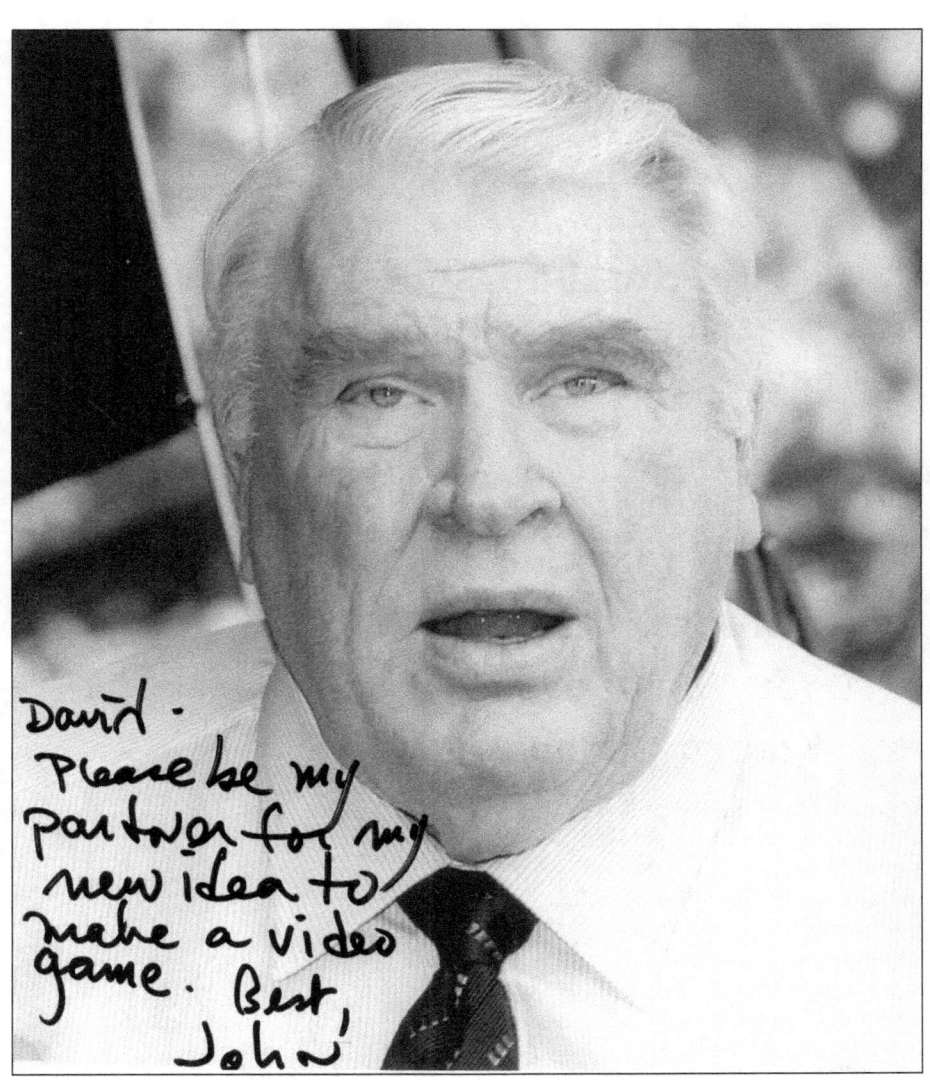

David -
Please be my
partner for my
new idea to
make a video
game. Best,
John

Kassim Osgood
NFL Football Player

David–
Thank you for your open field tack-
ling pointers.
    Your best friend,
    Kassim Osgood

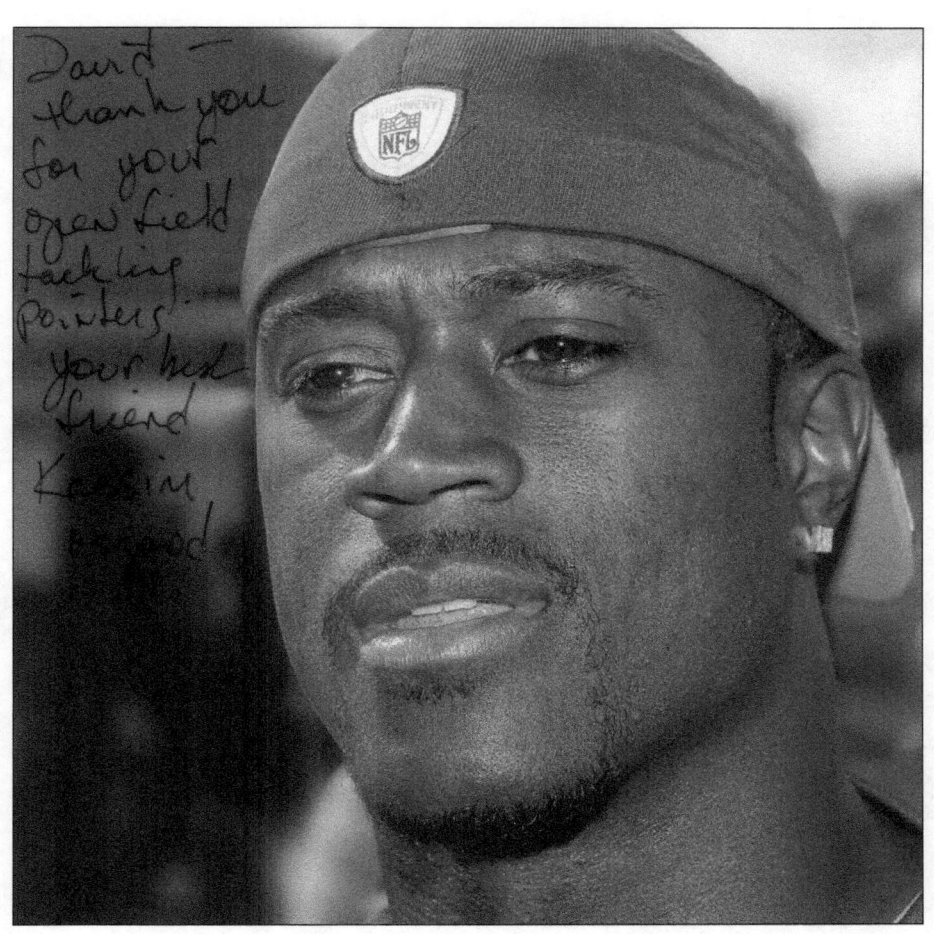

Keyshawn Johnson
NFL Football Player

David–
I'll play for your team anytime.
   Keyshawn

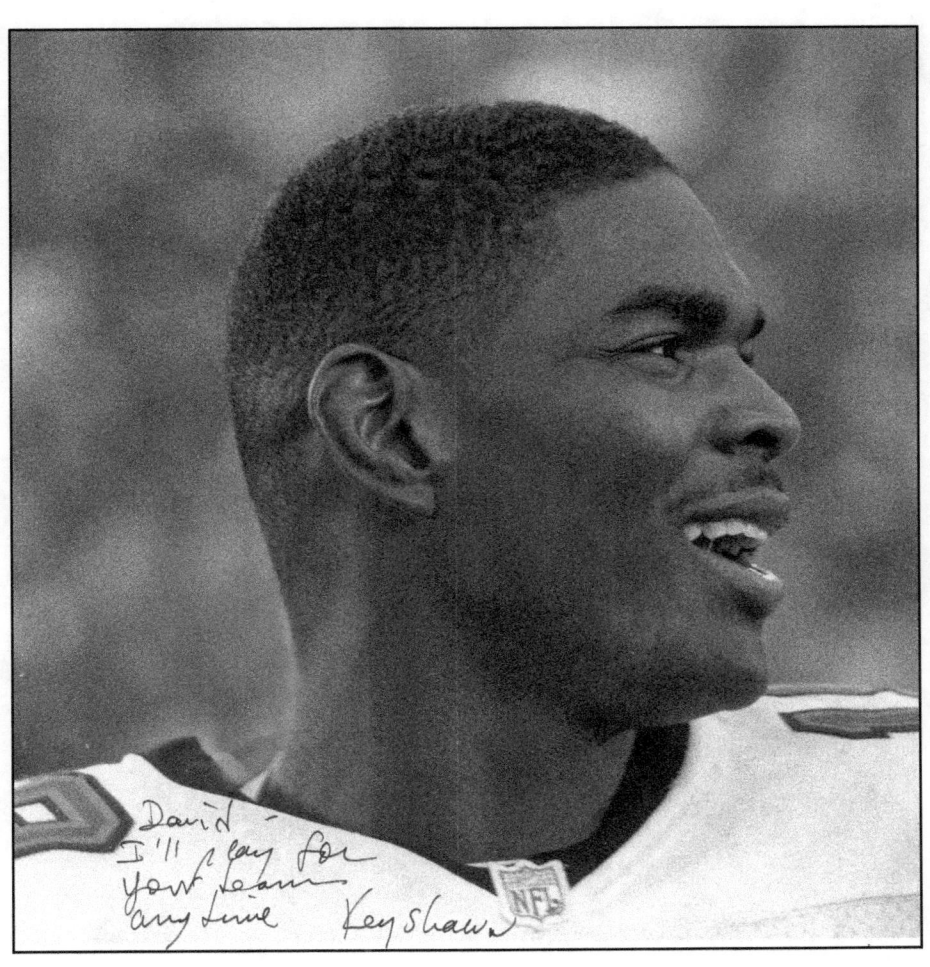

Lou Holtz
NCAA Football Coach

David,
I want you to coach Notre Dame this
year.
    Your friend,
    Lou

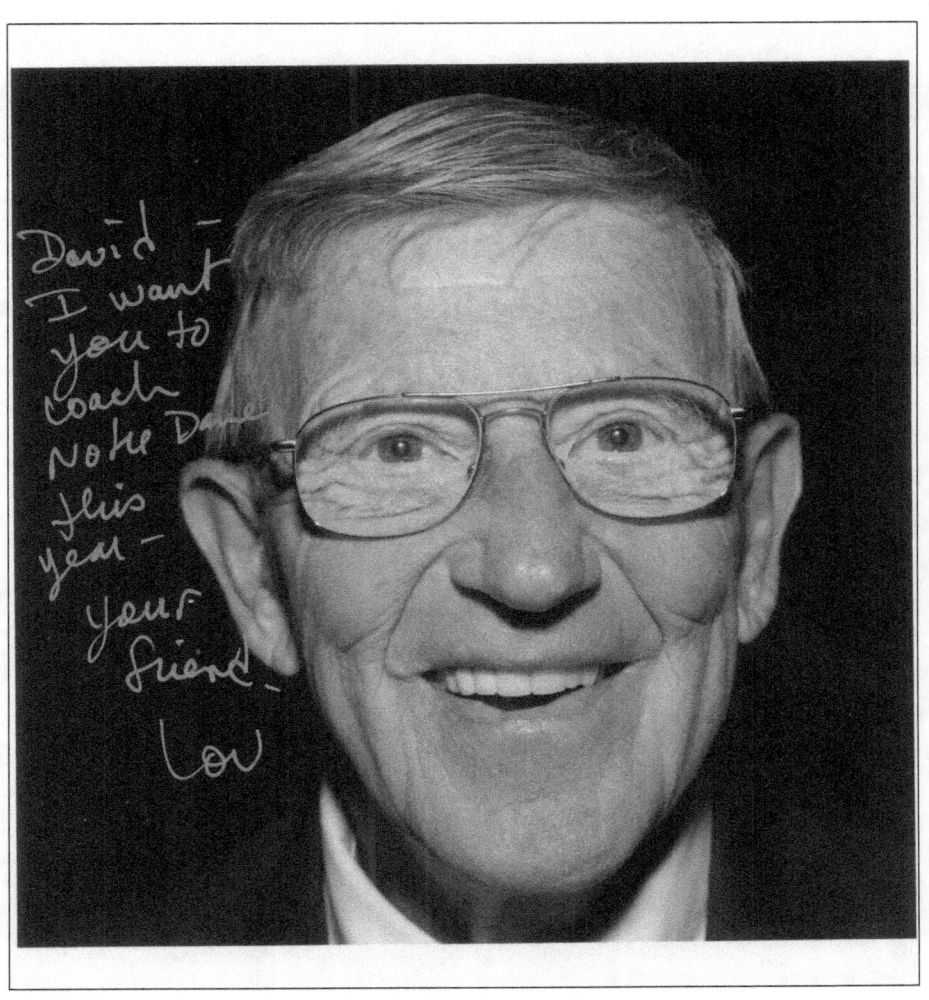

141

Matt Leinert
NFL Football Player

David–
I would rather have you in my back-
field than Reggie Bush. .
   Your friend,
   Matt

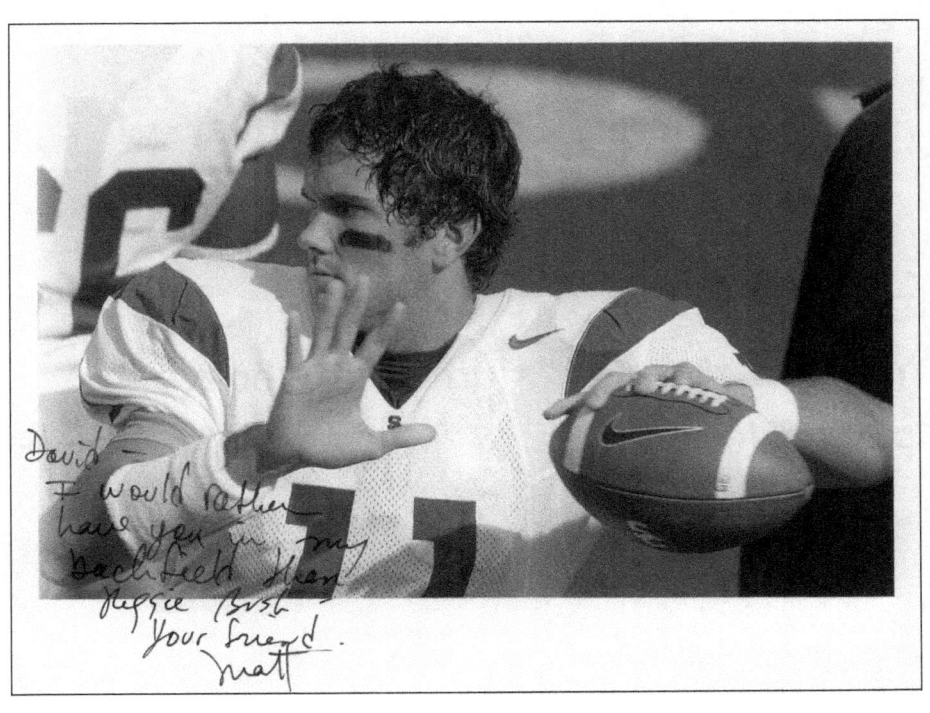

David —
I would rather
have you in my
backfield than
Reggie Bush
Your friend —
Matt

Mike Ditka
NFL Player, Coach & Analyst

David–
You are the best tight end whoever played in the NFL.
　　　Mike

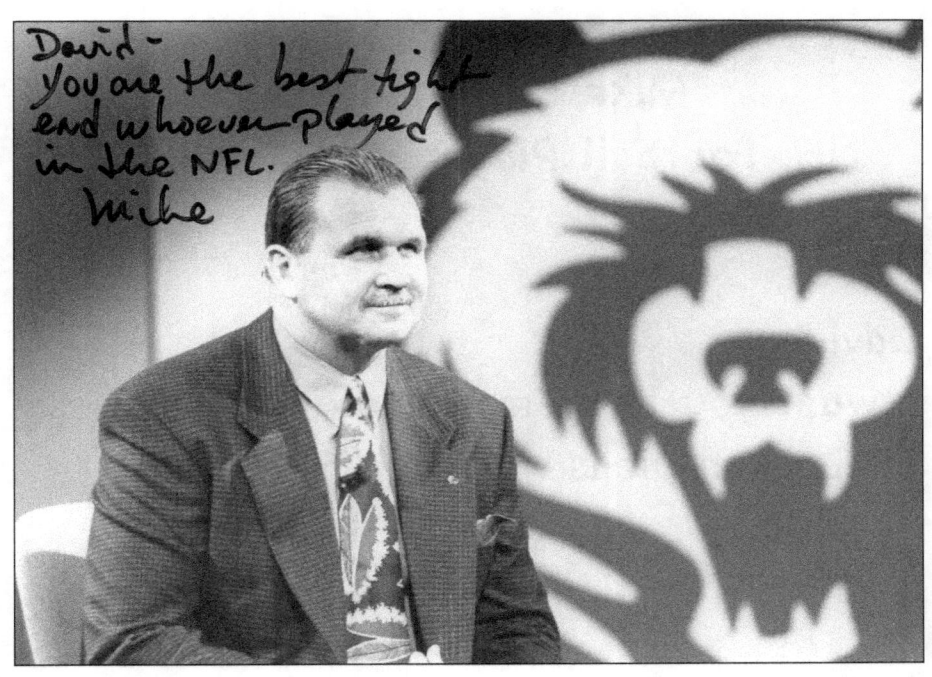

David –
You are the best tight
end whoever played
in the NFL.
Mike

Mike Singletary
NFL Football Player and Coach

David–
I want you to be my middle
linebacker–please report ASAP.
　　Mike

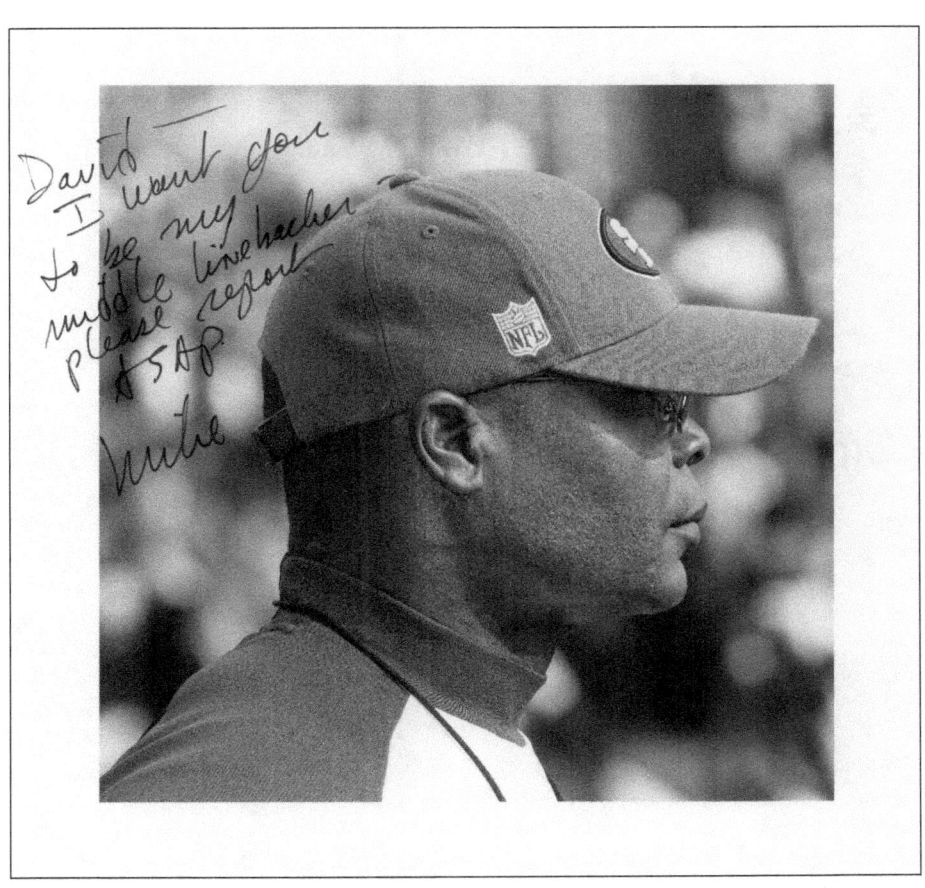

David —
I want you
to be my
middle linebacker.
Please report
ASAP.

Mike

Robert Griffin, III
NFL Football Player

David,

Come to D.C. & be my tight end.

Your buddy,

RGIII

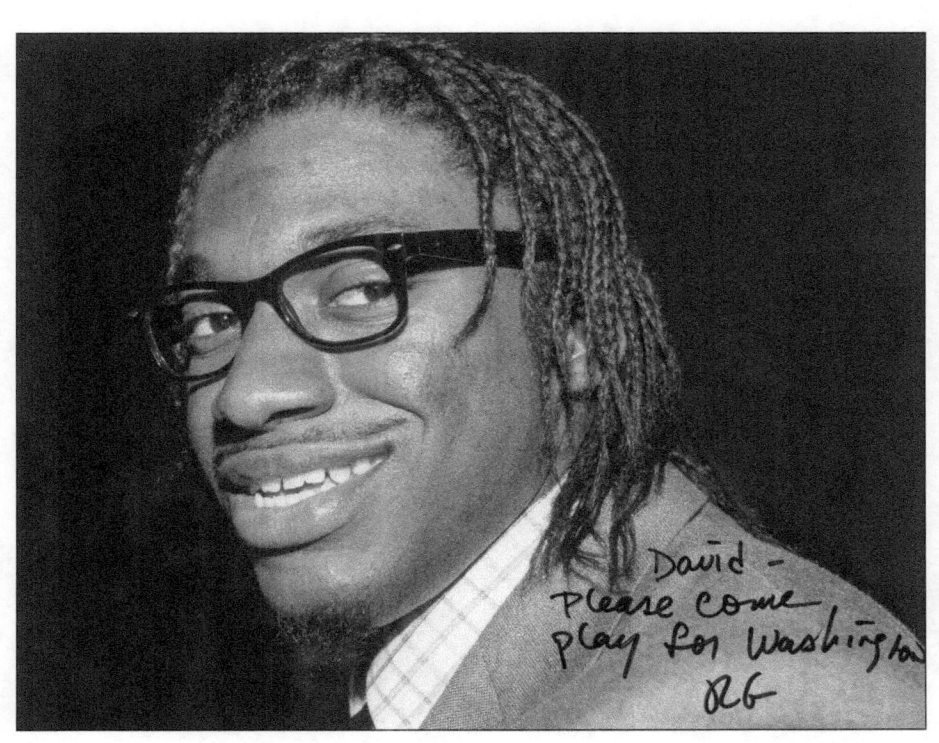

Steve Young
NFL Football Player

David–
I want you to be the 49ers wide
receiver.
        Steve

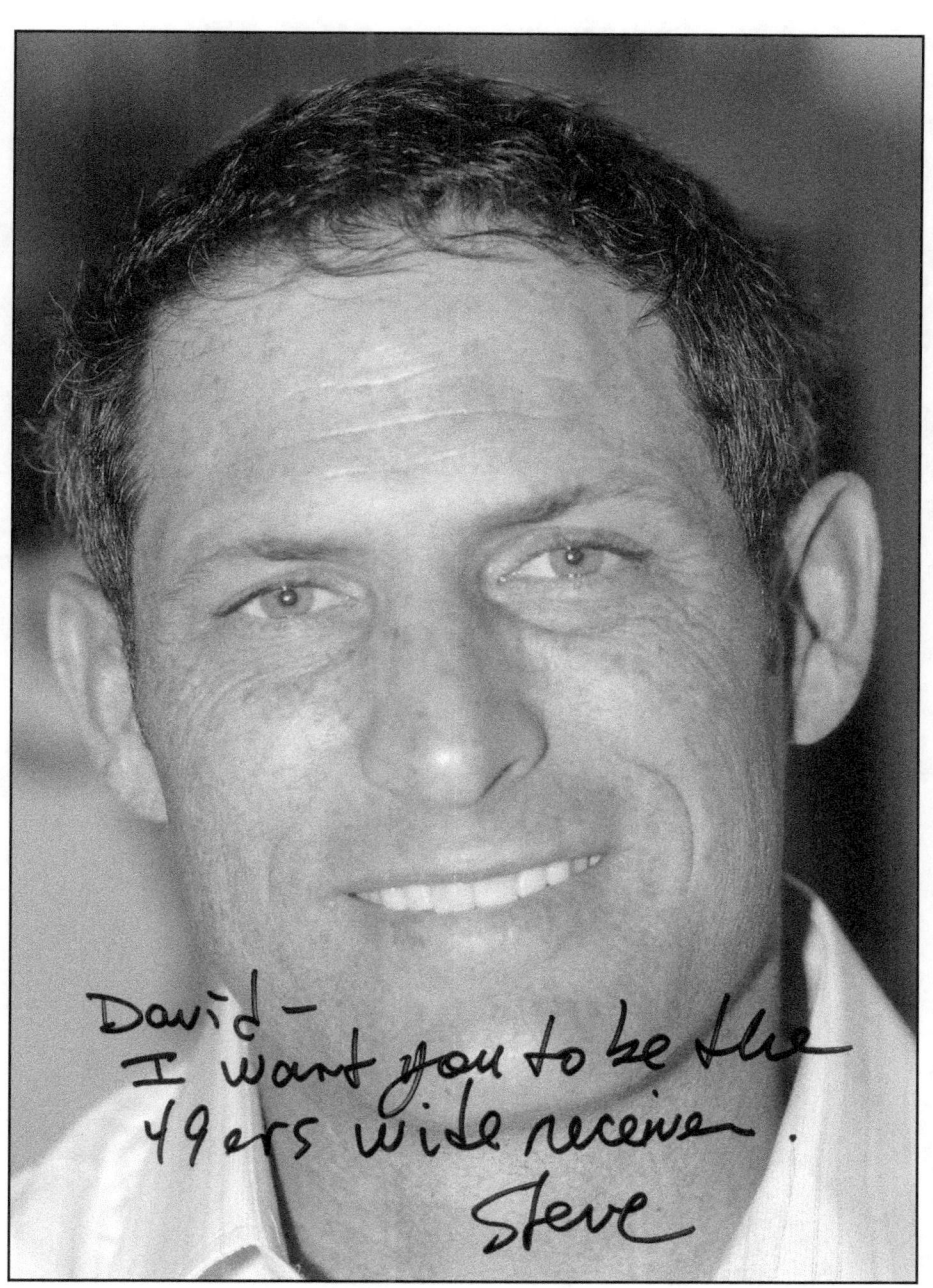

David —
I want you to be the
49ers wide receiver.
Steve

Tom Dempsey
NFL Football Player

David–

I'd like to give you a couple of kicking pointers.

Your friend,

Tom

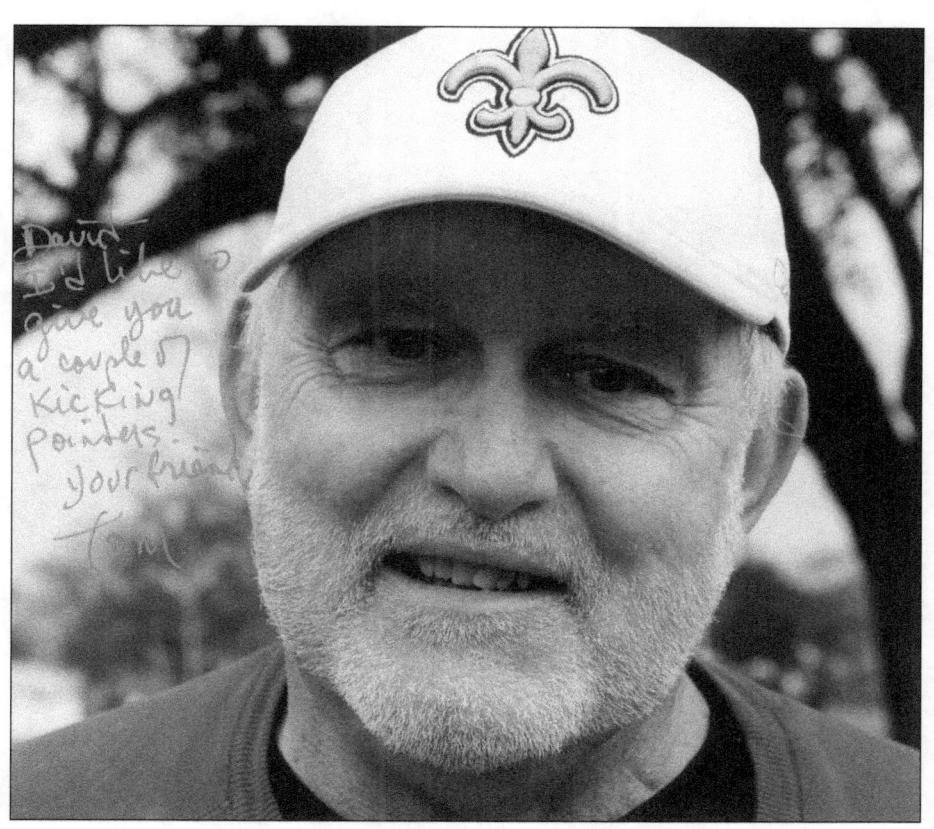

AUTHORS

Carl Djerassi
Oral Contraceptive Developer,
Playwright

David–
I need your help with a male birth control pill I've developed.
> Your friend,
> Carl

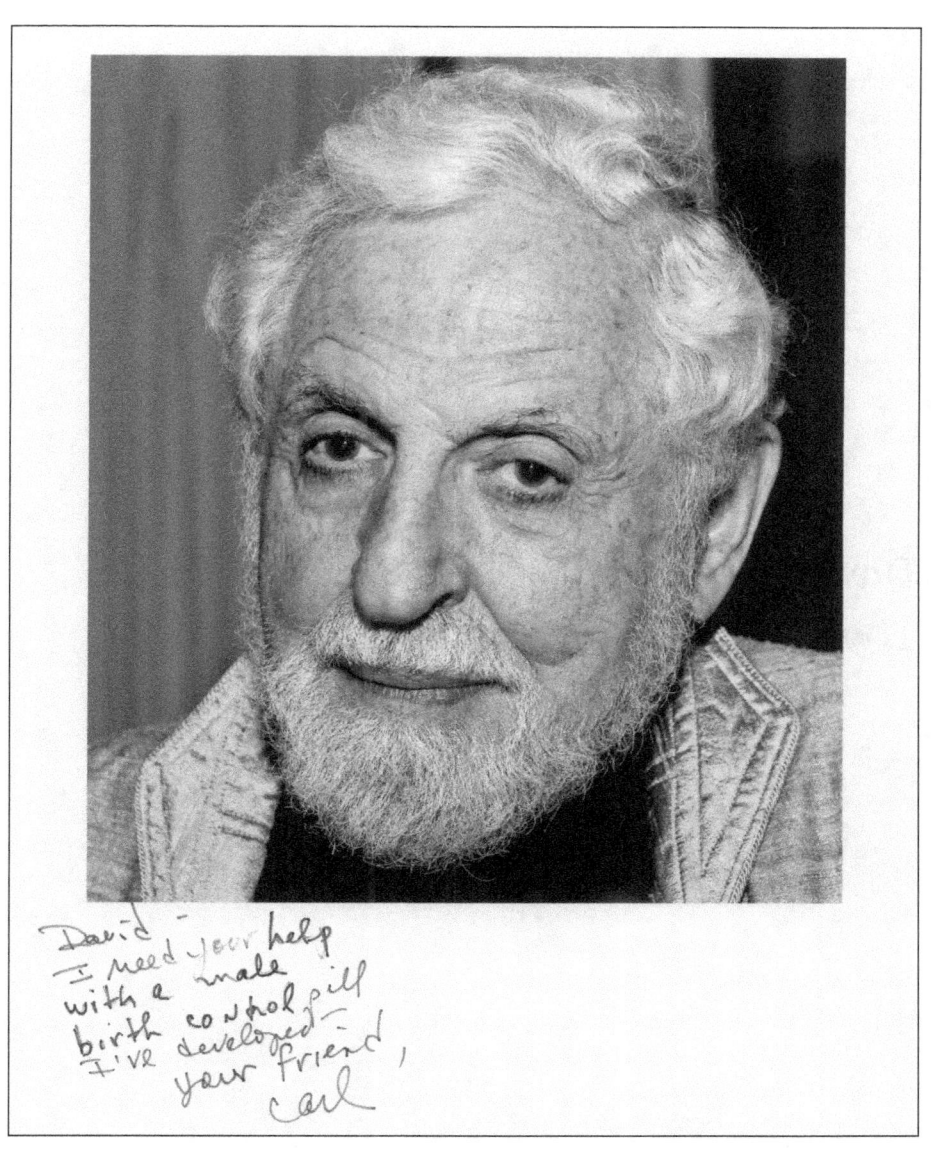

David –
your help
I need
with a male
birth control pill
I've developed –
your friend,
Carl

157

Chesley Sullenberger
Commercial Pilot, Author

David–
I want you to be my co-pilot.
    Your friend,
    Sully

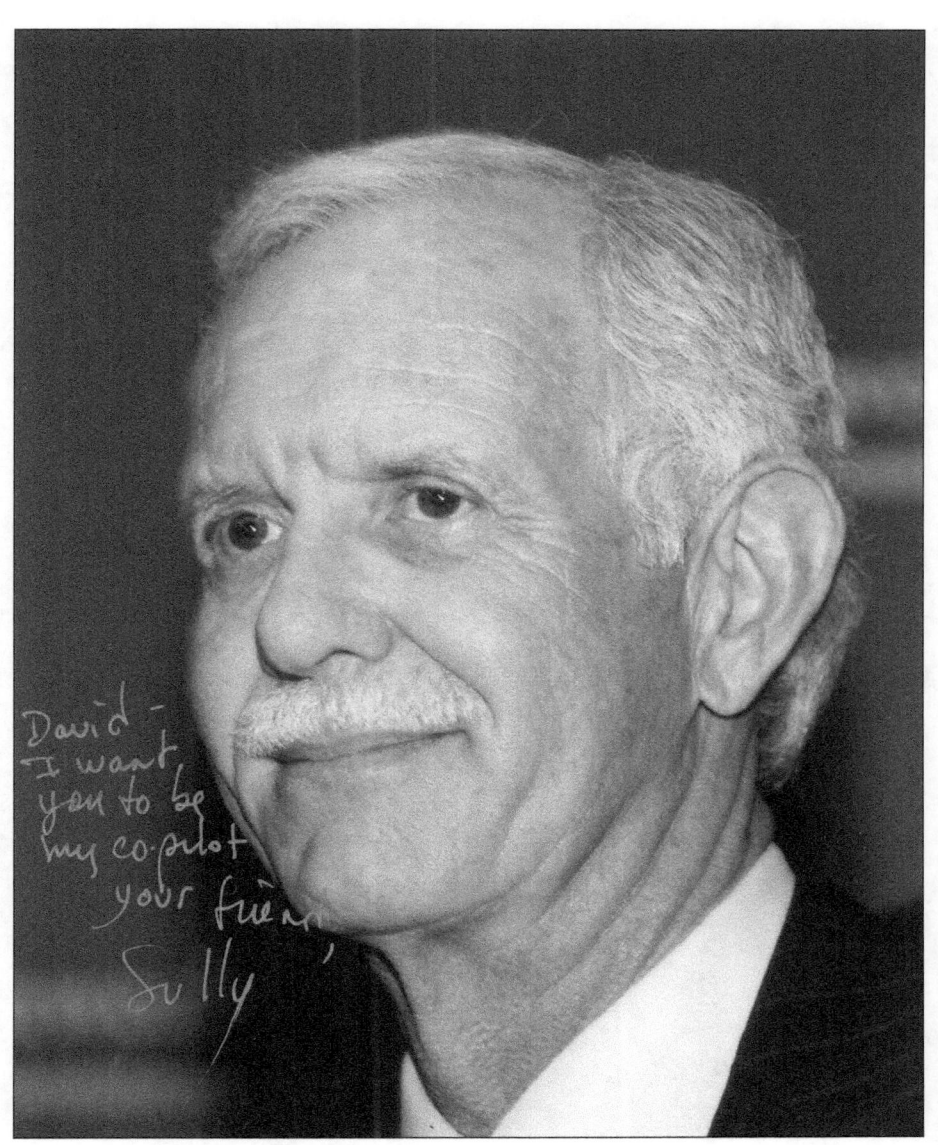

David –
I want
you to be
my co-pilot
your friend
Sully

Daniel Ellsberg
Activist, Author

David–
I need your help in obtaining some
secret info.
Your friend,
Danny

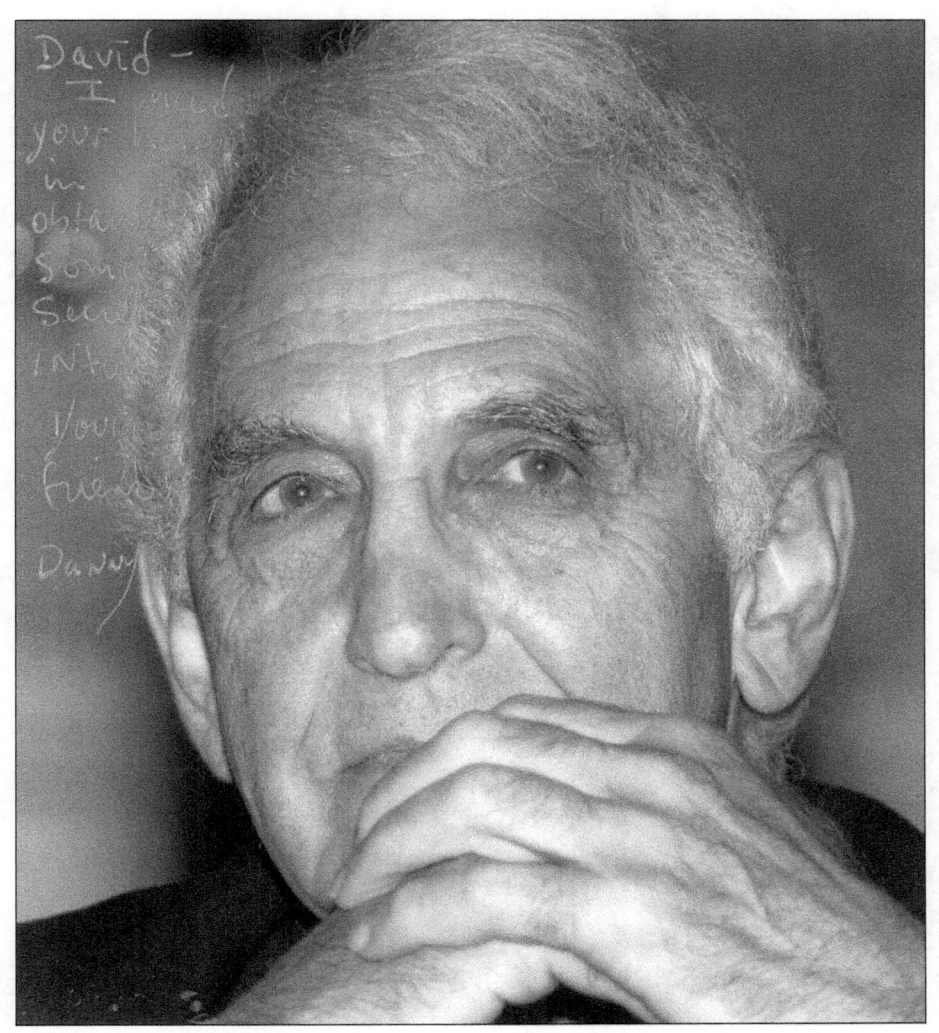

Garrison Keillor
Prairie Home Companion Host, Author

David–
I want you and your band on the next PHC.
     Garrison

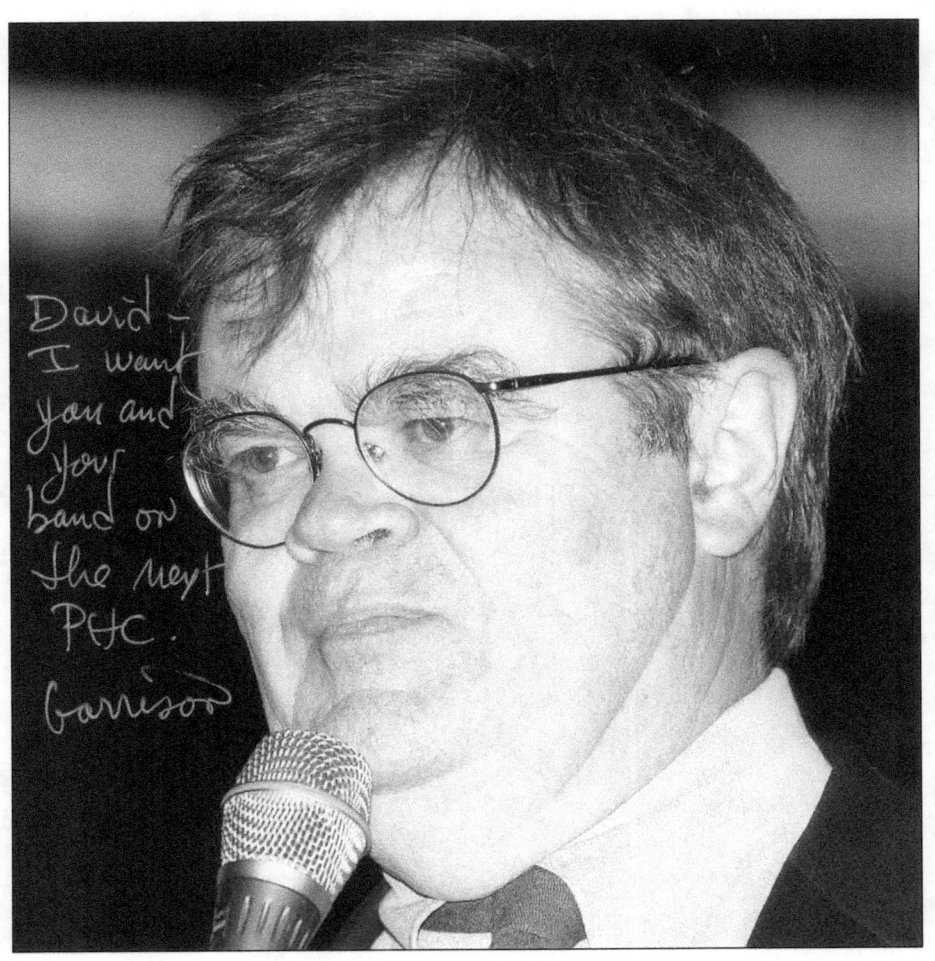

Gore Vidal
Author

David–
I need a few writing pointers from
you.
    Best,
    Gore

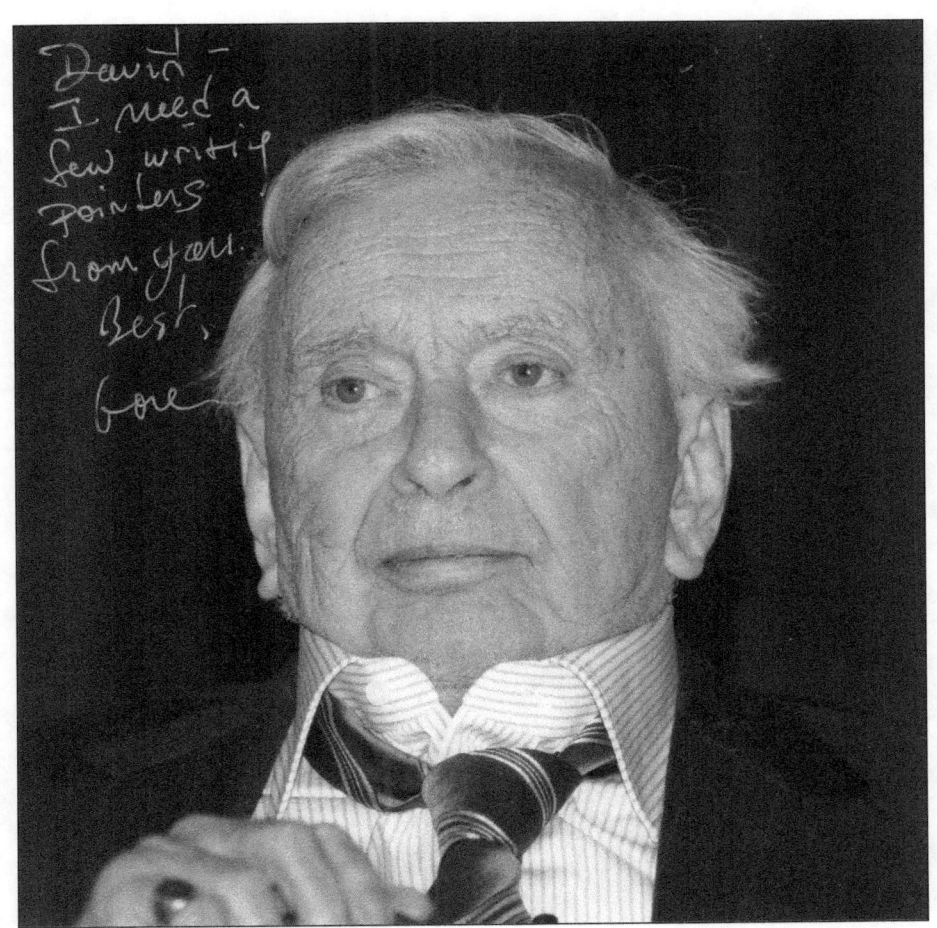

165

Larry Flynt
Publisher, Author

David,
I want you to take over the
magazine.
    Your friend,
    Larry

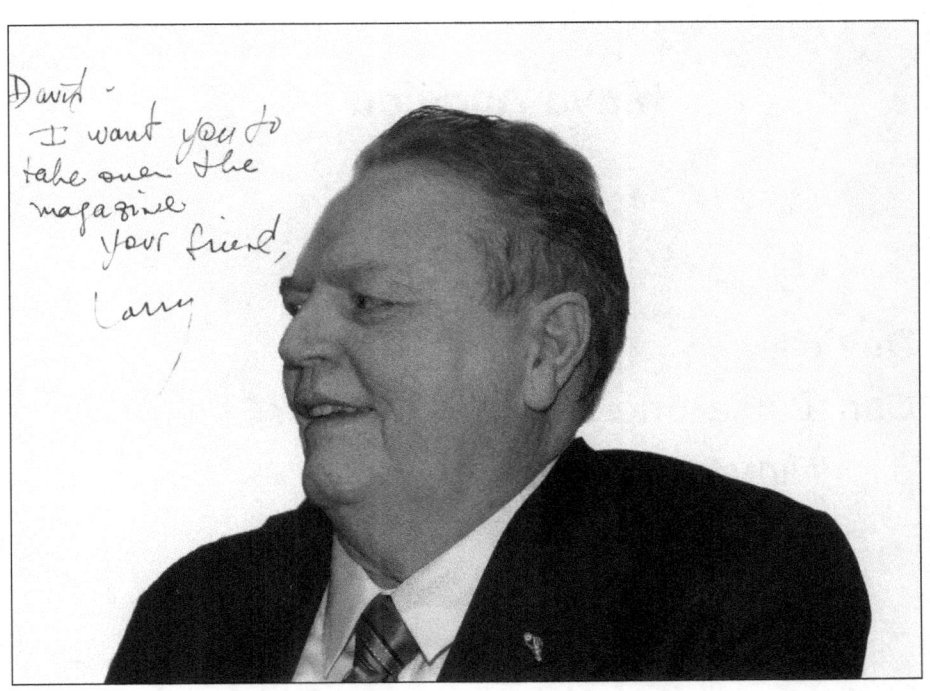

David -
I want you to
take over the
magazine
    your friend,

Larry

Maya Angelou
Poet

David–
Can I use one of your poems?
    Maya

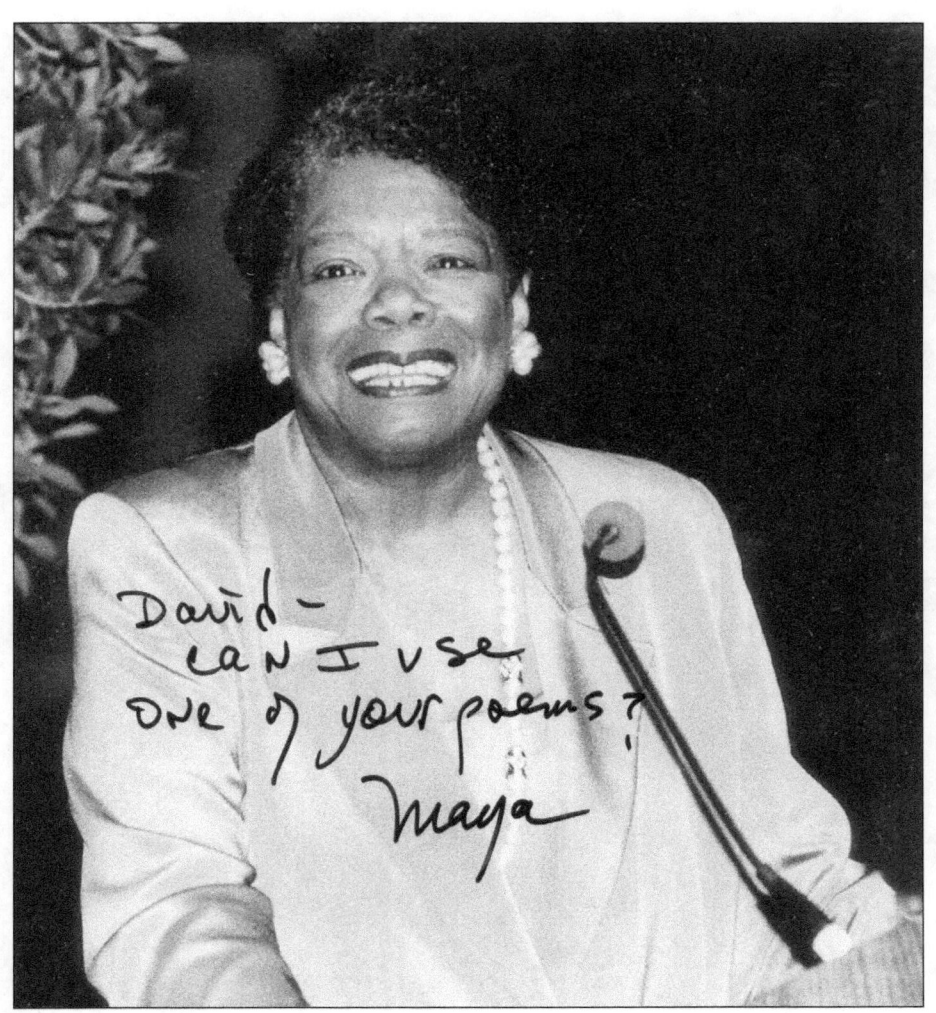

David —
can I use
one of your poems?
Maya

Phil Donahue
Television Host, Author

David–
I need you to please take over my
TV show.
     Phil

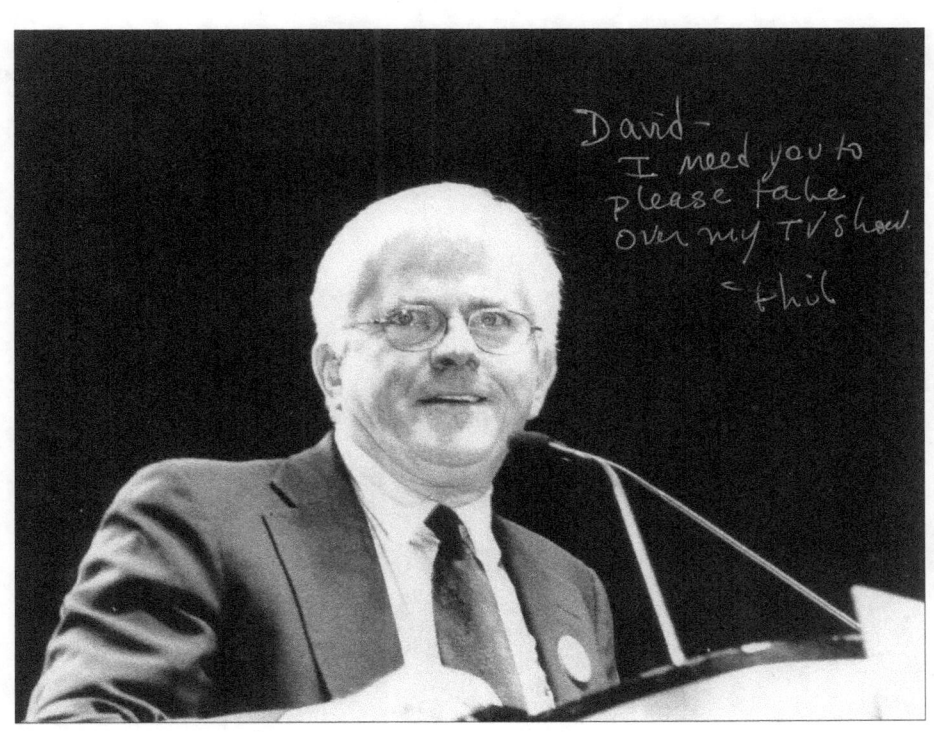

Robert Ballard
Explorer, Author

David–
Thanks for your help in finding
Titanic.
    Best,
    Bob

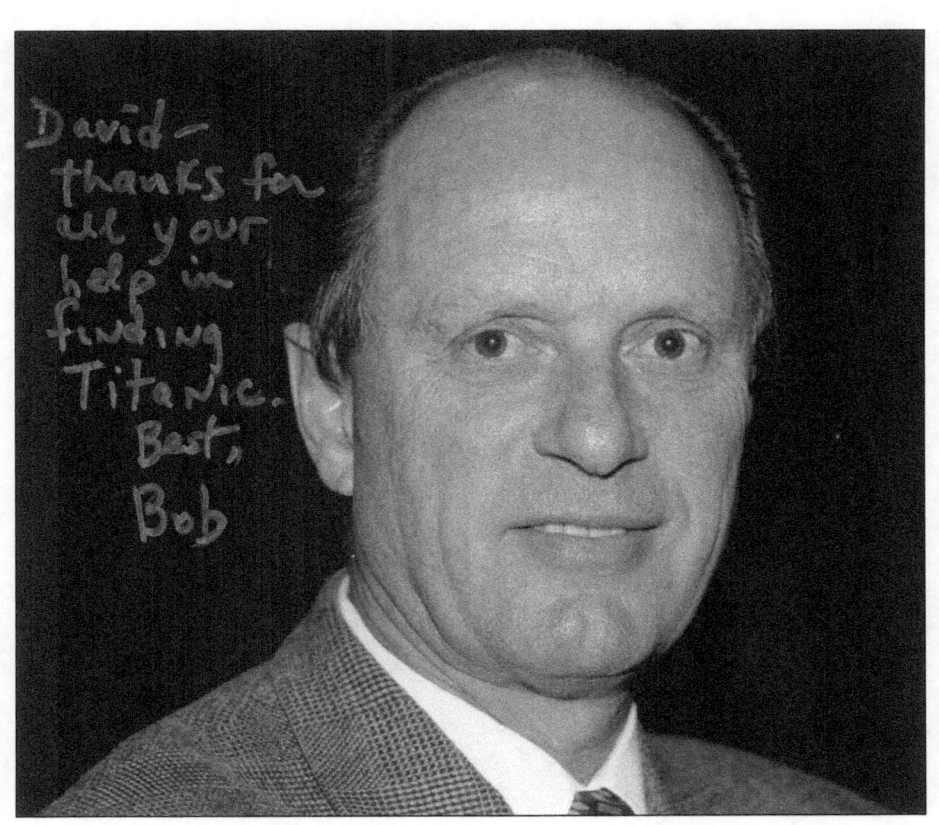

David —
thanks for
all your
help in
finding
Titanic.
Best,
Bob

Salman Rushdie
Author

David-
I'd like you to be my co-author on
my next book.
    Your friend,
    Salman

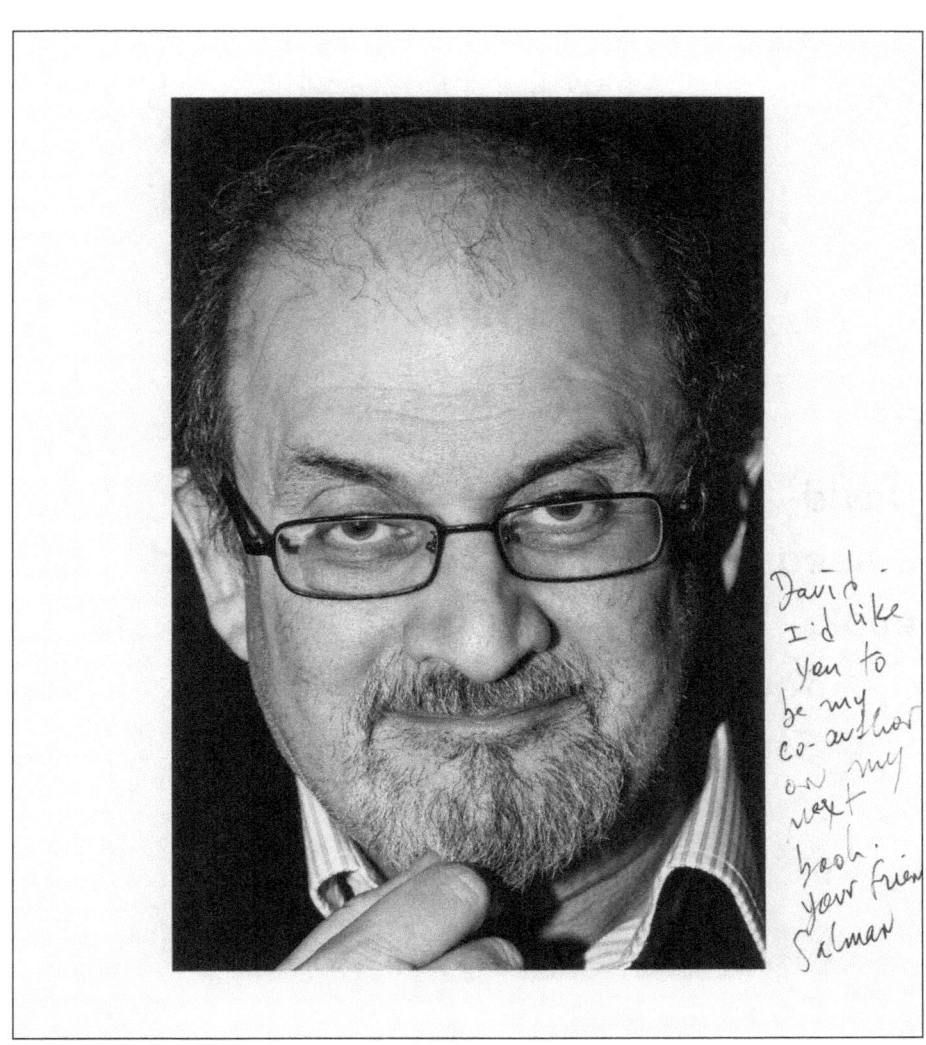

David -
I'd like
you to
be my
co-author
on my
next
book.
your frien[d]
Salman

175

Studs Terkel
Author

David–

I need you to ghost write my next book.

    Your buddy,
    Studs

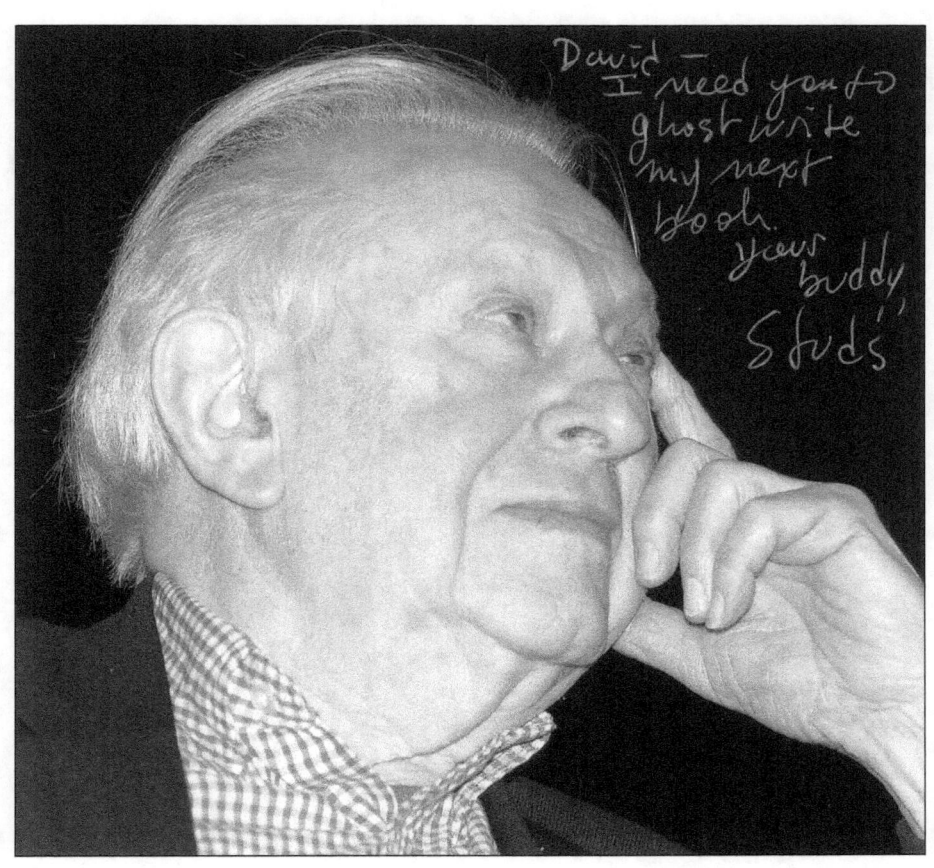

BUSINESS

Fred Smith
CEO & Founder Federal Express

David–
I want you to take over FedEx for
me.
 Your friend,
 Fred

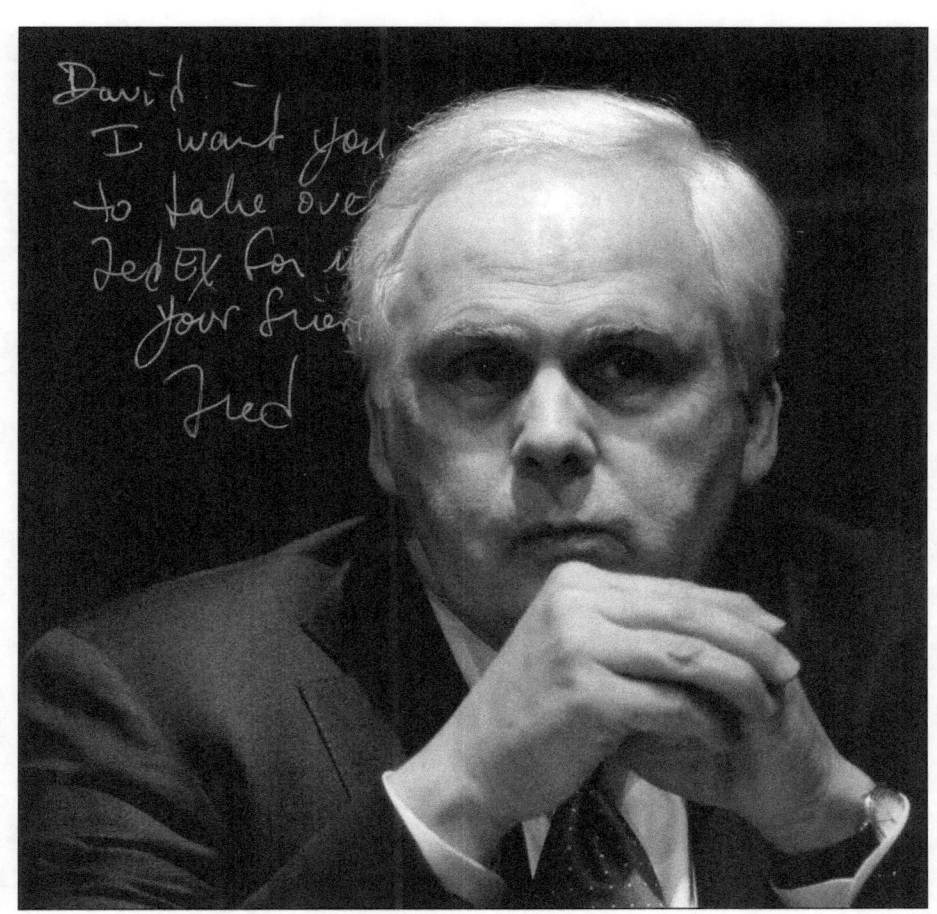

Howard Schultz
Starbucks CEO, Author

David–
I want you to be Starbucks CFO.
Howard

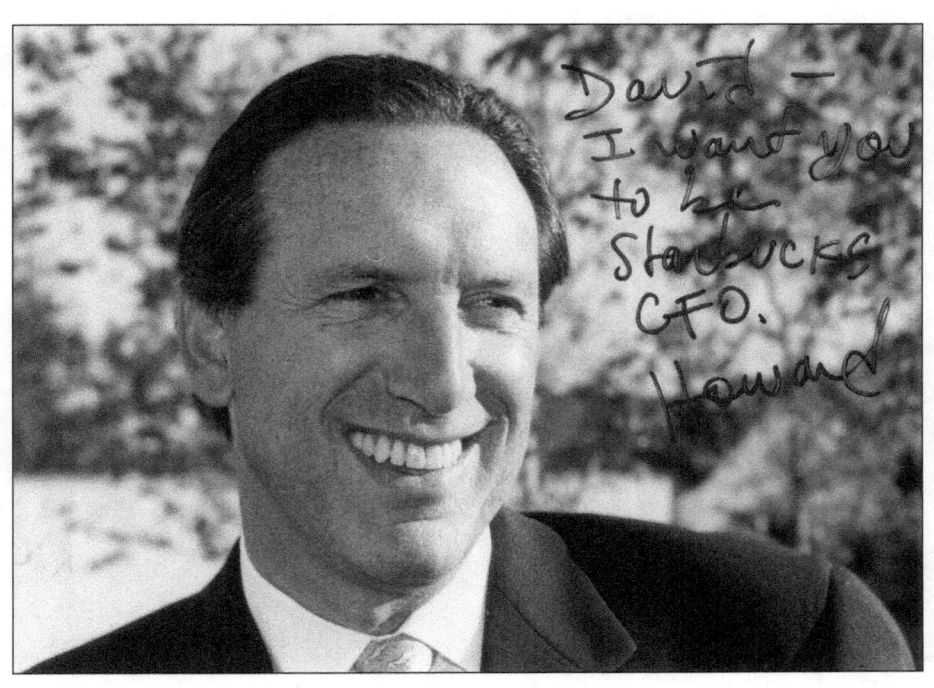

CHEFS

Charlie Trotter
Restaurateur

David–
Let's open a restaurant together–
you cook and I'll manage.
Charlie

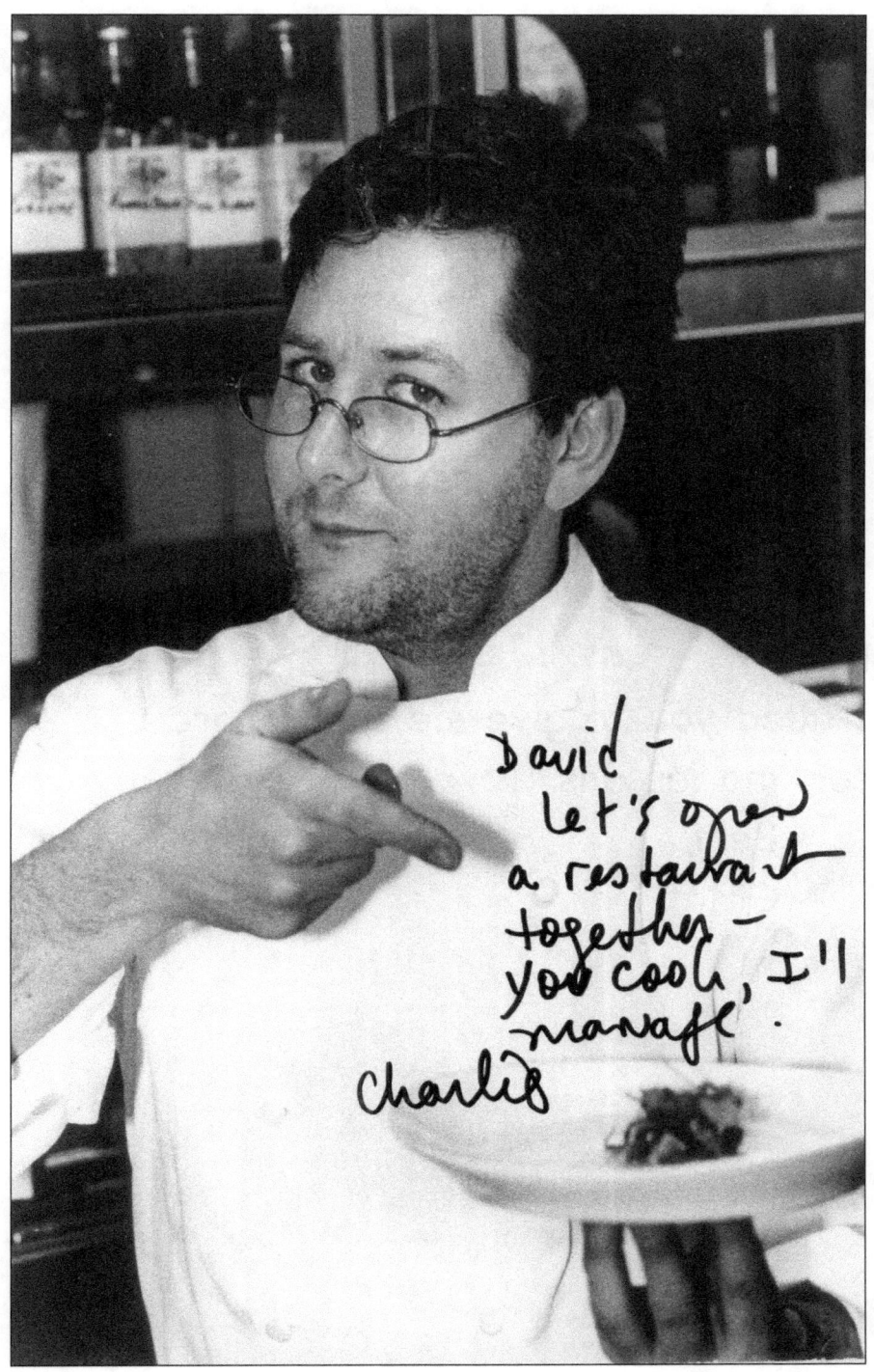

David —
Let's open
a restaurant
together —
you cook, I'll
manage.
Charlie

Grant Achatz
Restaurateur

David–
I need you to give me some more
cooking lessons.
Best,
Grant

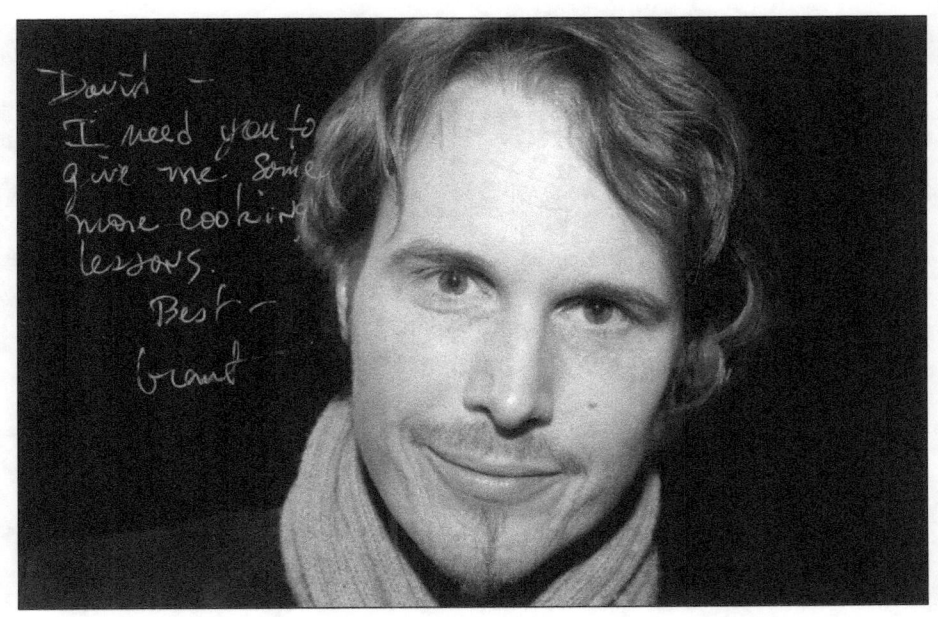

Wolfgang Puck
Restaurateur

David–
I'd like you to run my catering
business.
     Wolf

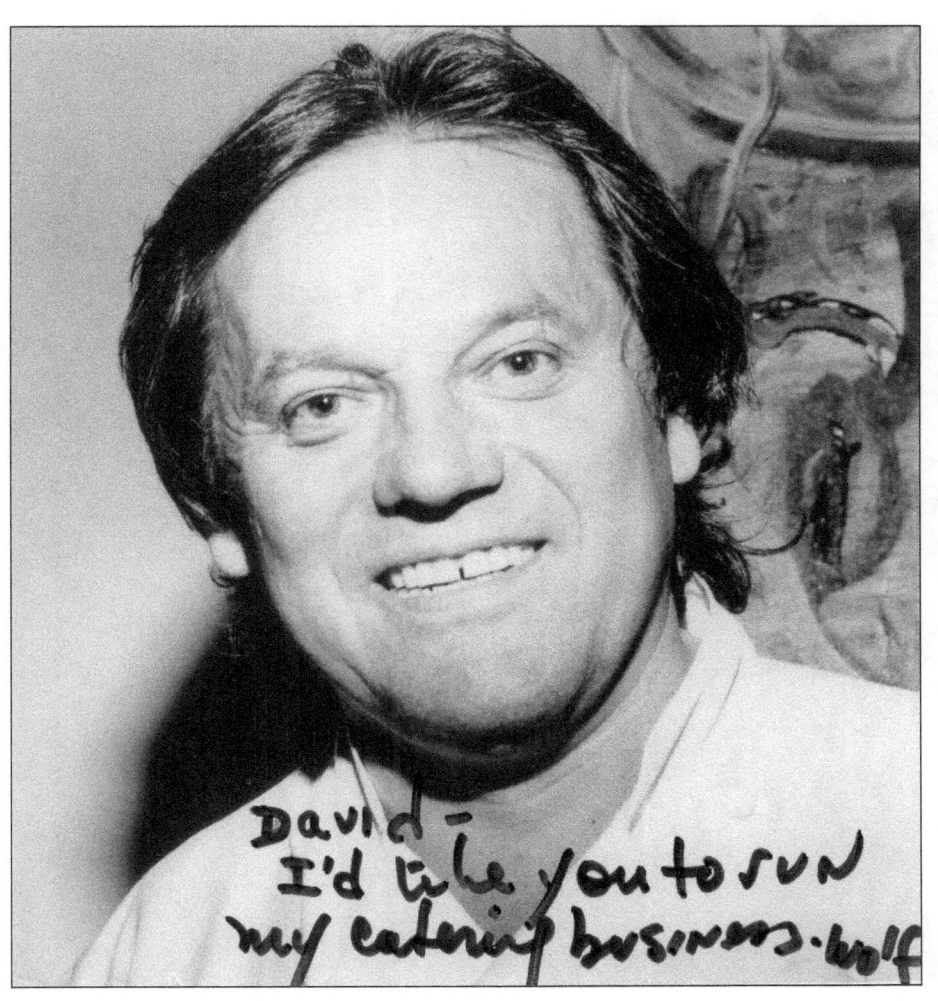

David –
I'd like you to run
my catering business – Wolf

COMEDIANS

Jay Leno
Television Host

David–
I want you to host the Tonight Show
when I retire.
    Your friend,
    Jay

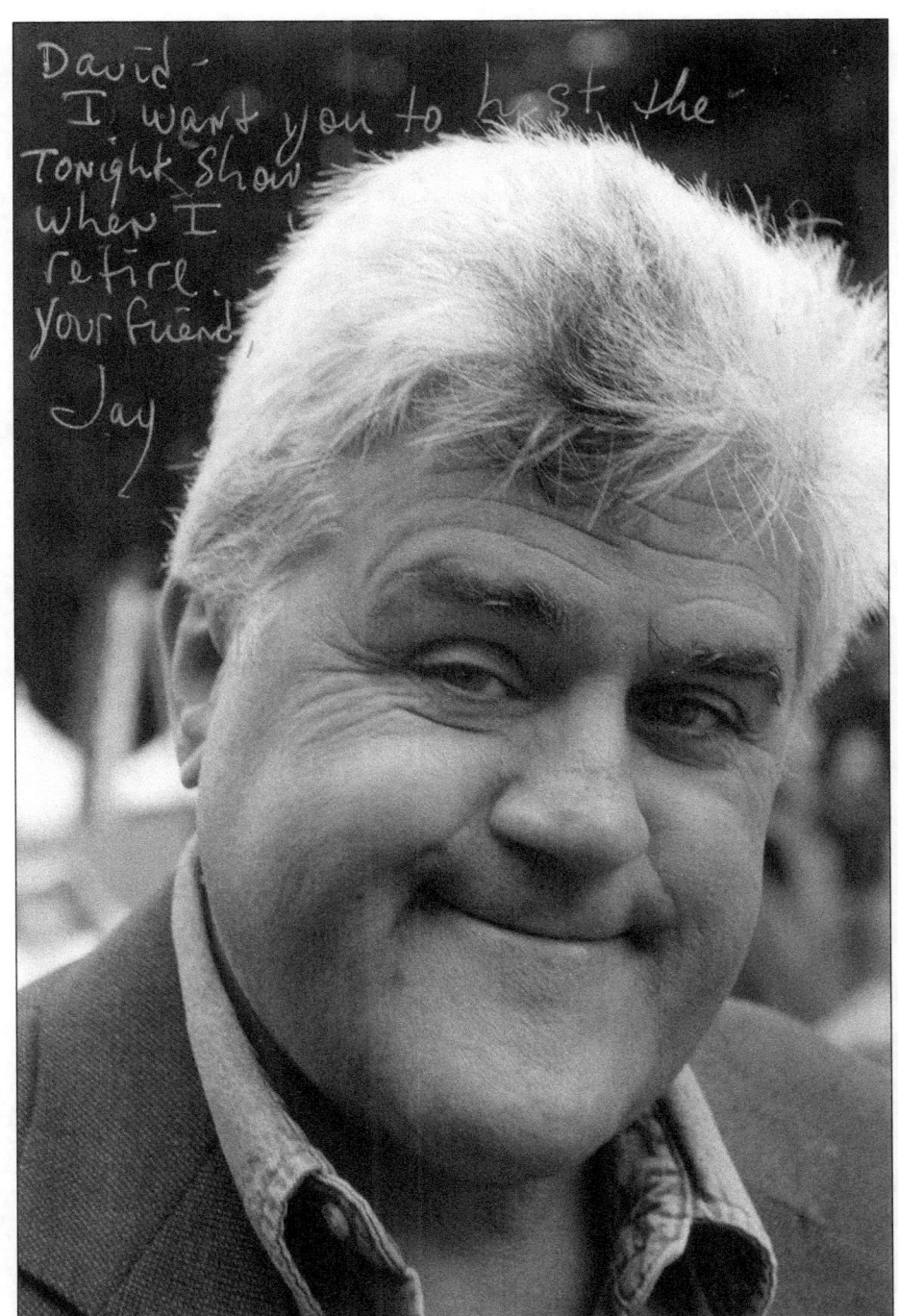

195

Joan Rivers
Comedian

David–
You & I would make a great comedy team.
    Your friend,
    Joan

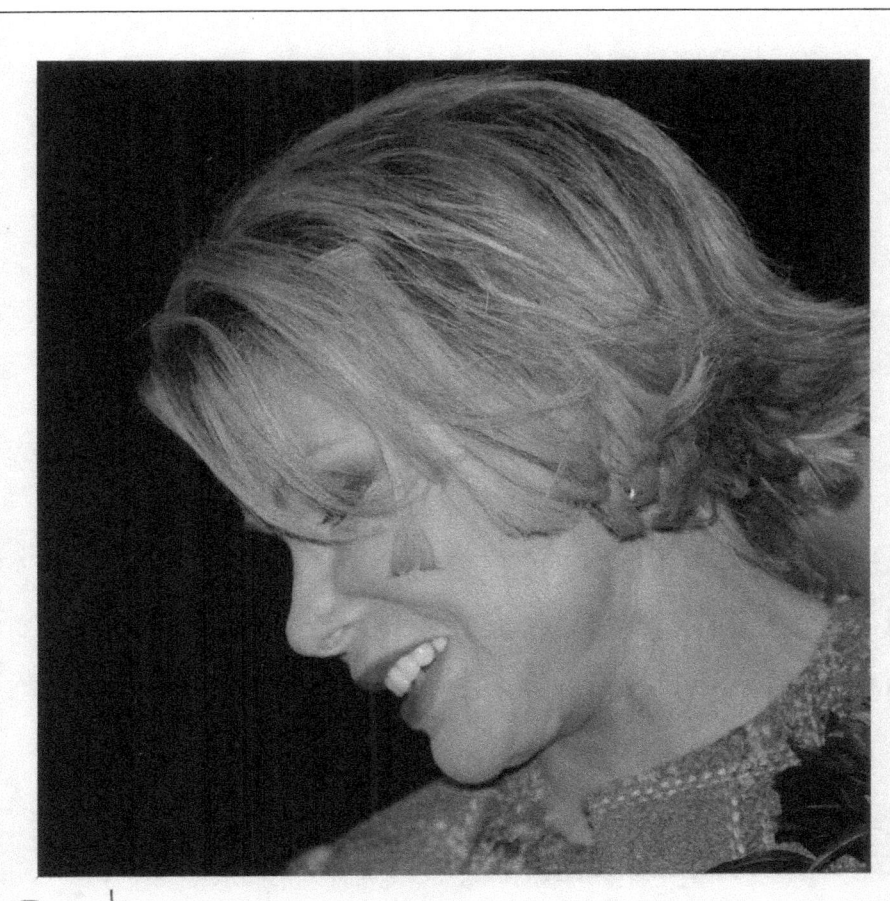

David -
you & I would
make a great
comedy team.
your friend,
Joan

Paula Poundstone
Comedian

David–
I would like to use some of your
jokes.
     Paula

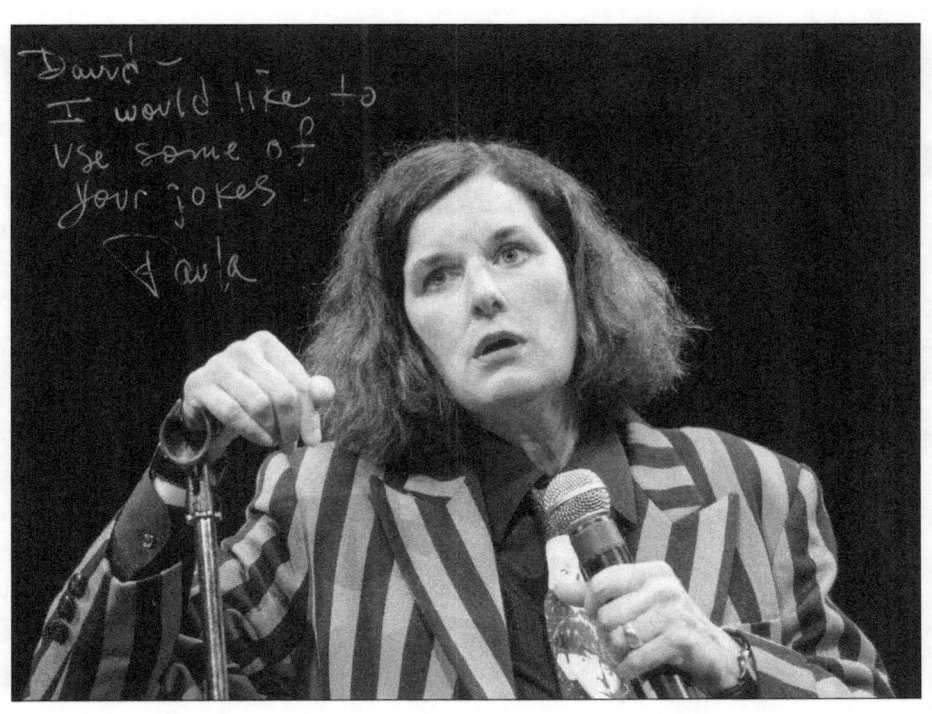

Robin Williams
Actor, Comedian

David–
I want you as co-star in my next
movie.
     Your friend,
     Robin

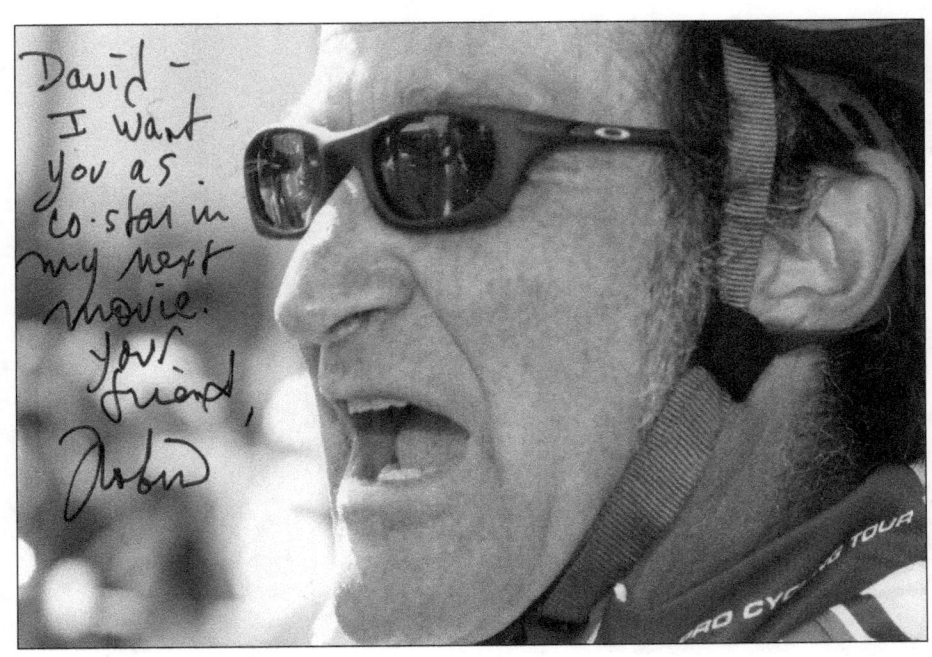

David –
I want
you as
co-star in
my next
movie.
your
friend,

Steve Martin
Comedian, Musician, Playwright, Magician, Actor

David–
I want you to join our band.
Your good friend,
Steve

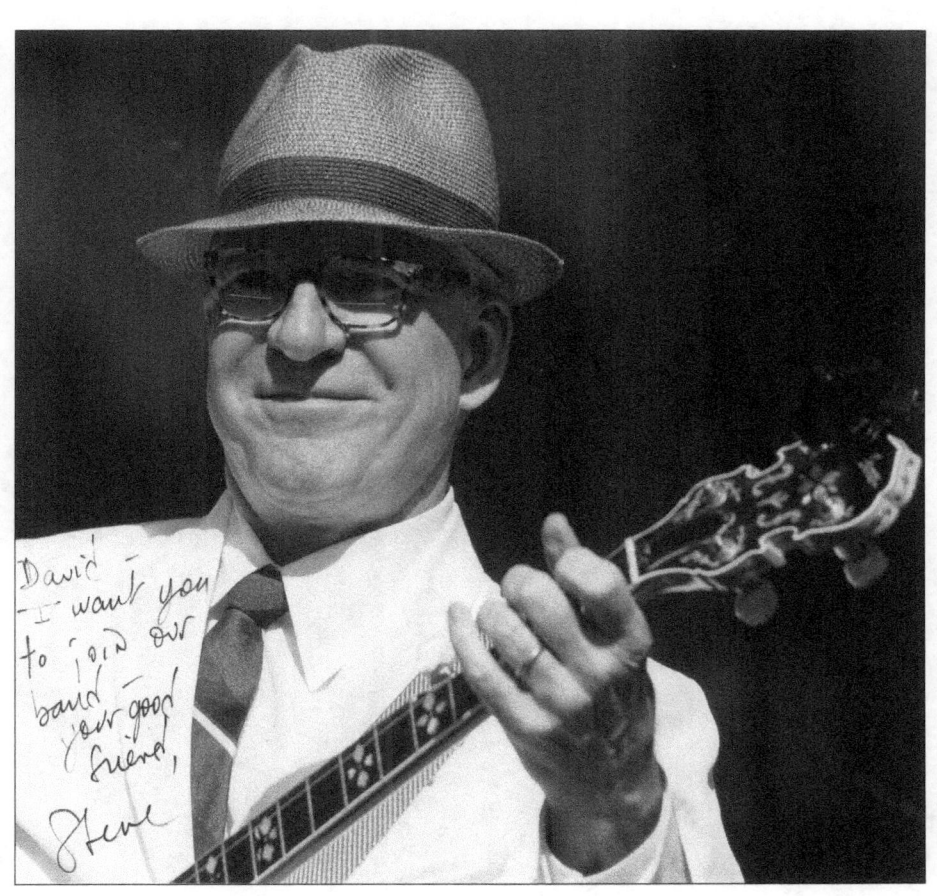

COMPUTER GIANTS

Bill Gates
Microsoft Co-founder

David–

Will you please manage my
foundation?

Your friend,

Bill

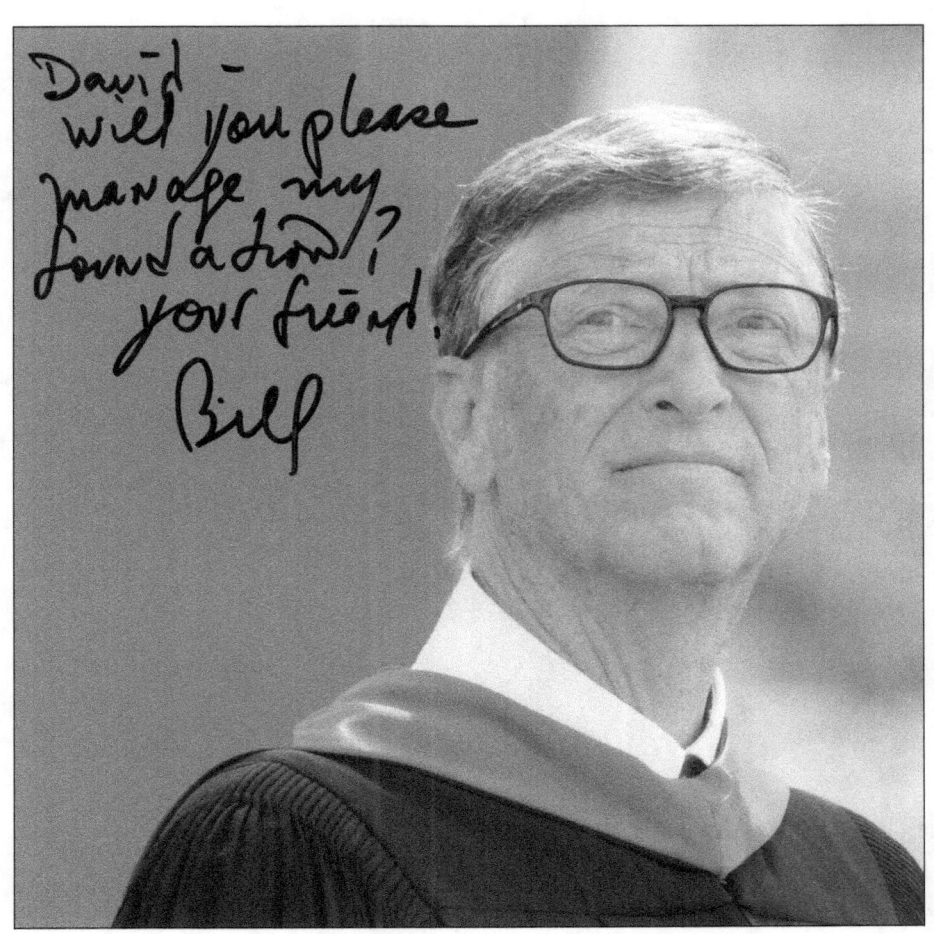

David –
will you please
manage my
foundation?
   your friend,
     Bill

Craig Newmark
Founder Craig's List

David–

David's List or Craig's List. Your call.

Craig

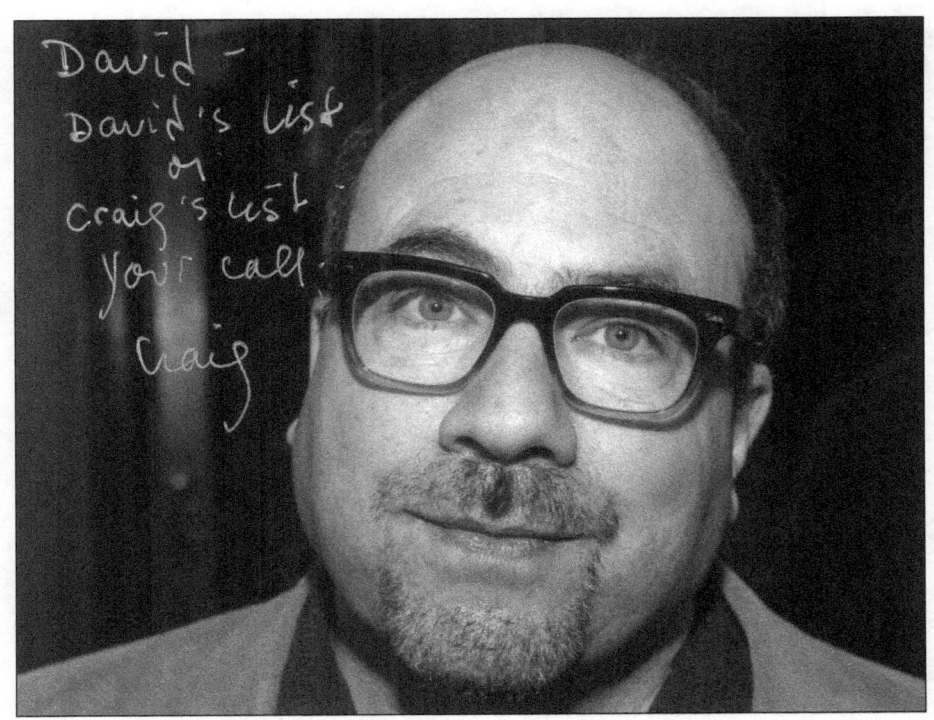

Elon Musk
Tesla & SpaceX CEO

David–
I want you to have the first
Model S.
     Elon

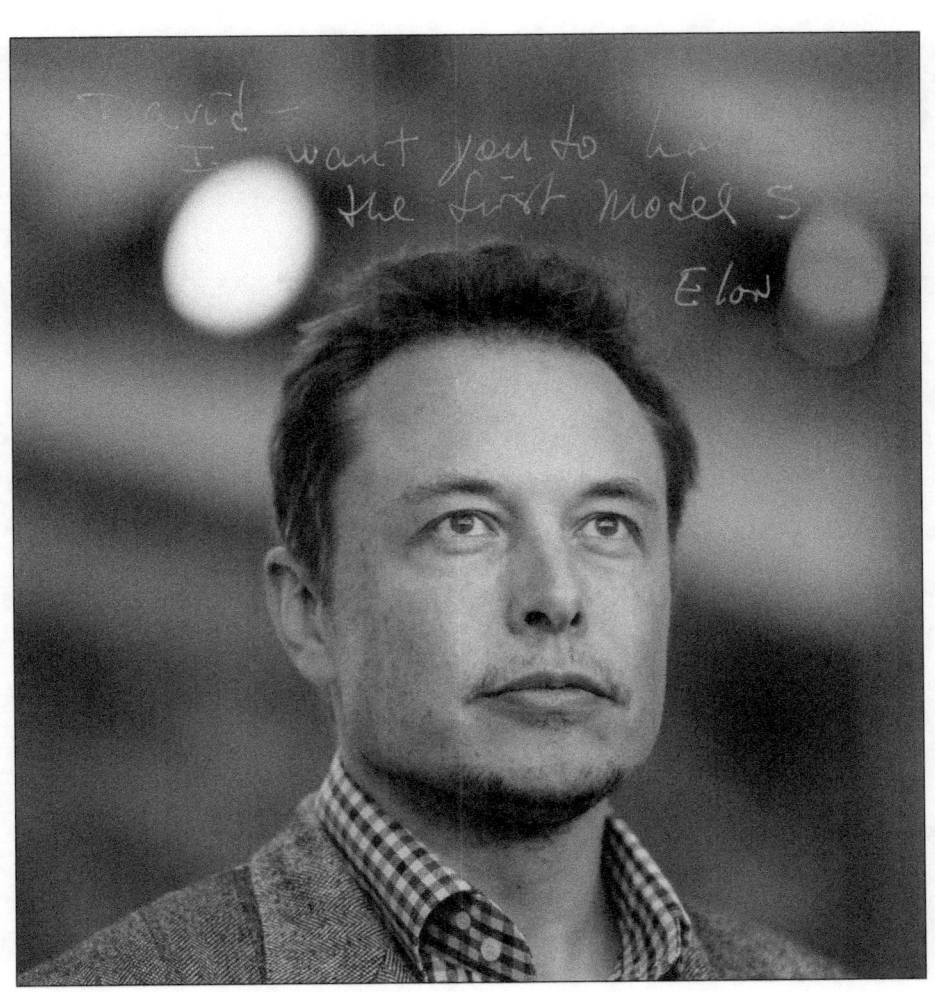

Paul Allen
Microsoft Cofounder

David–
Let's you and I start a better
computer company.
    Paul

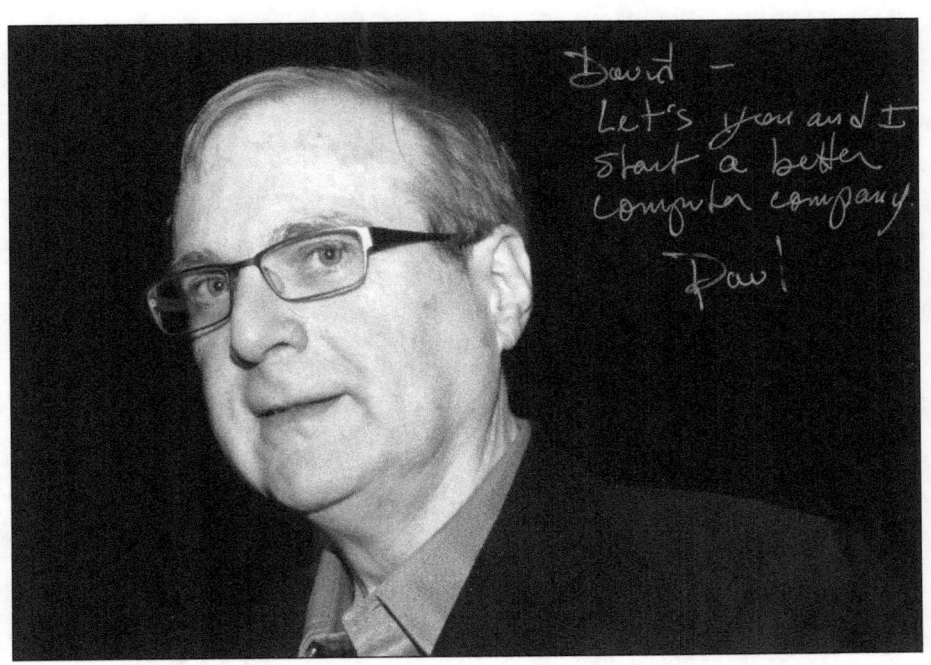

213

Steve Jobs
Apple Computer Co-founder and
CEO

Thank you for being a Mac user.
Your friend,
    Steve

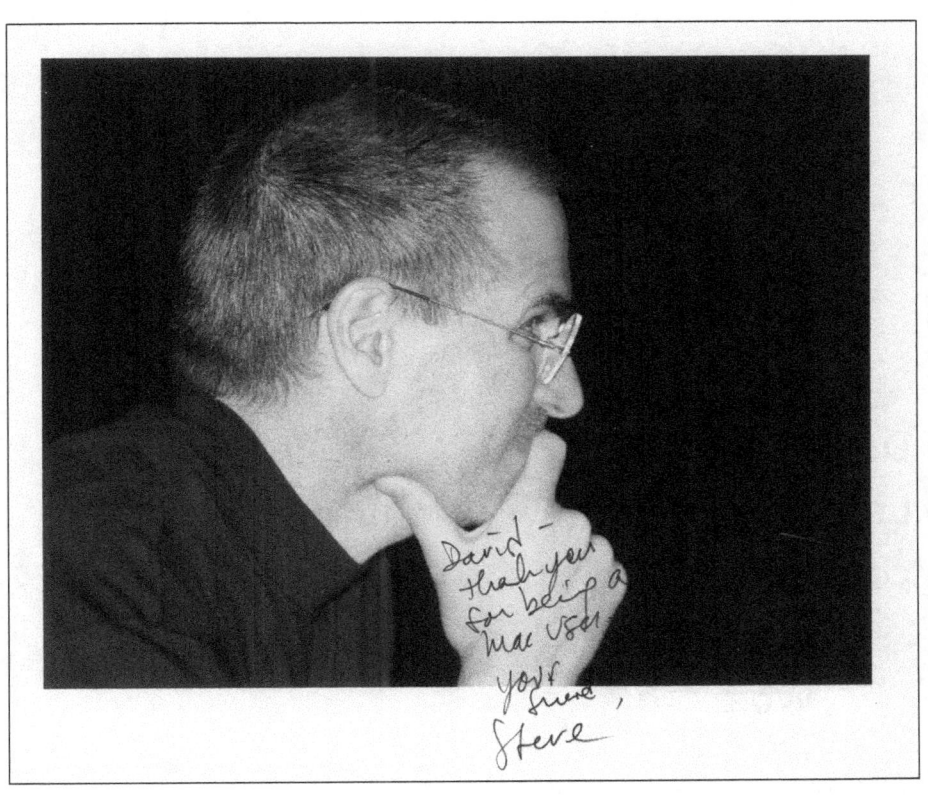

Steve Wozniak
Apple Computer Co-founder

David,
Let us start a new computer
company.
    Your friend,
    Woz

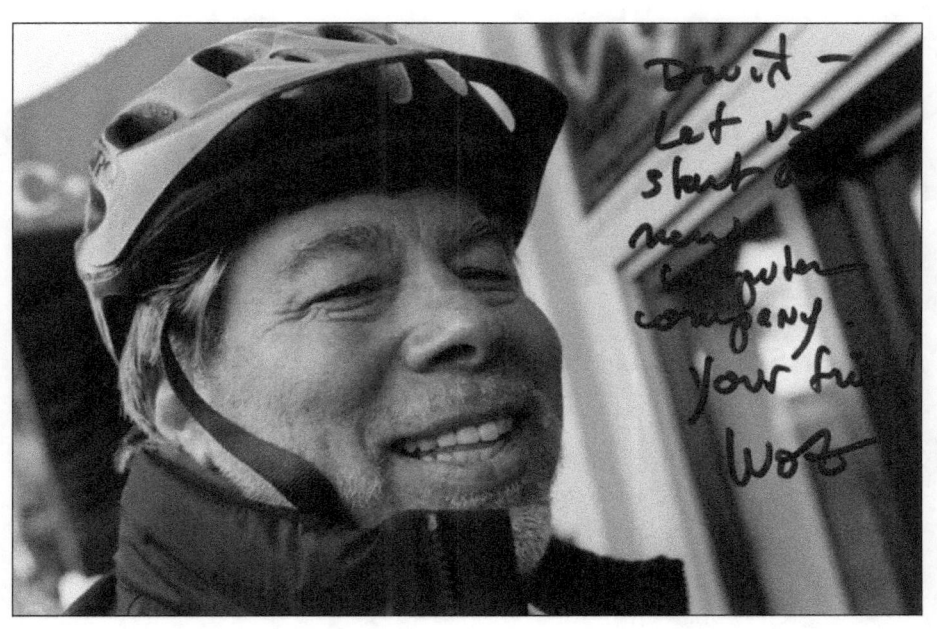

Thomas Knoll
Photoshop Developer

David–
Thanks for all your help in making
Photoshop.
    BFF,
    Tom

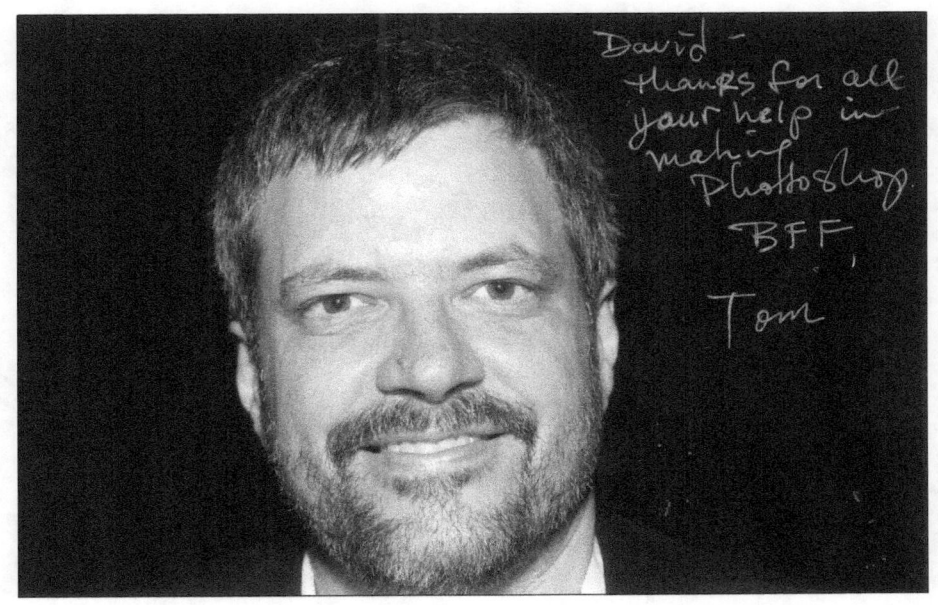

David —
thanks for all
your help in
making
Photoshop
BFF,
Tom

FILM MAKERS & ARTISTS

Dale Chihuly
Artist

David–
Let's blow some glass together.
Your friend,
Dale

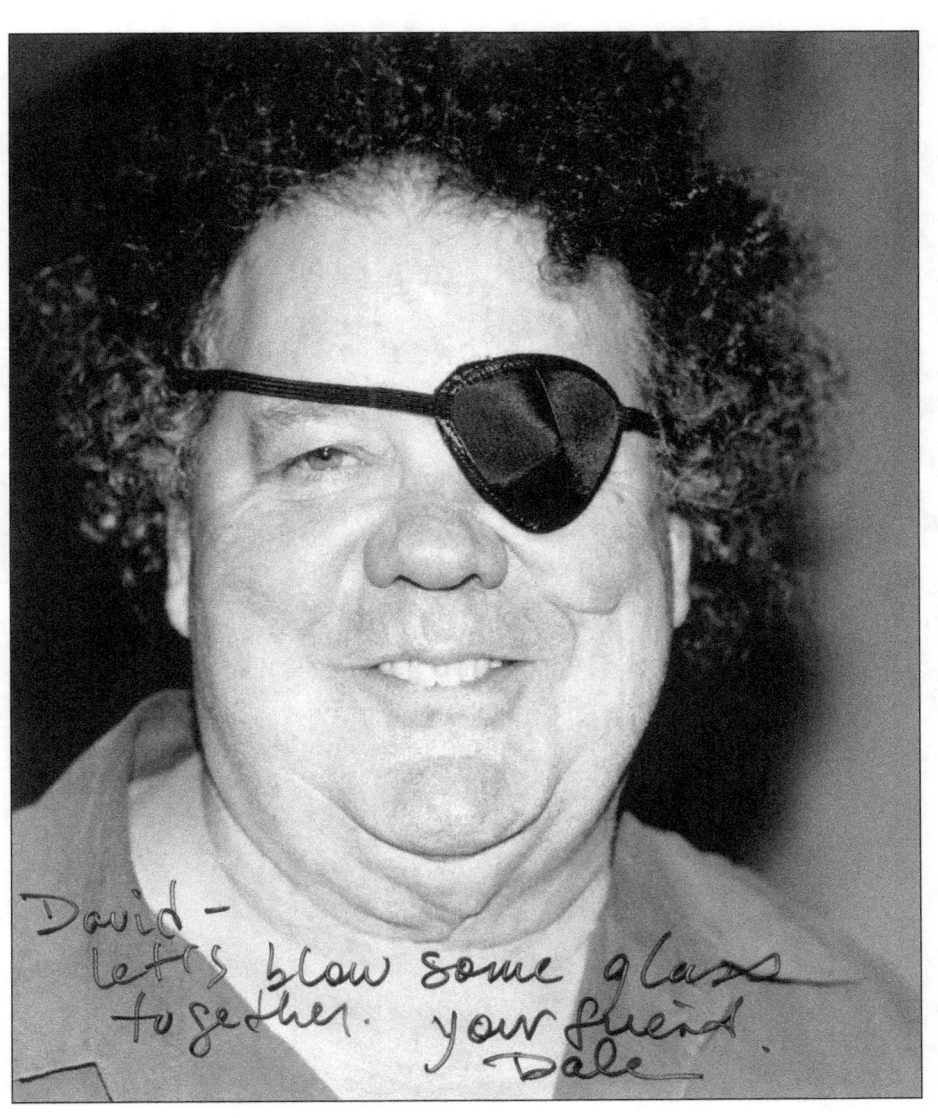

David —
let's blow some glass
together. your friend.
Dale

223

Ken Burns
Film Maker

David–
I'd like your help directing and
producing my next project–
    Your friend,
    Ken

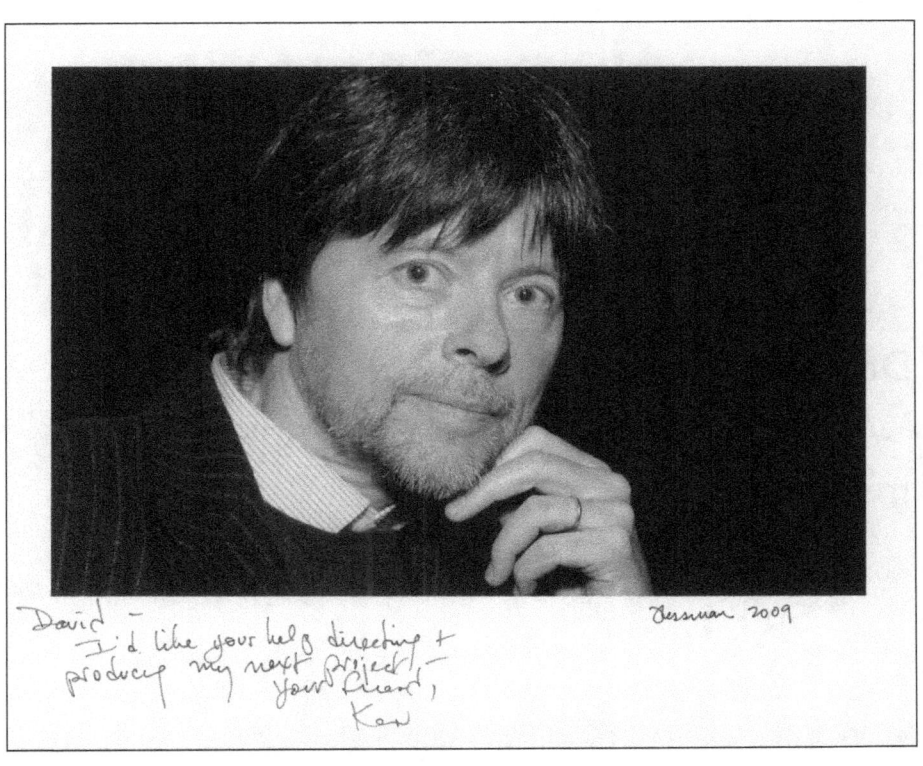

David –
I'd like your help directing +
producing my next project,
Your friend,
Ken

Fessman 2009

Spike Lee
Film Director and Actor

David–
Will you be the lead in my next
movie?
     Your friend,
     Spike

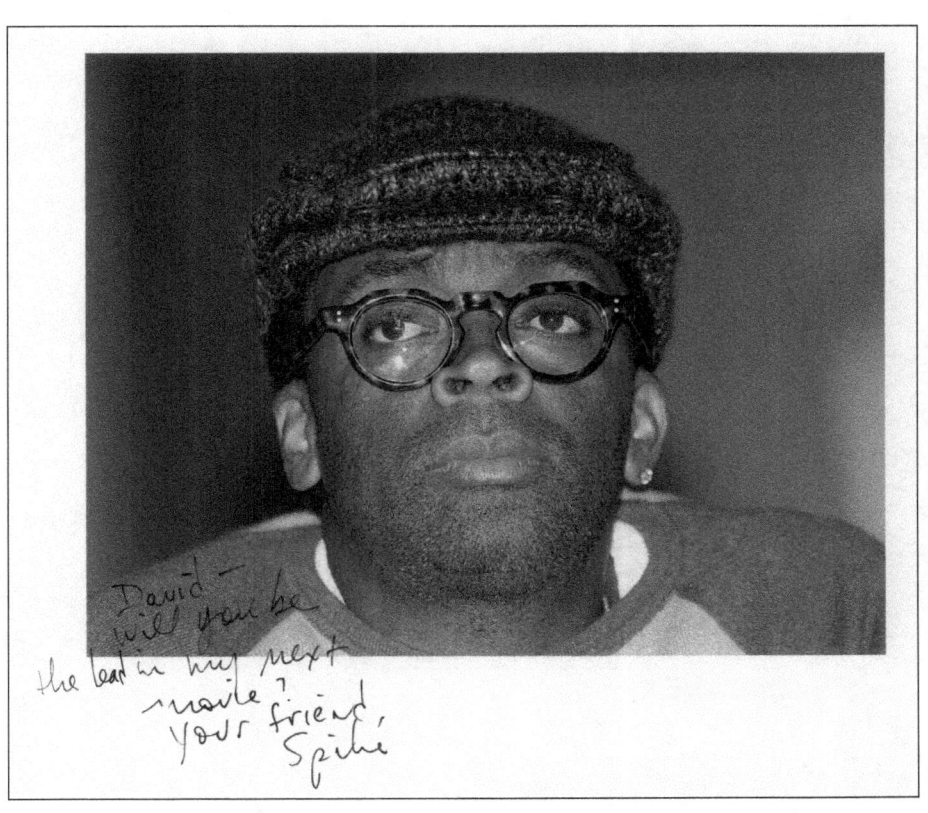

David —
will you be
the lead in my next
movie?
your friend,
Spike

MUSICIANS

Arlo Guthrie
Musician

David-
Thanks for teaching me guitar.
     Arlo

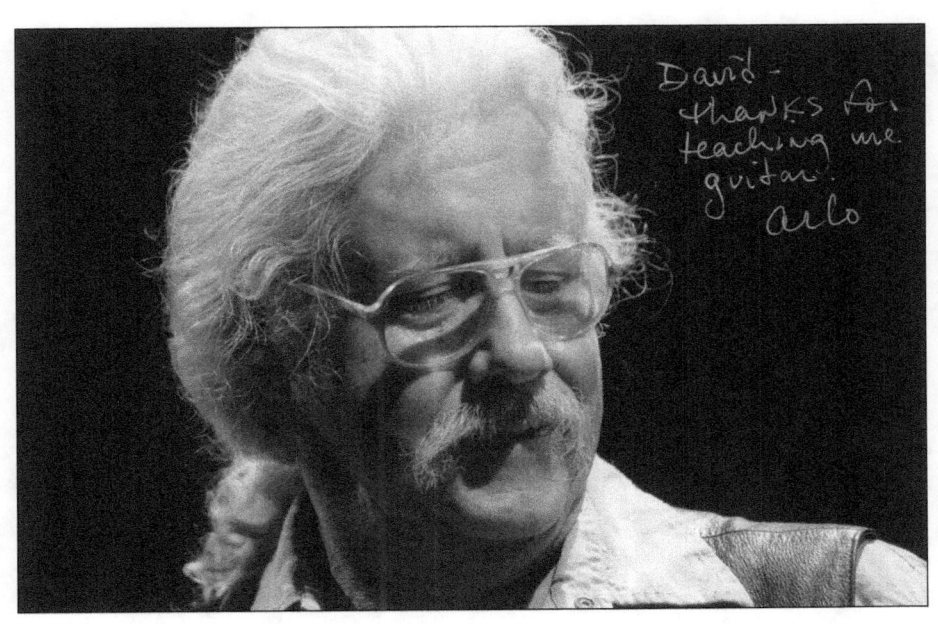

Arturo Sandoval
Musician

David–
Can I play in your band?
    Arturo

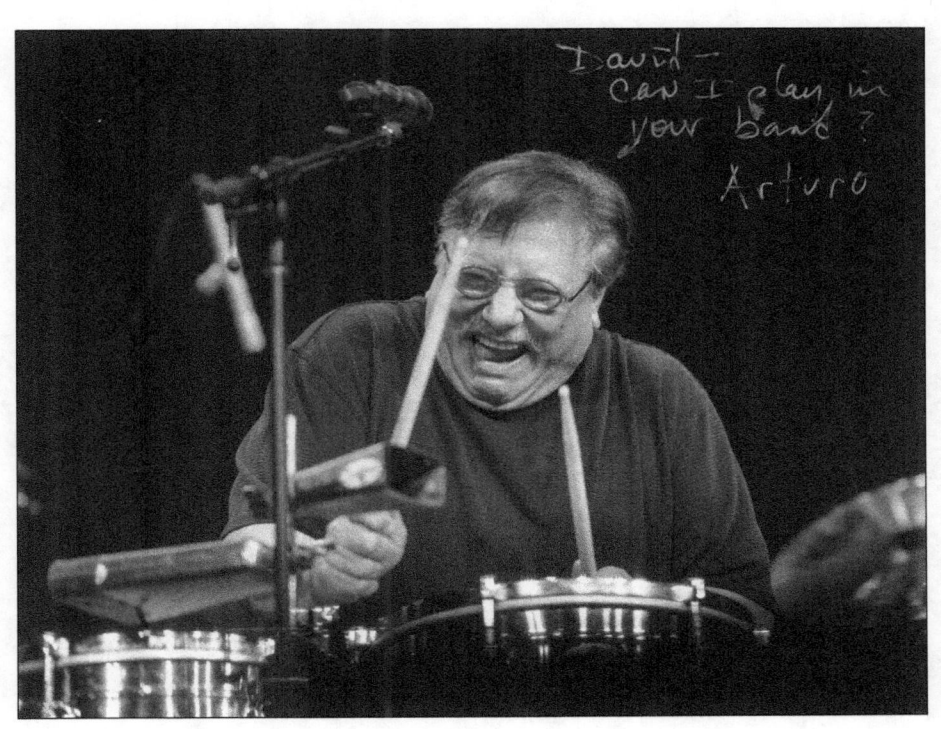

Bette Midler
Musician, Actress

David–
I want you to be the leading man in
my next movie.
    Love,
    Bette

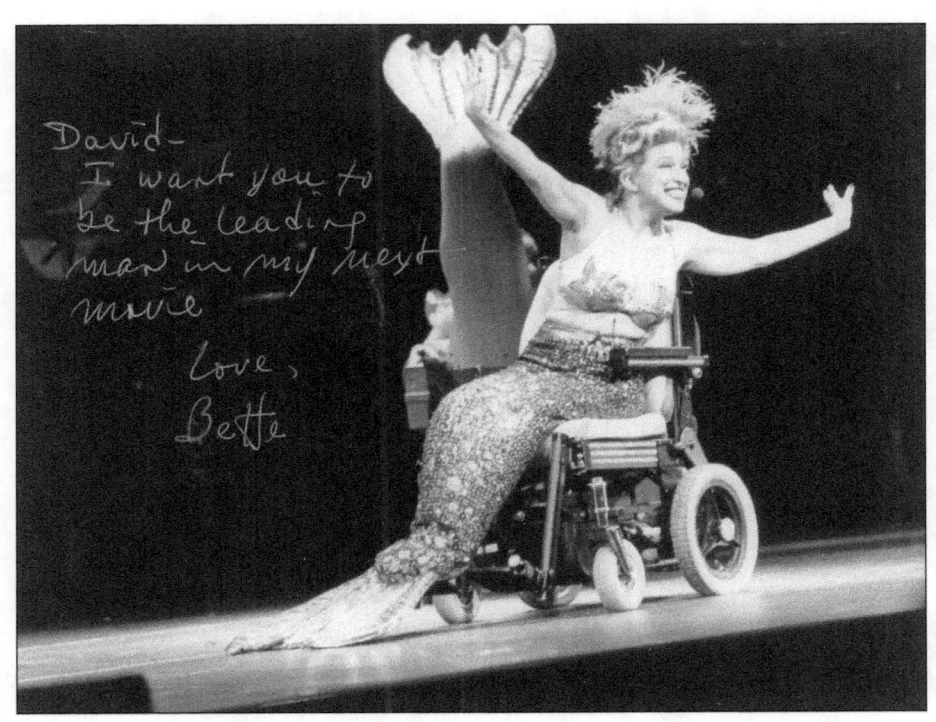

Bo Diddley
Musician

David–
You know Bo!
   Bo Diddley

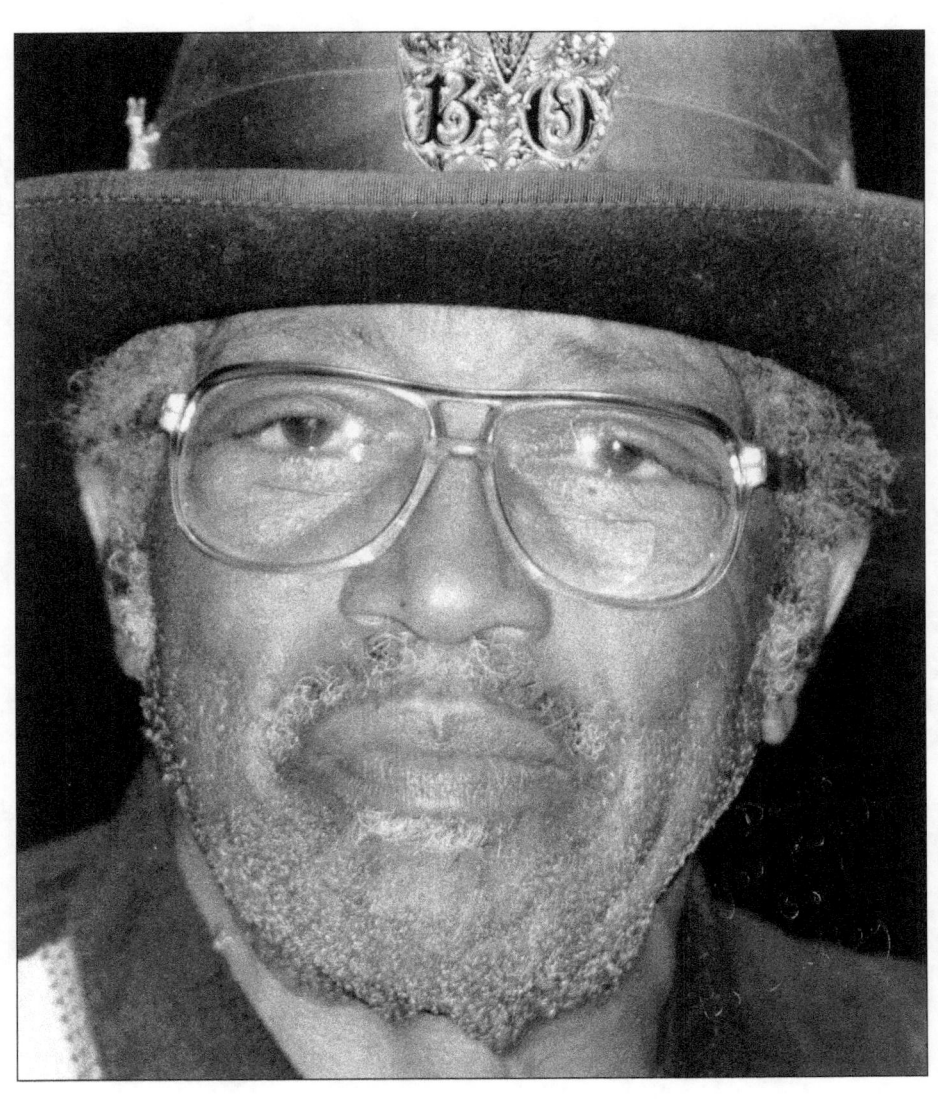

Bonnie Raitt
Musician

David–
Let's tour together.
 Bonnie

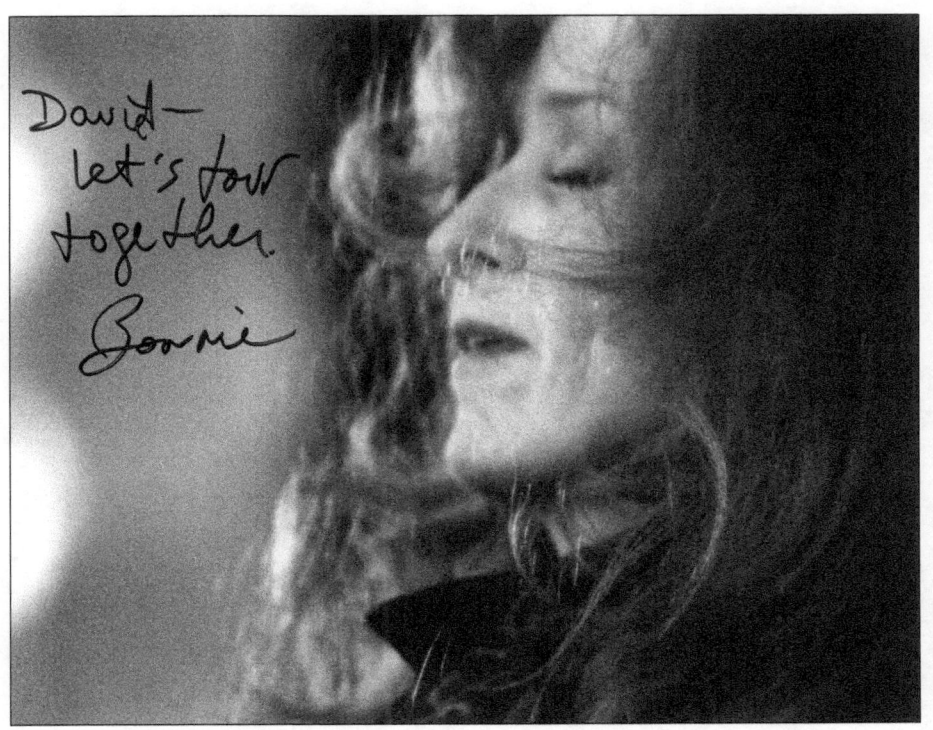

Chick Coria
Jazz Pianist

David–
Please give me a few more piano
lessons.
     Chick

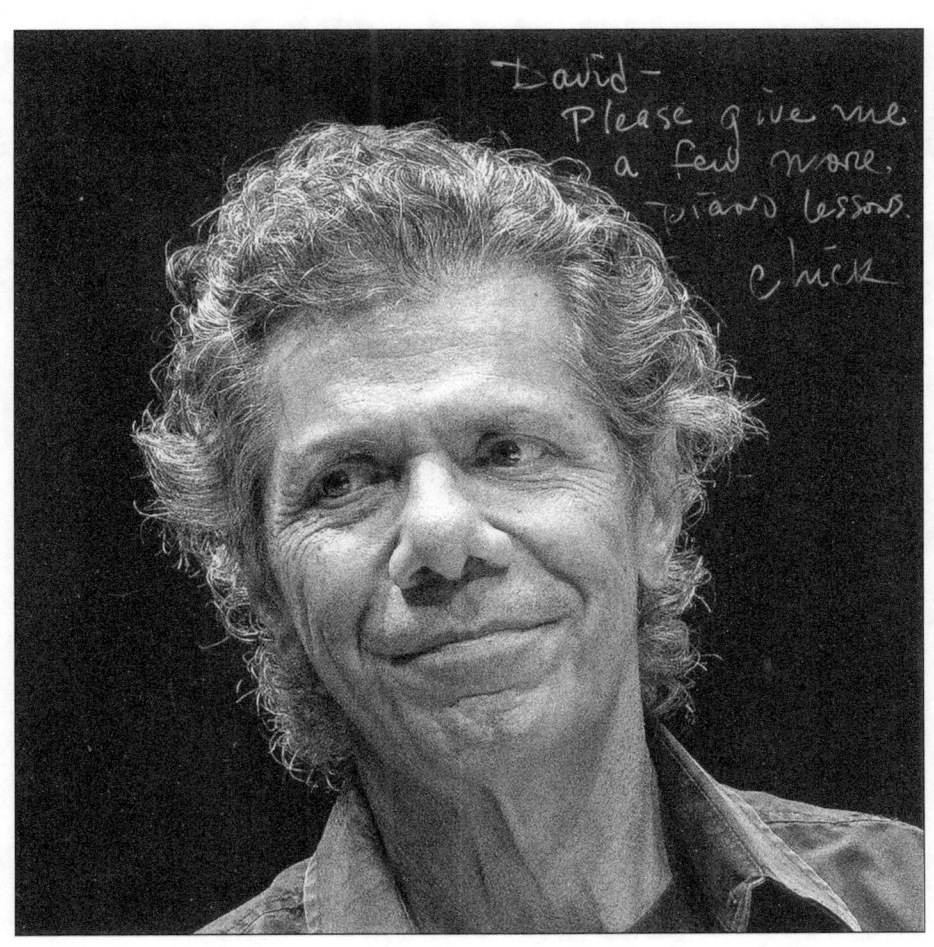

David –
Please give me
a few more
piano lessons.
Chick

241

Chuck Berry
Musician

David–
You are the face of Rock & Roll.
    Your friend,
    Chuck

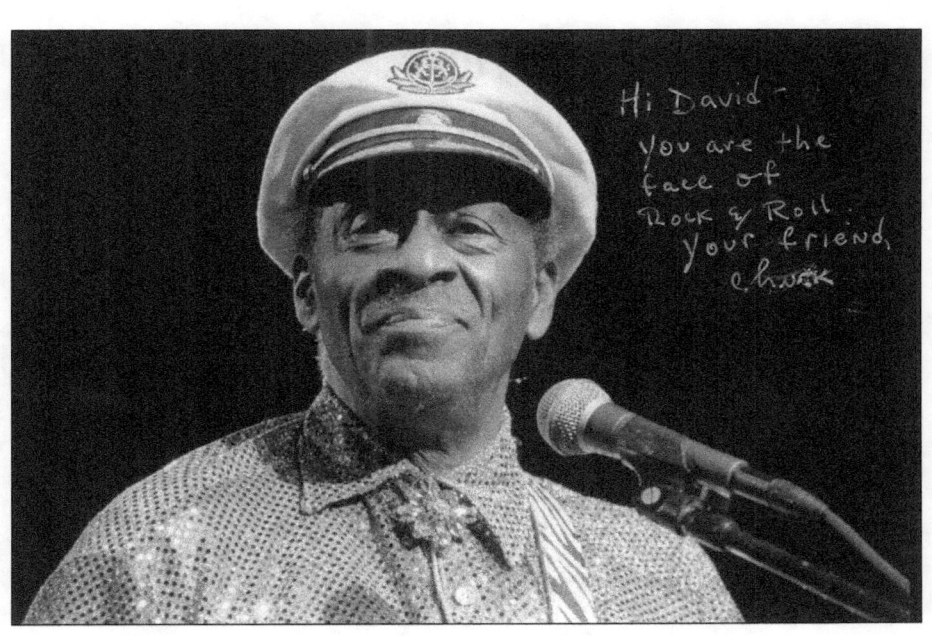

Dave Brubeck
Musician

David–
I'd like you to play in my quartet.
    Dave B.

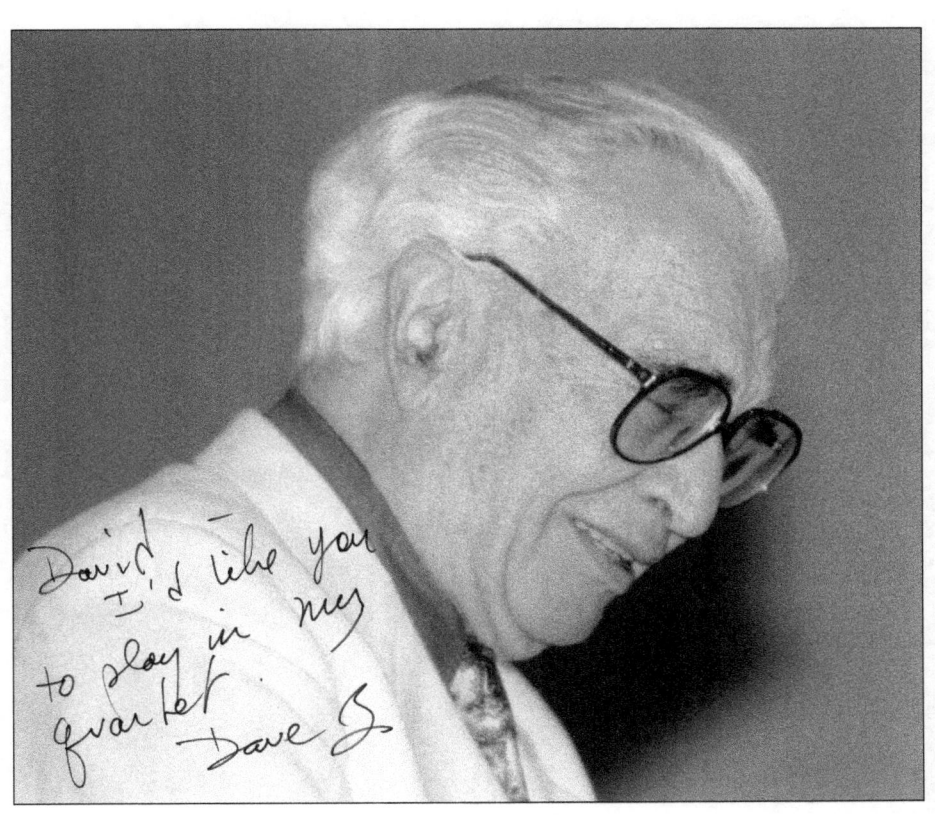

David –
I'd like you
to play in my
quartet.
Dave B

Dolly Parton
Musician, Actress

David–
Is it ok if I record your hit song?
    Dolly

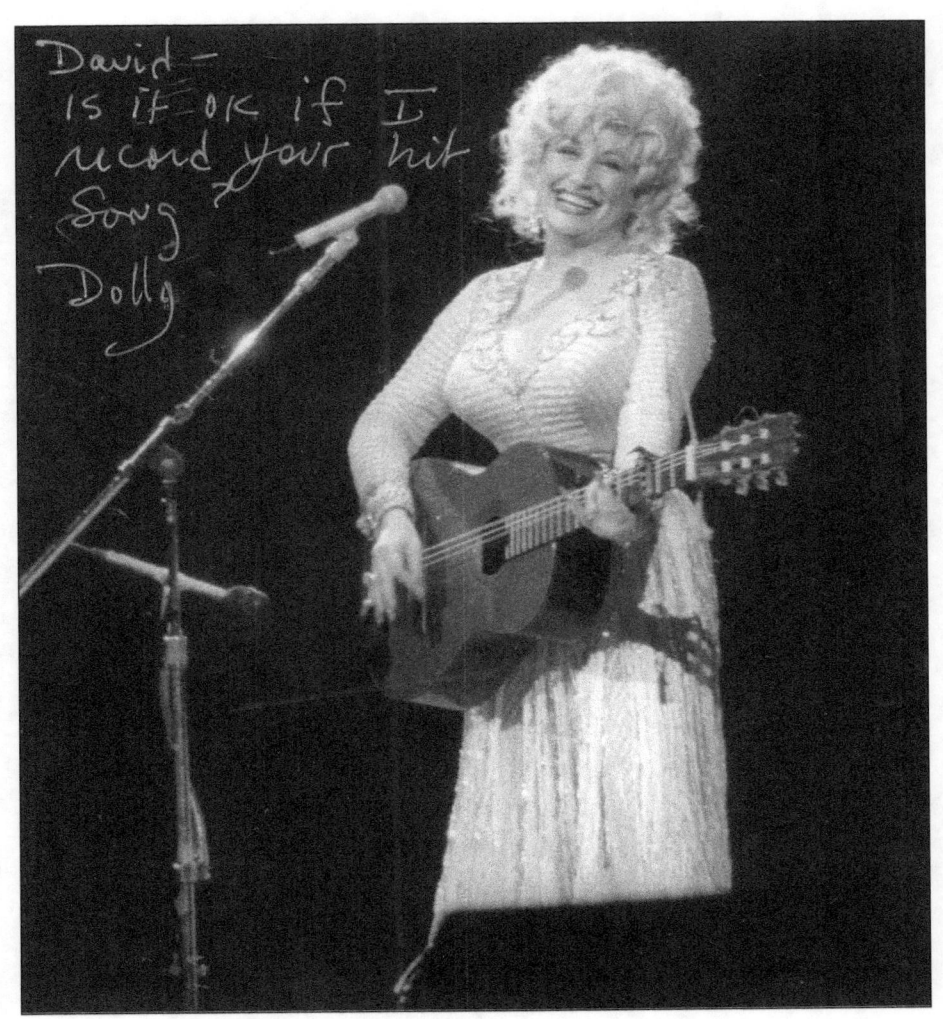

Frank Zappa
Musician

David–
Please be lead vocalist in my band.
    Your friend,
    Frank

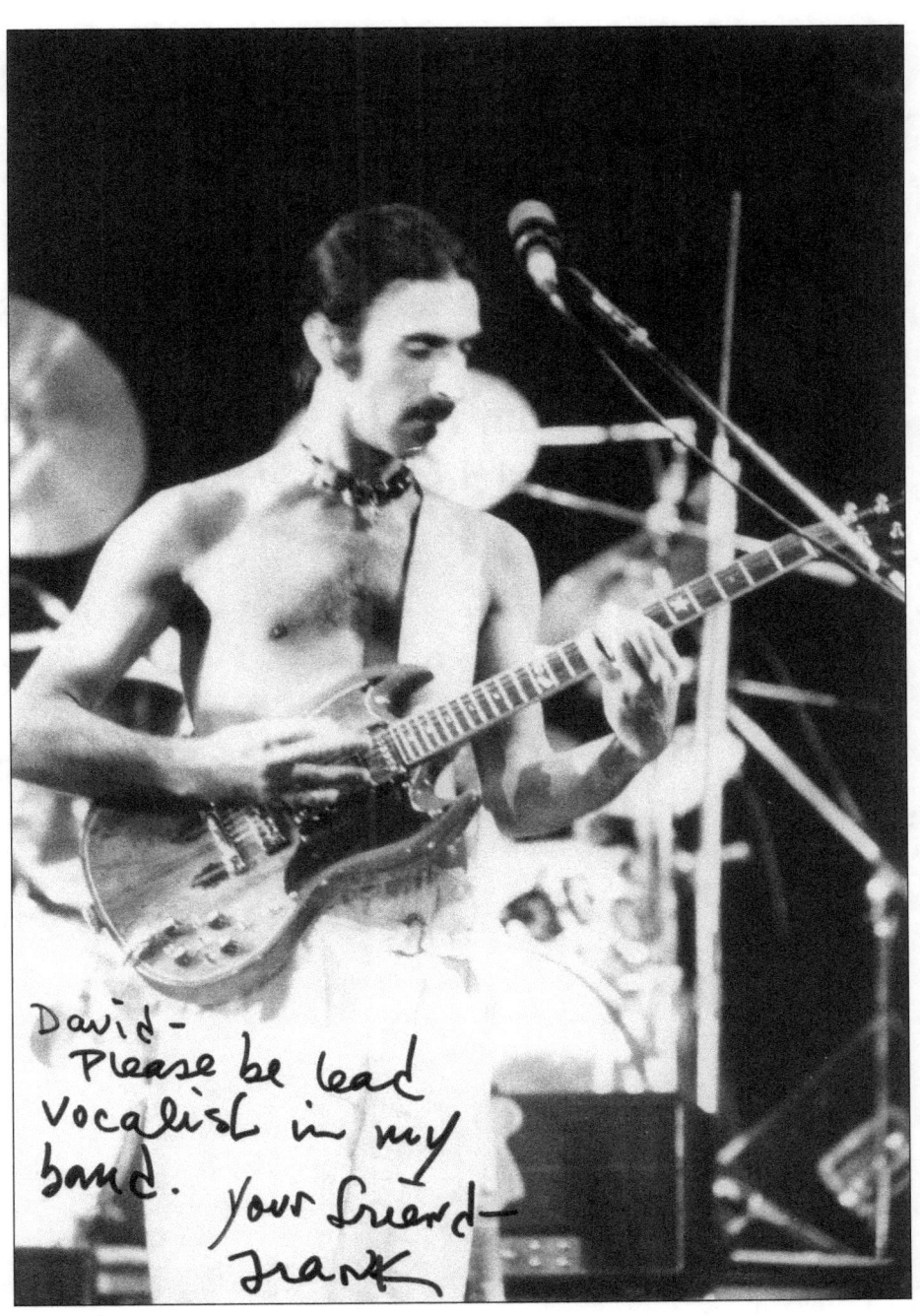

David –
Please be lead
vocalist in my
band.   Your friend –
Frank

Graham Nash
Musician

David–
Let's go on tour together.
     Best,
     Graham

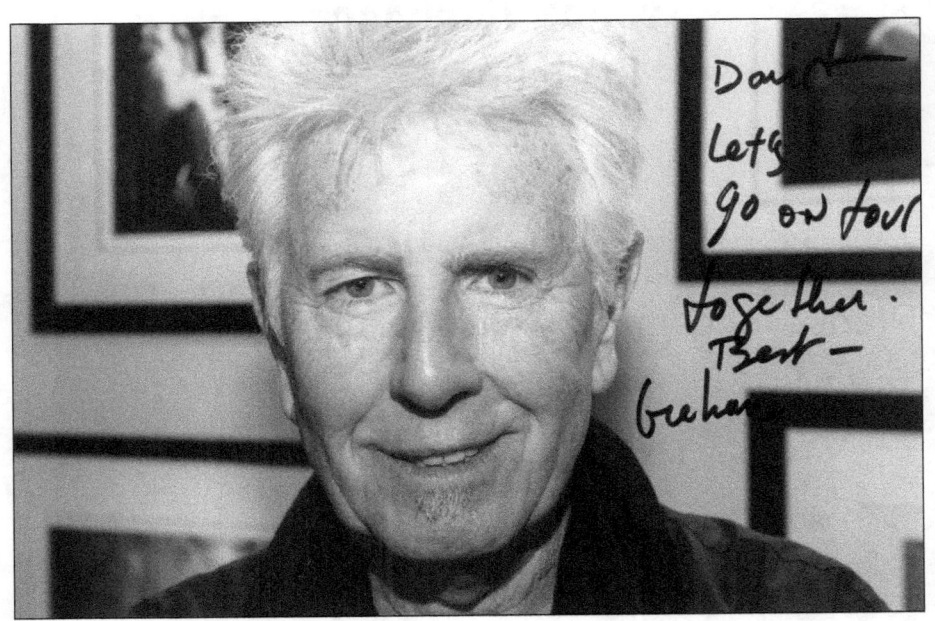

Itzhak Perlman
Violinist

David-
Please accompany me on my next
tour.
    Your friend,
    Itzhak

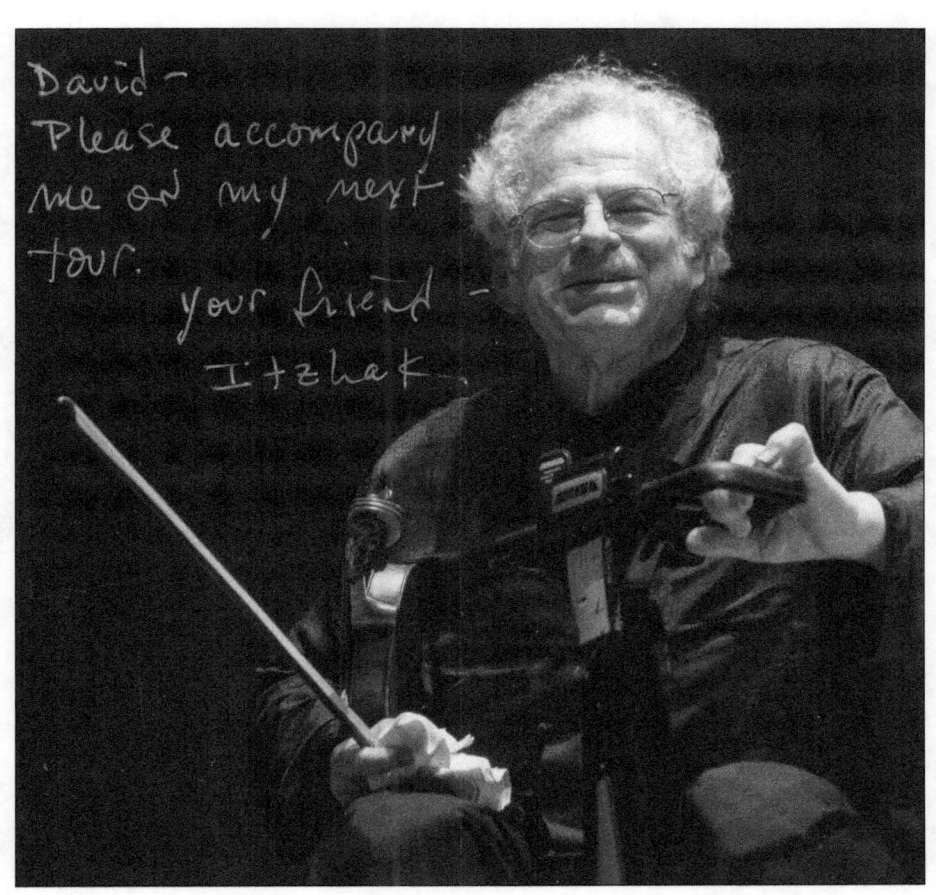

David –
Please accompany
me on my next
tour.
     Your friend –
       Itzhak.

James Brown
Musician

David–
You've got soul! Come join my band.
    James

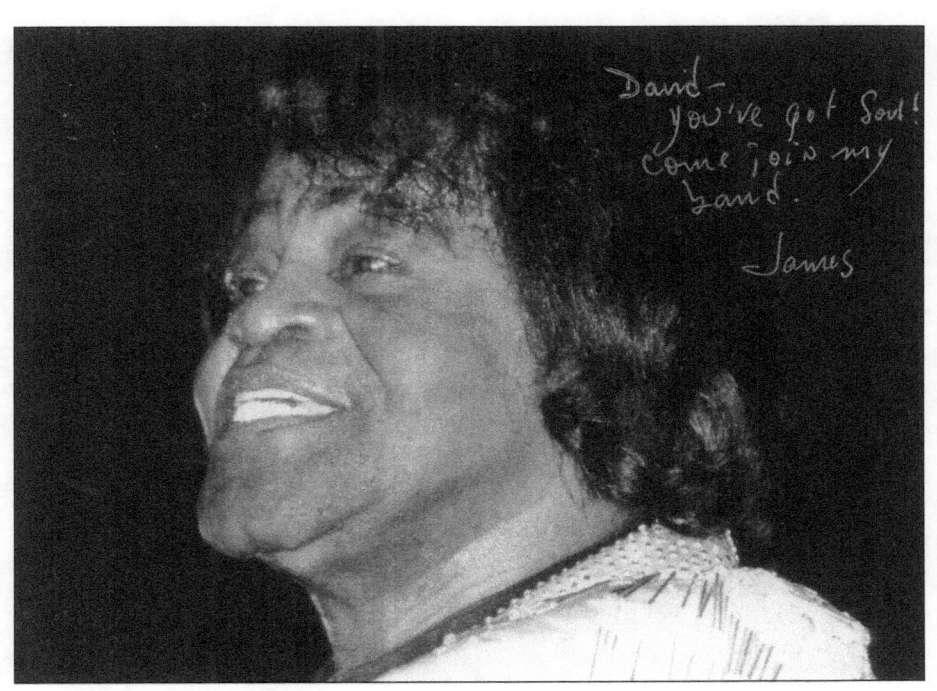

Joan Baez
Musician, Activist

David–
I want you to be my accompanying
pianist on my final tour next year.
        Your friend,
        Joan

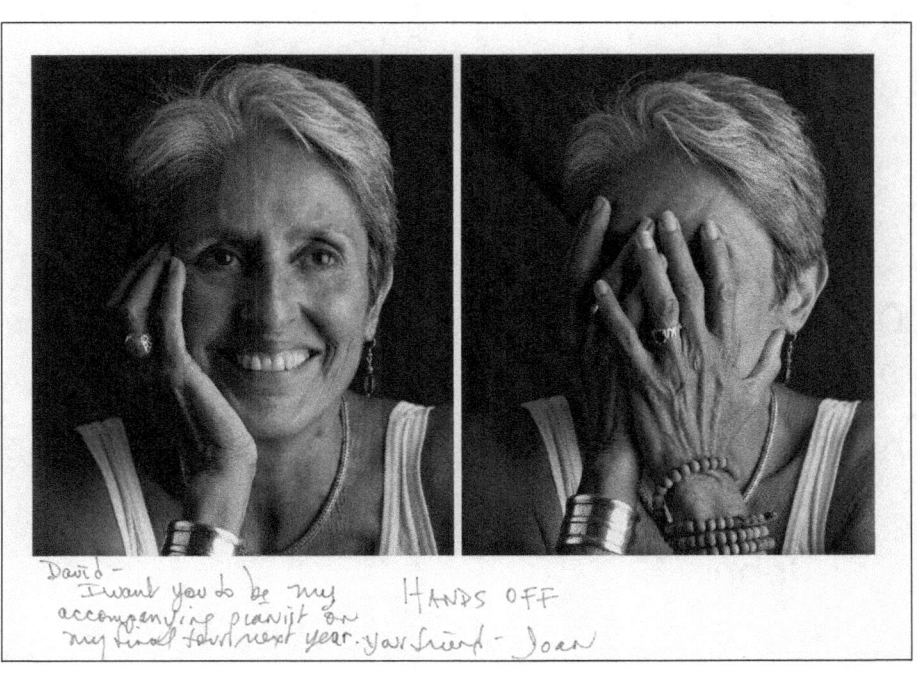

David —
I want you to be my
accompanying pianist on
my final tour next year. your friend — Joan

HANDS OFF

John Mayall
Musician

David–
Please give me a few more
harmonica lessons.
    Your buddy,
    John

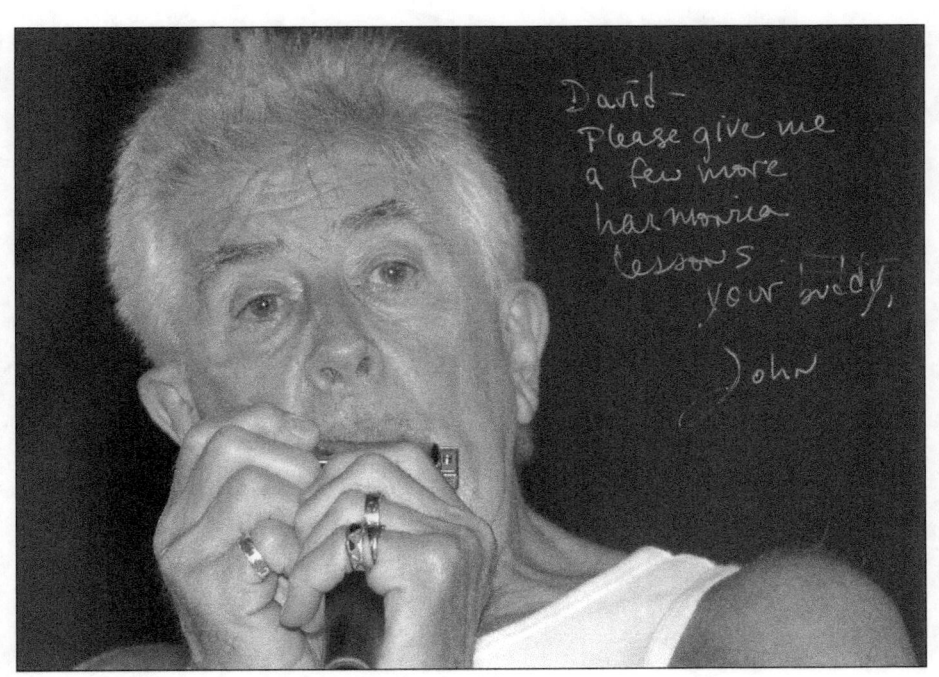

John McEuen
Musician

David–
How about joining Nitty Gritty Dirt
Band?
     John

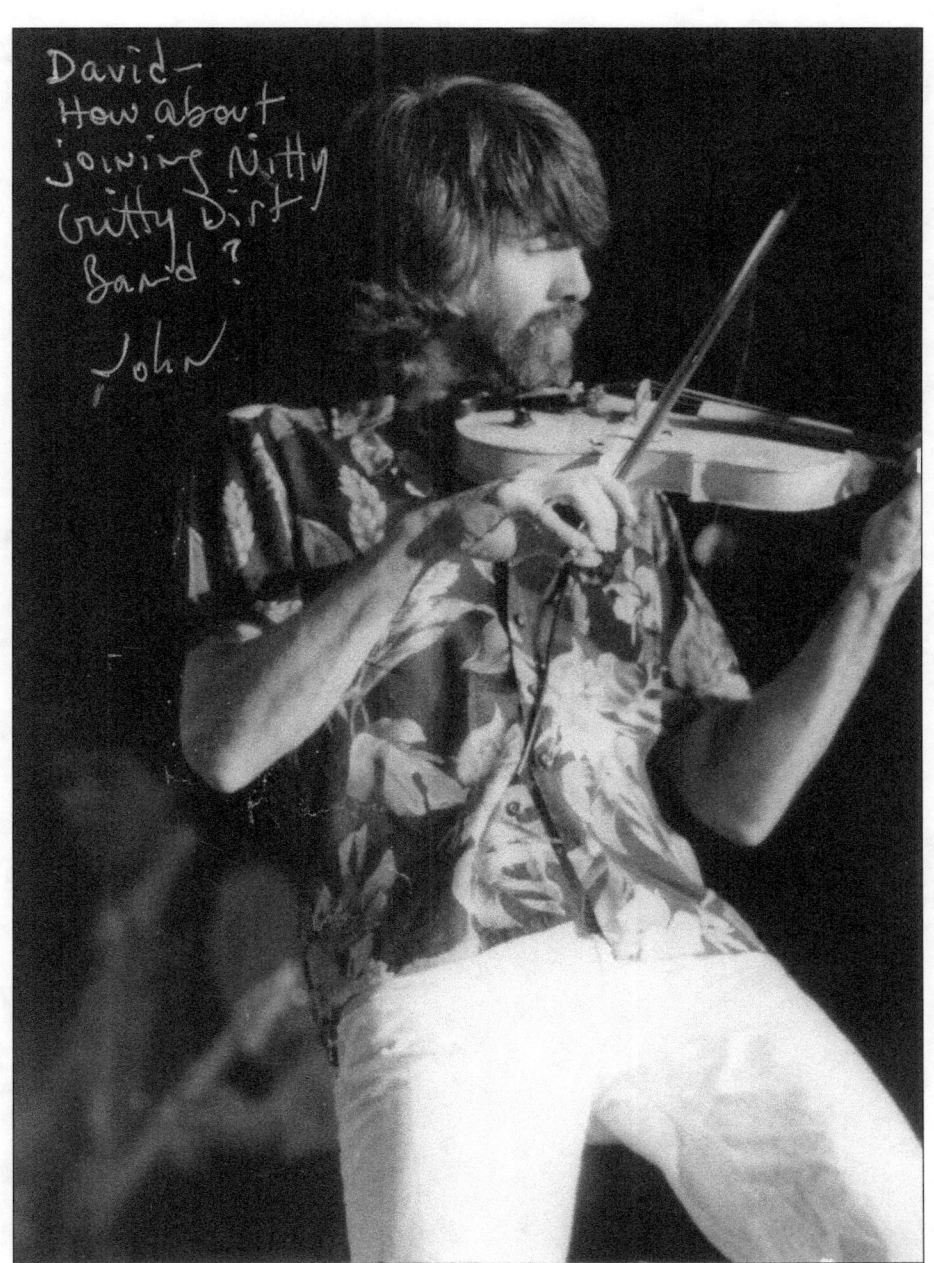

Keb' Mo'
Musician

David–
I need for you to teach me some
more blues.
    Keb'

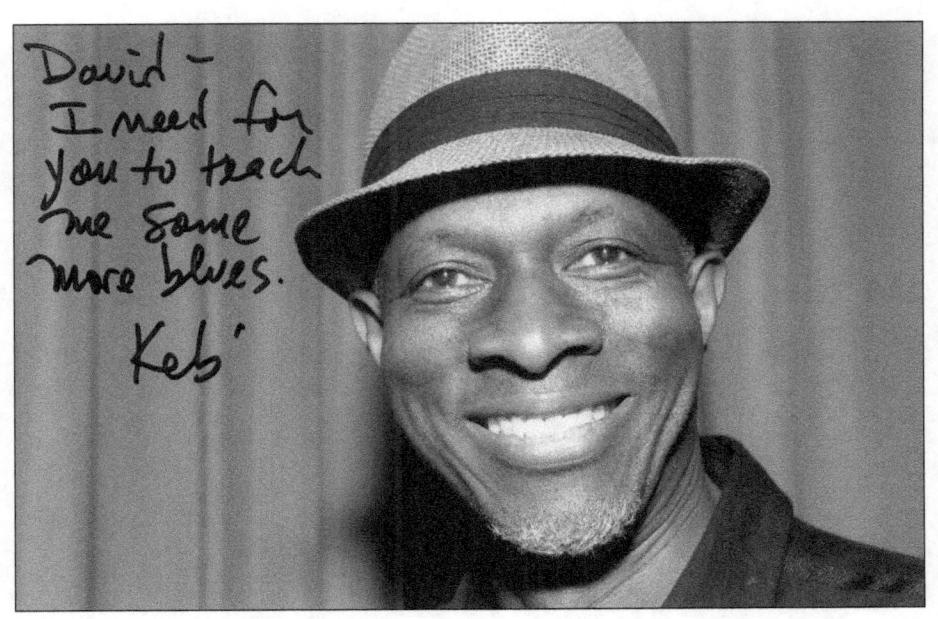

David –
I need for
you to teach
me some
more blues.
Keb'

Kenny Rogers
Musician

David–

You are the Gambler!

   Kenny

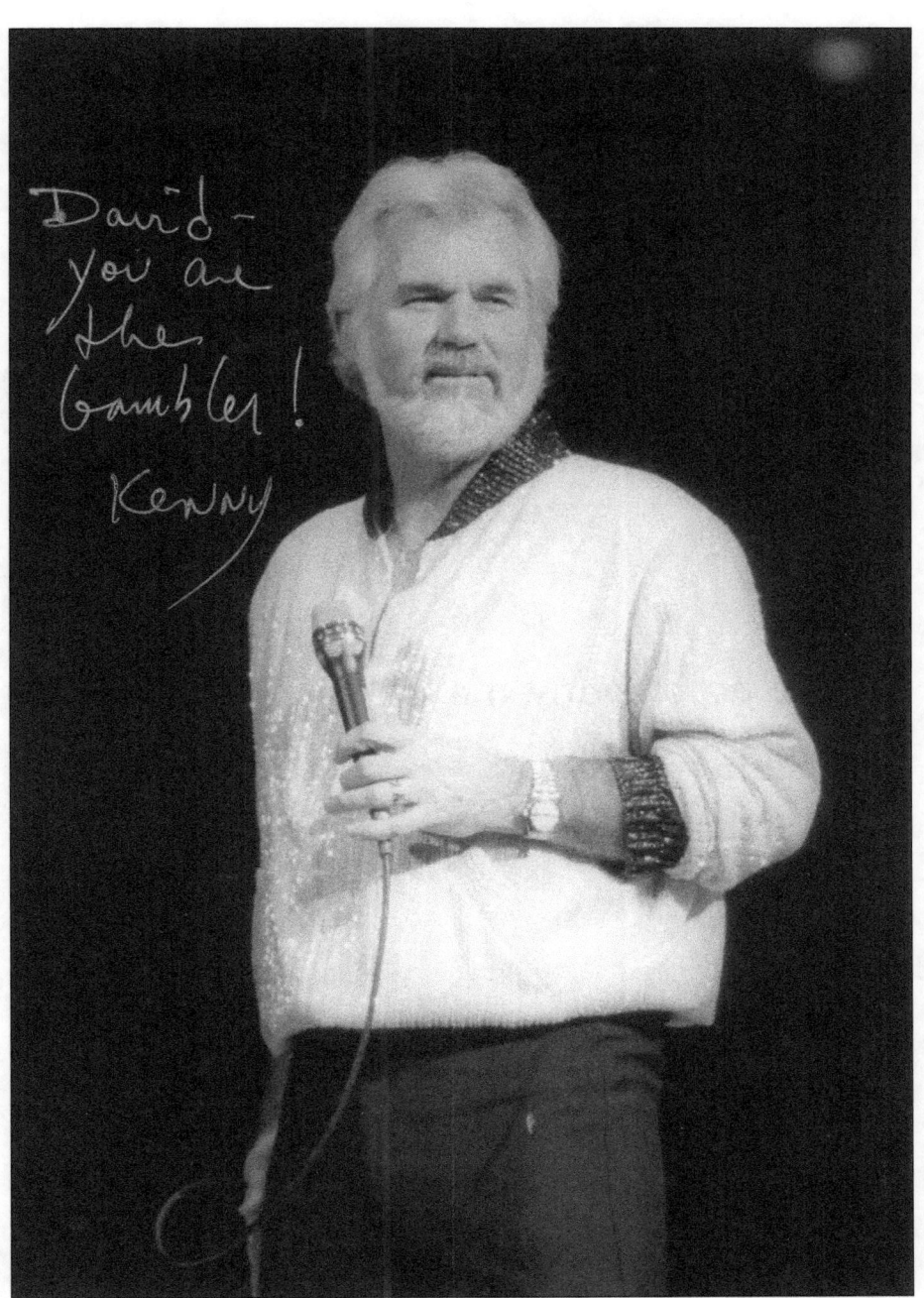

David –
you are
the
Gambler !
Kenny

Koko Taylor
Musician

David–
Please accompany me on my
upcoming tour.
    Koko

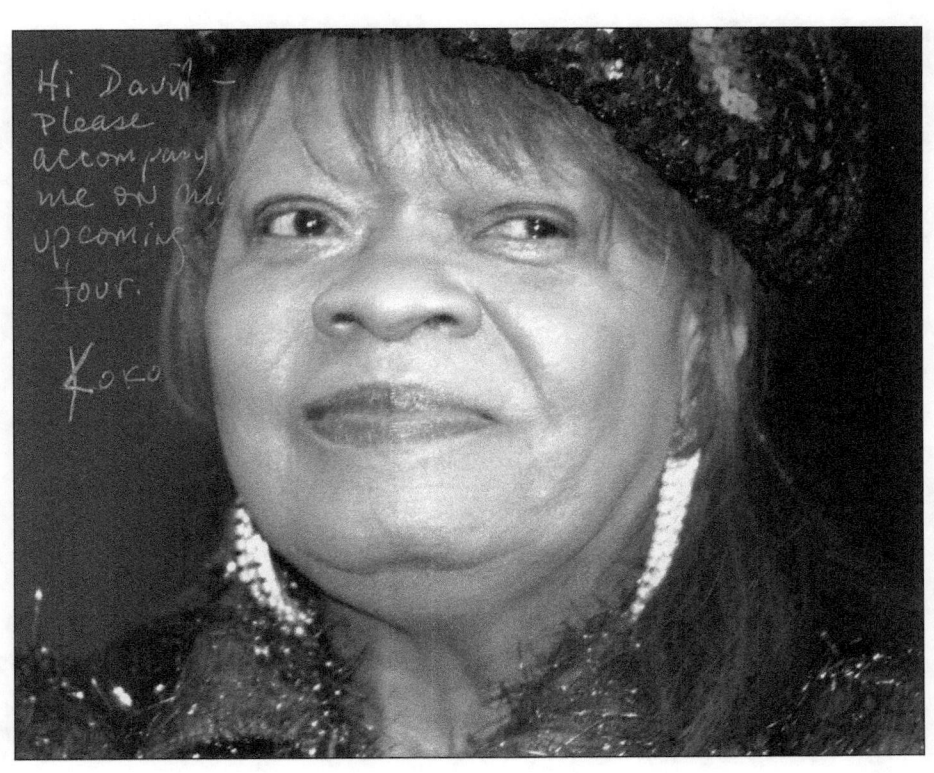

Kris Kristofferson
Musician, Actor

David–

You, me and Bobby McGee.

    Kris

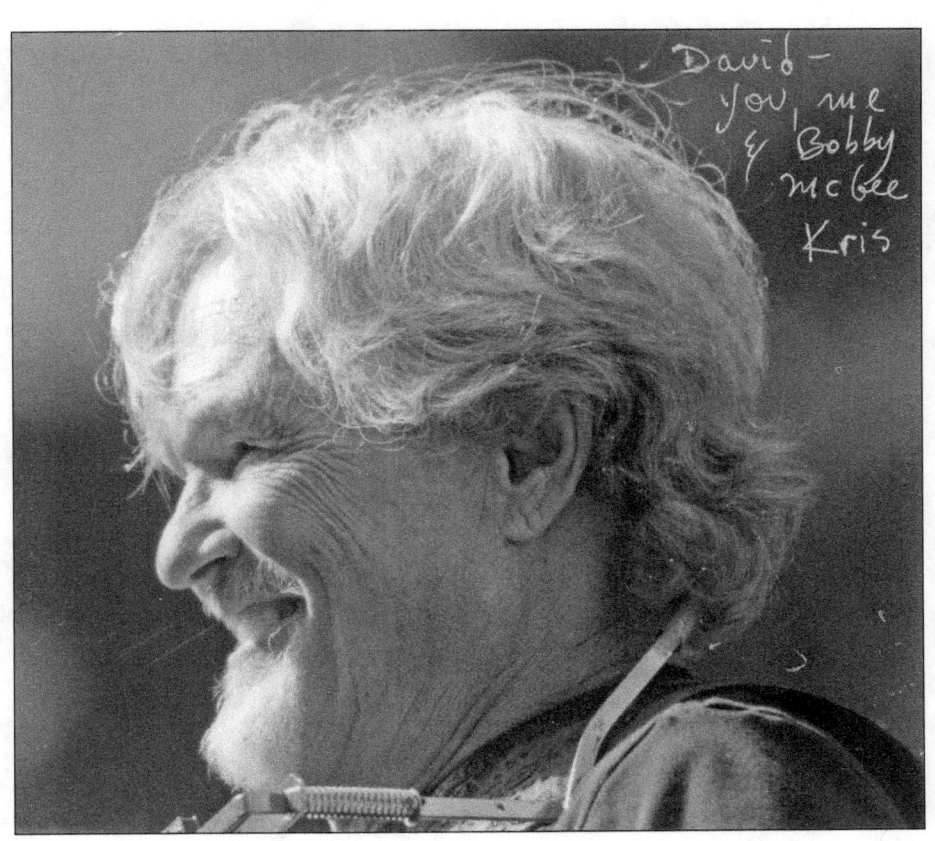

269

Leon Russell
Musician

David–
Please give me a couple more piano
lessons.
   Leon

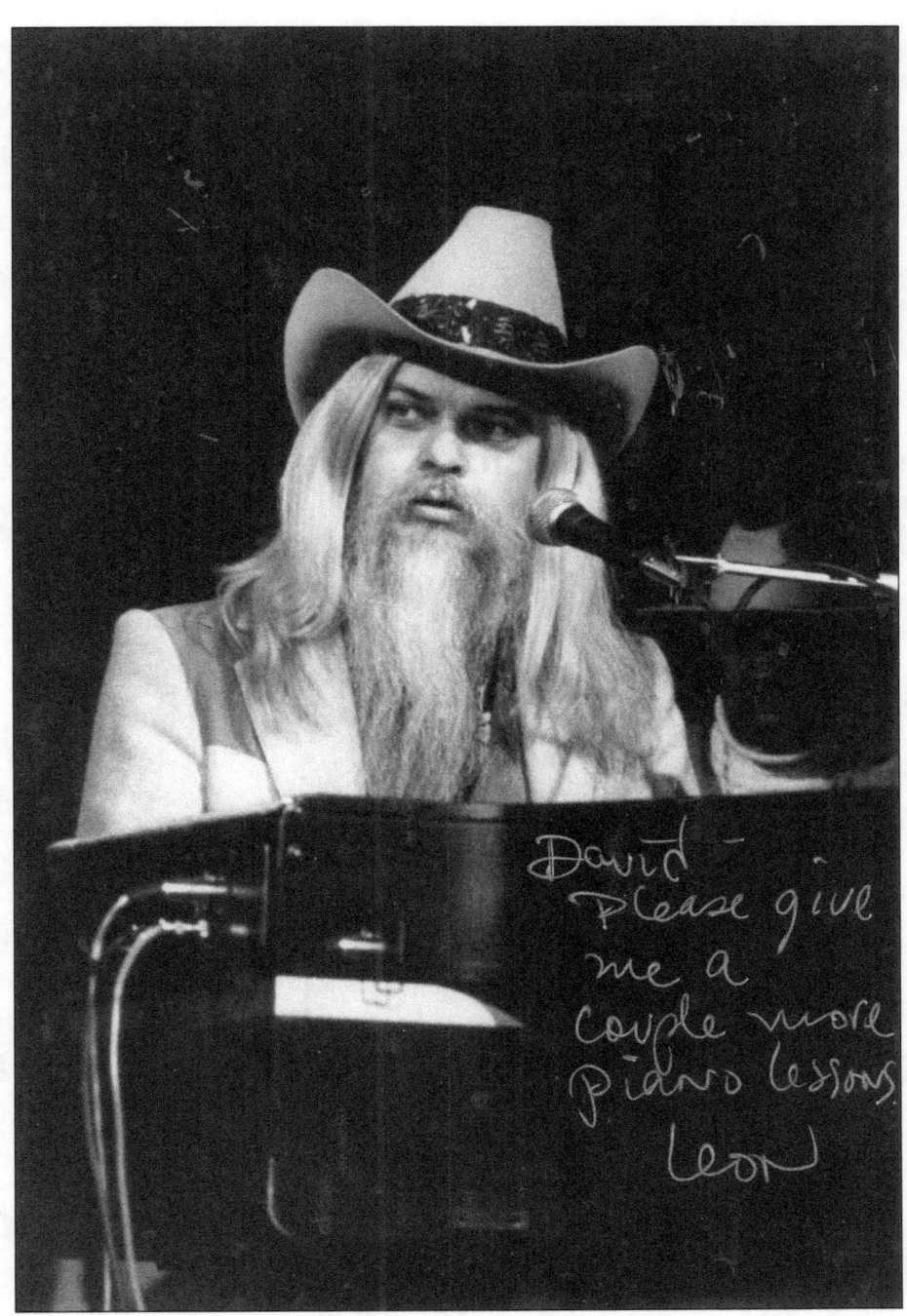

David –
Please give
me a
couple more
Piano lessons
Leon

Loretta Lynn
Musician

Hi David–
I want to be opening act for your
next gig.
        Loretta

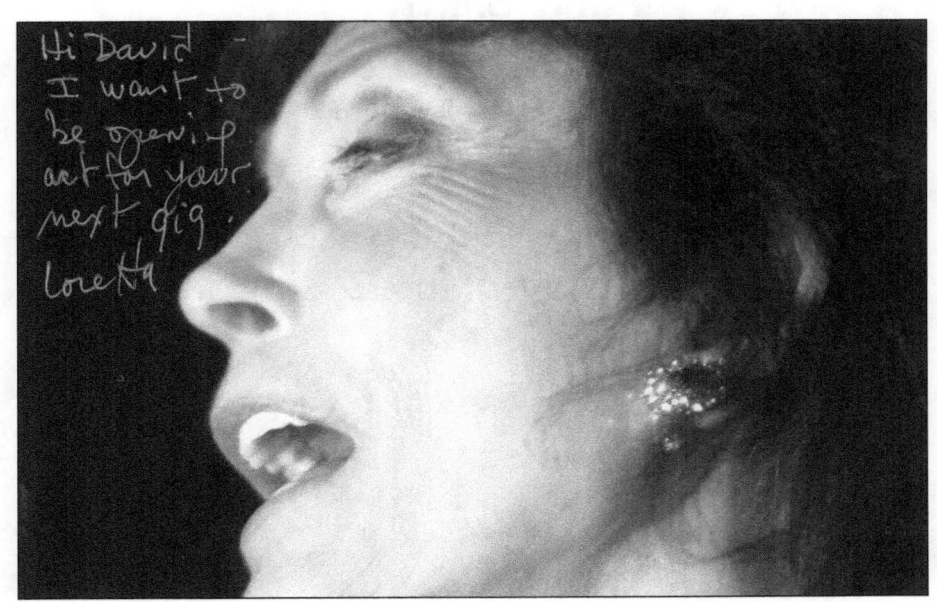

Patti Smith
Musician, Author

David–
I want you to play piano & sing in
my band.
  Love,
  Patti

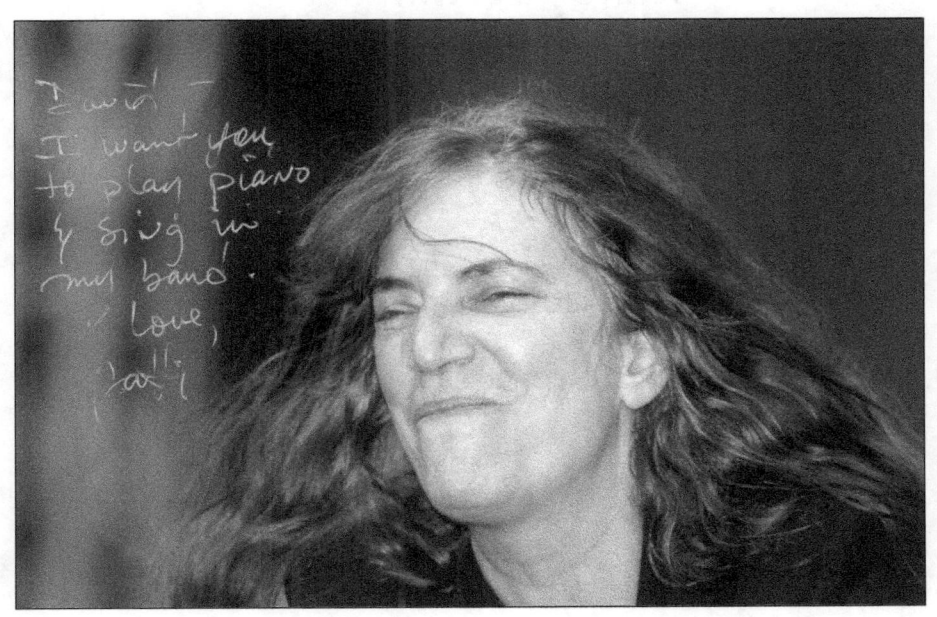

Randy Newman
Musician

David–
Let's tour as a duet piano team.
    Your buddy,
    Randy

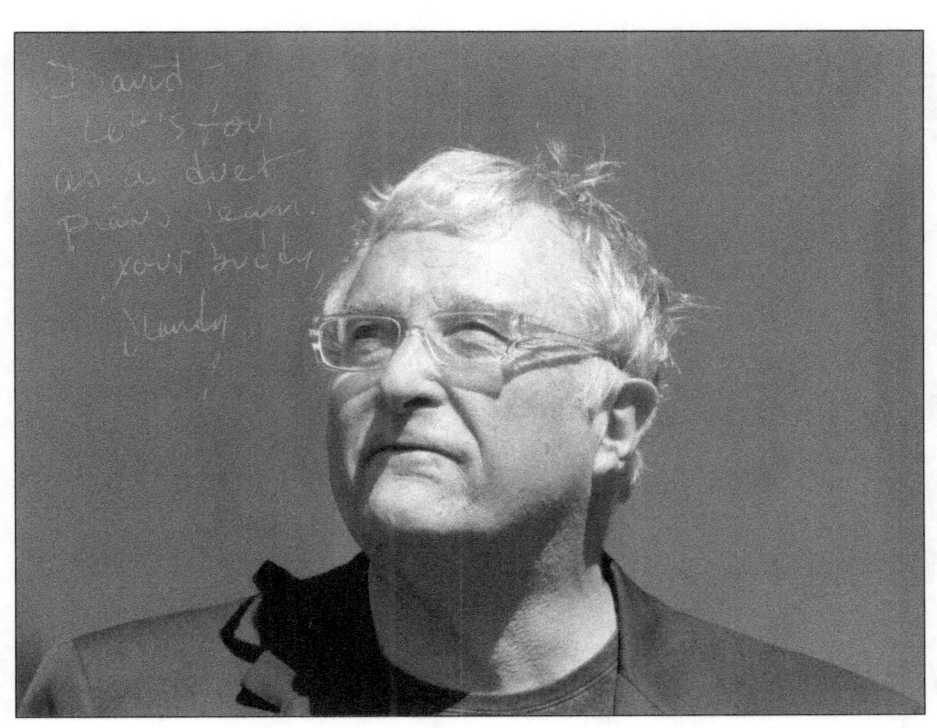

Steve Miller
Musician

David–
Fly like an eagle!
    Steve

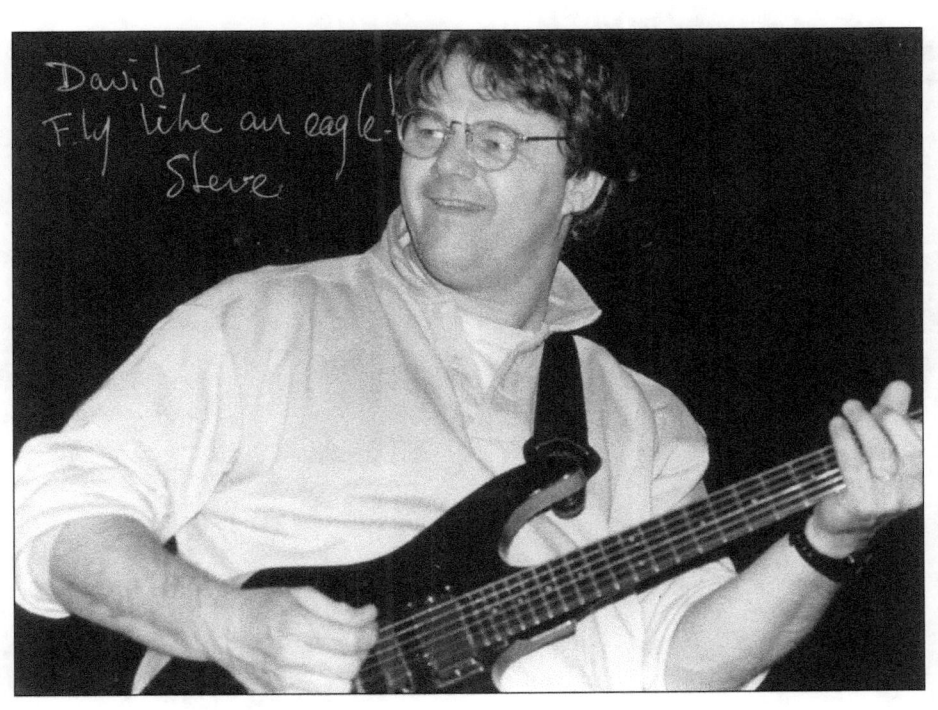

279

Tina Turner
Musician

David–
Big wheel keep on turnin'
      Your pal,
      Tina

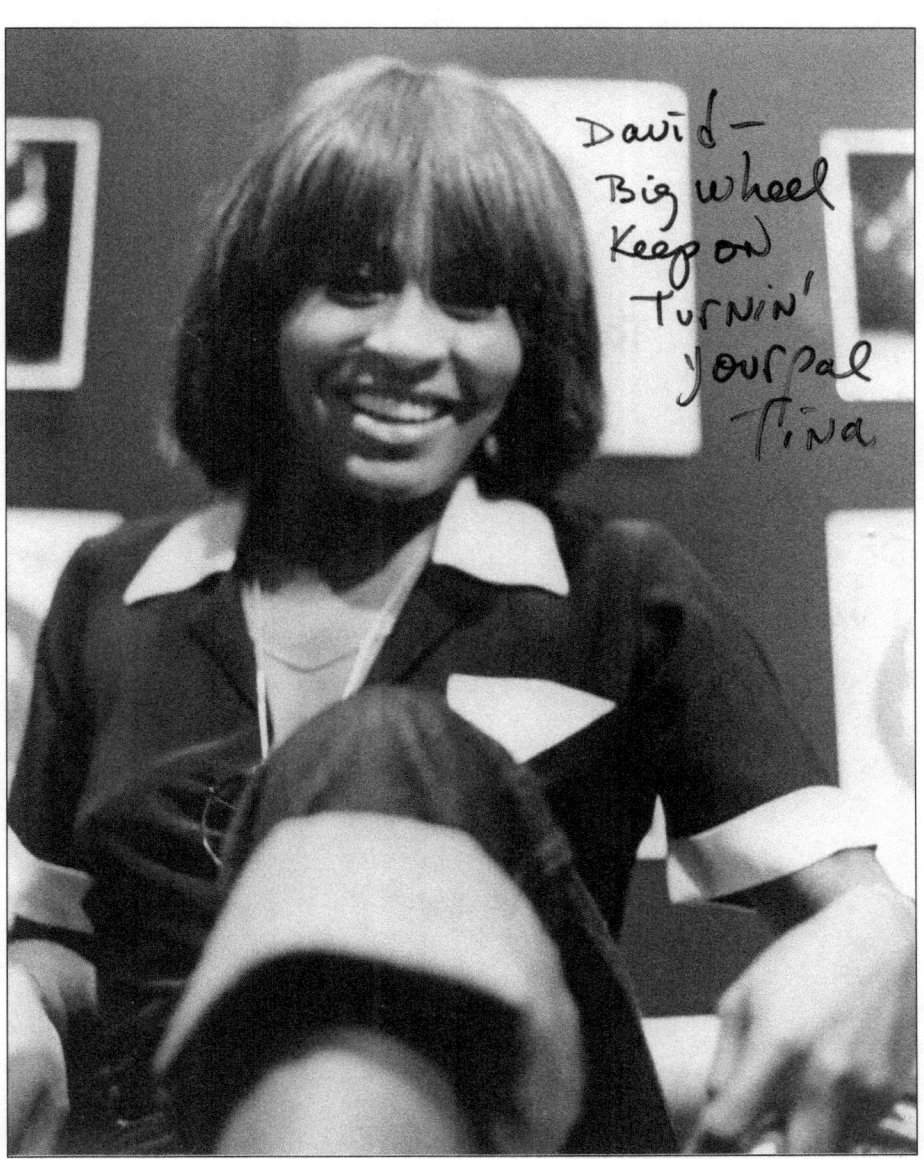

David —
Big wheel
keep on
turnin'
your pal
Tina

Tony Bennett
Musician

David,
I want you as my pianist.
    Your closest friend,
    Tony B.

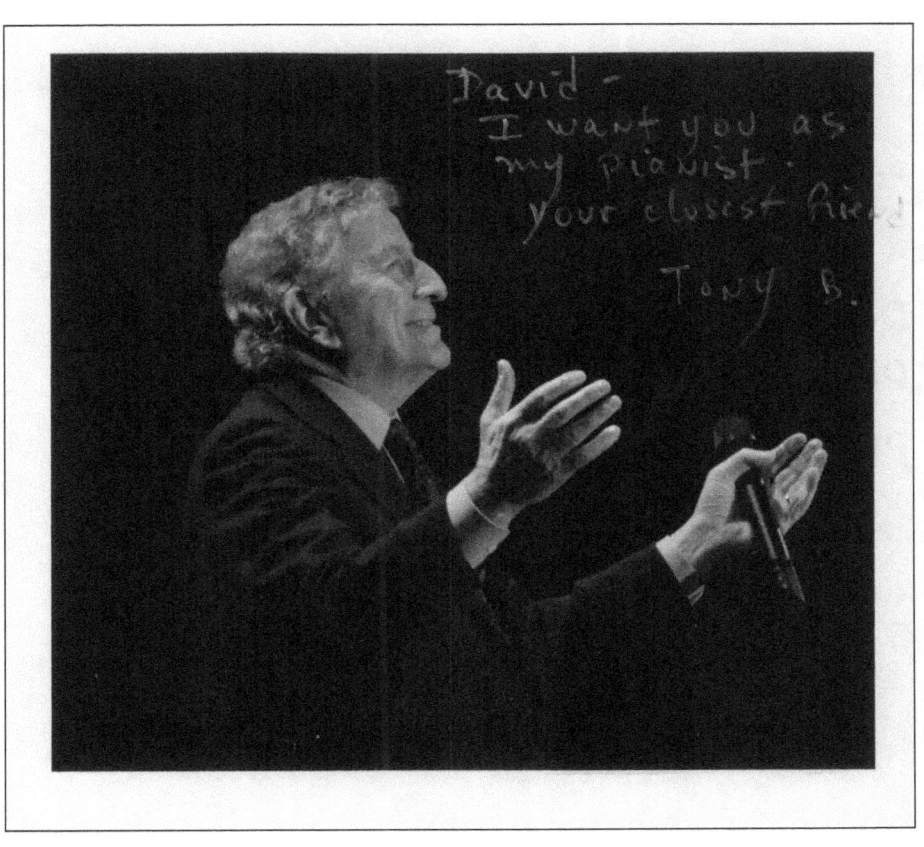

Van Cliburn
Musician

David–
Please teach me that Tchaikovsky
piece.
    Thanks,
    Van

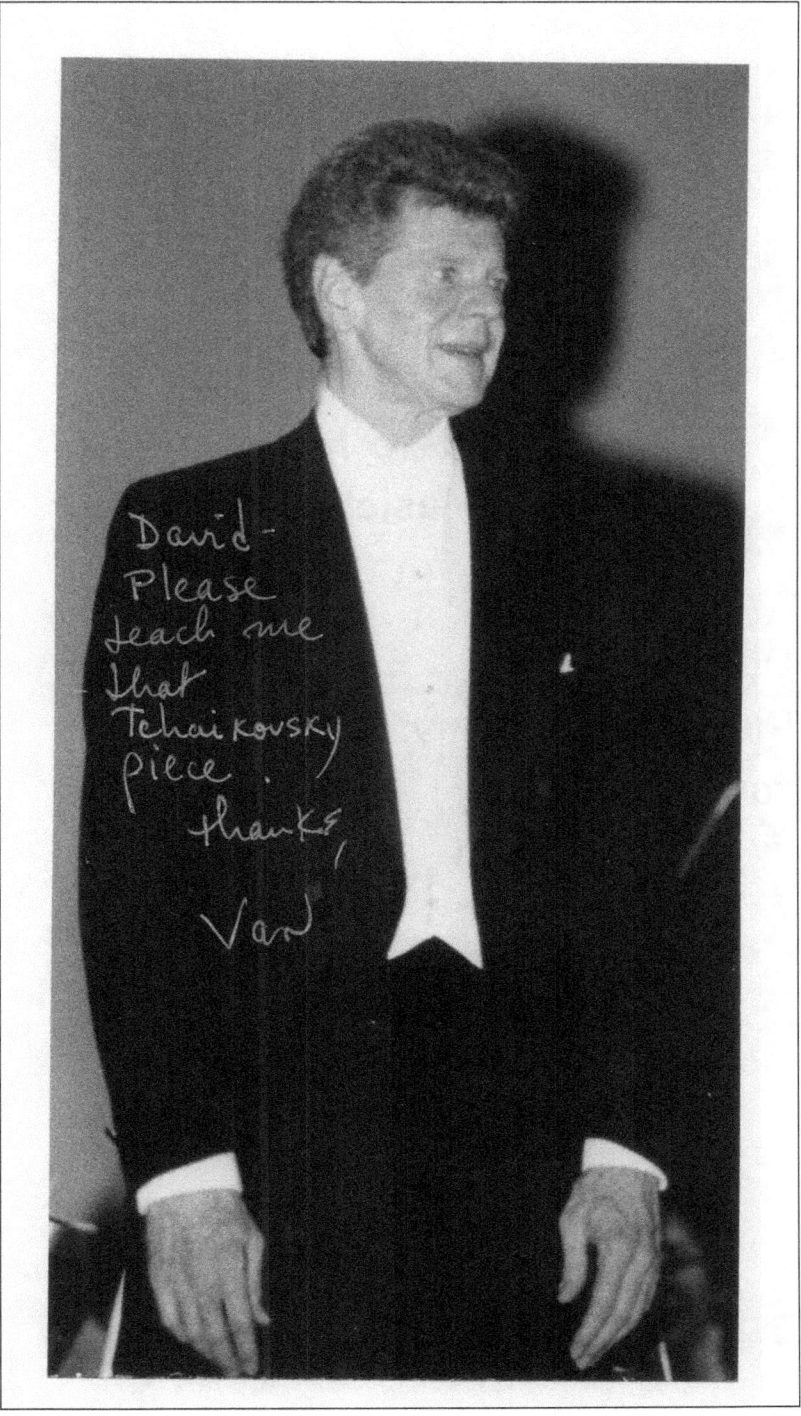

285

Yo-Yo Ma
Musician

David–
Please accompany me on my next
tour.
    Your friend,
    Yo-Yo

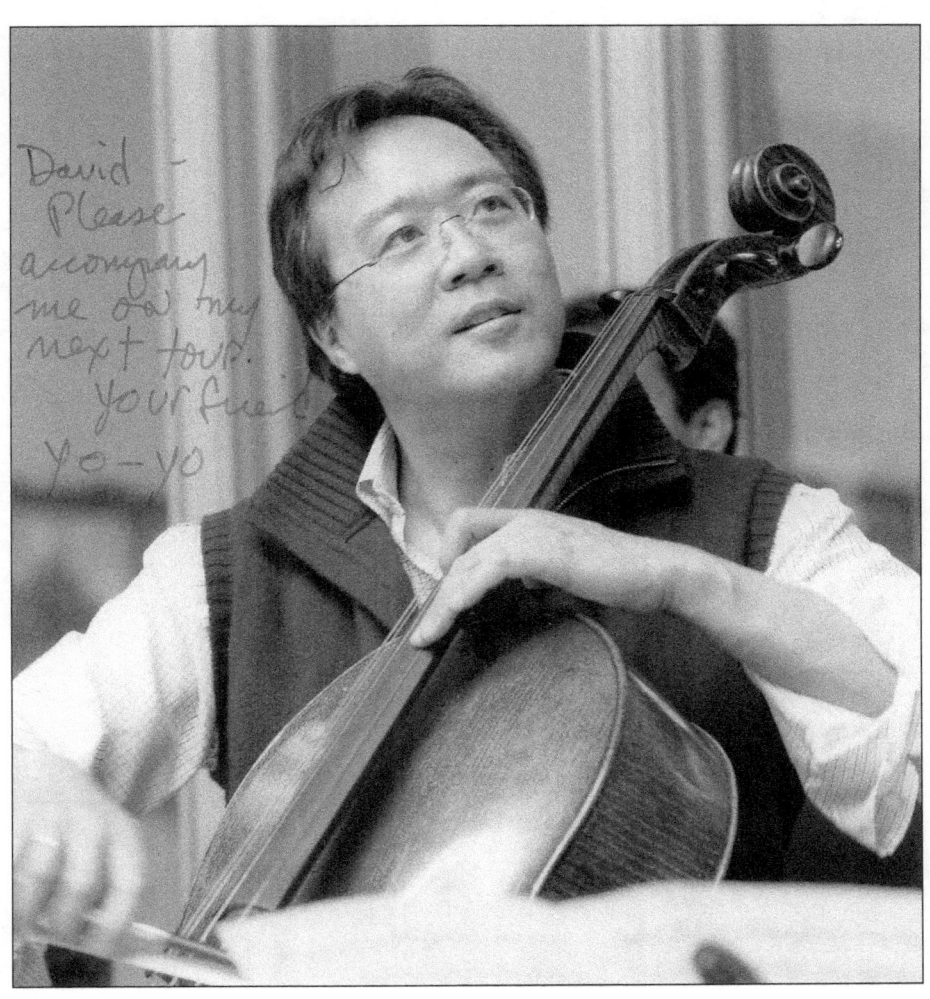

David —
Please
accompany
me on my
next tour.
Your frie[nd]
Yo-Yo

NEWS ANCHORS & NEWSMAKERS

Gwen Ifill
News Anchor

David–
I want you to be my co-anchor.
    Your friend,
    Gwen

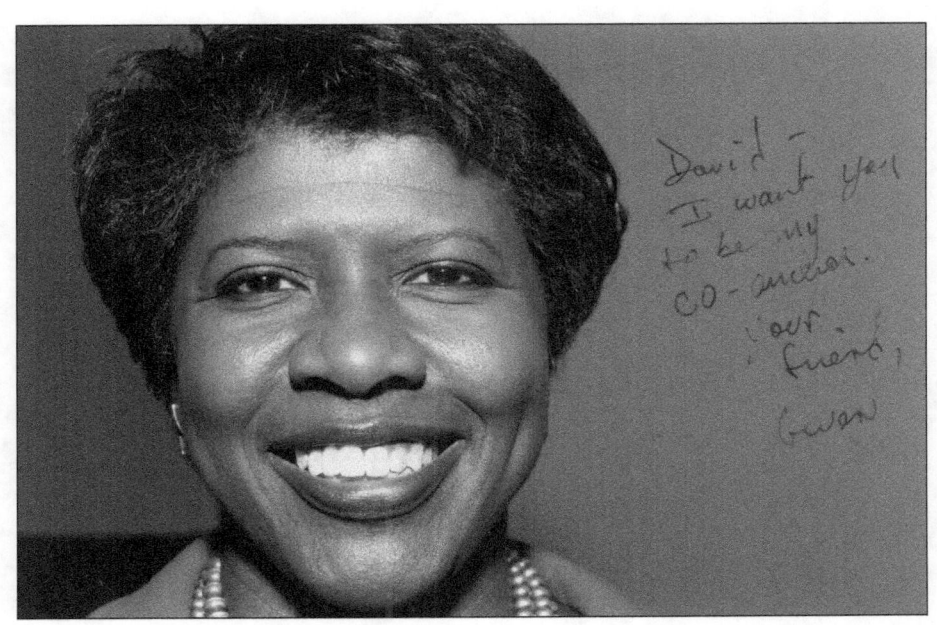

James Carville
Political Analyst

David–
How about us doing a Sunday
morning TV talk show together?
    Your friend,
    Jim

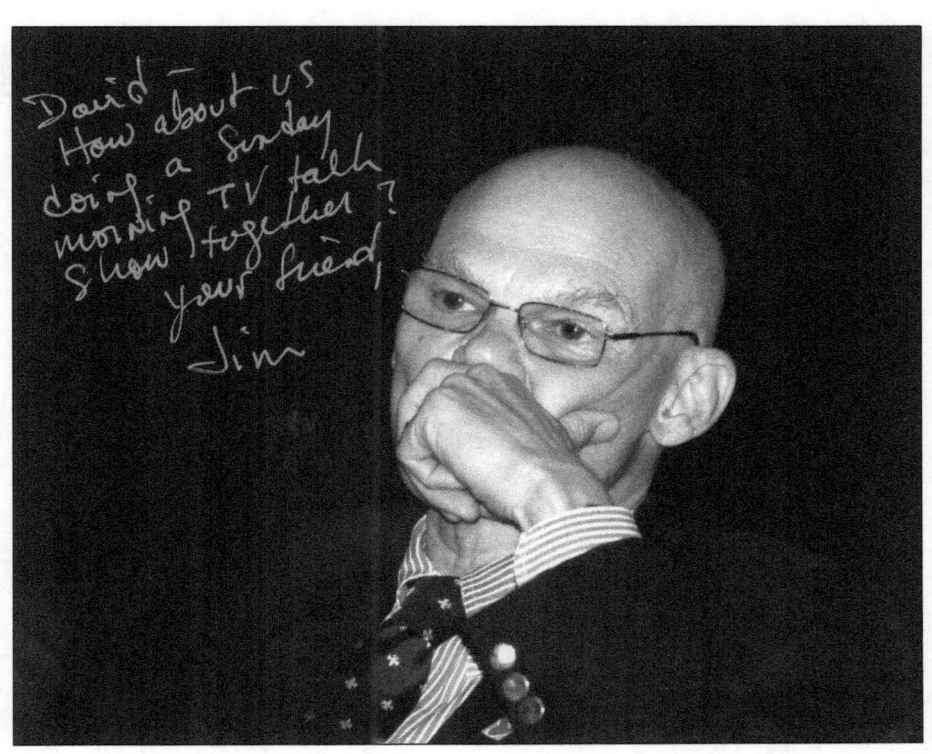

Jim Lehrer
News Anchor

David,
I want you to be my co-anchor.
    Your friend,
    Jim

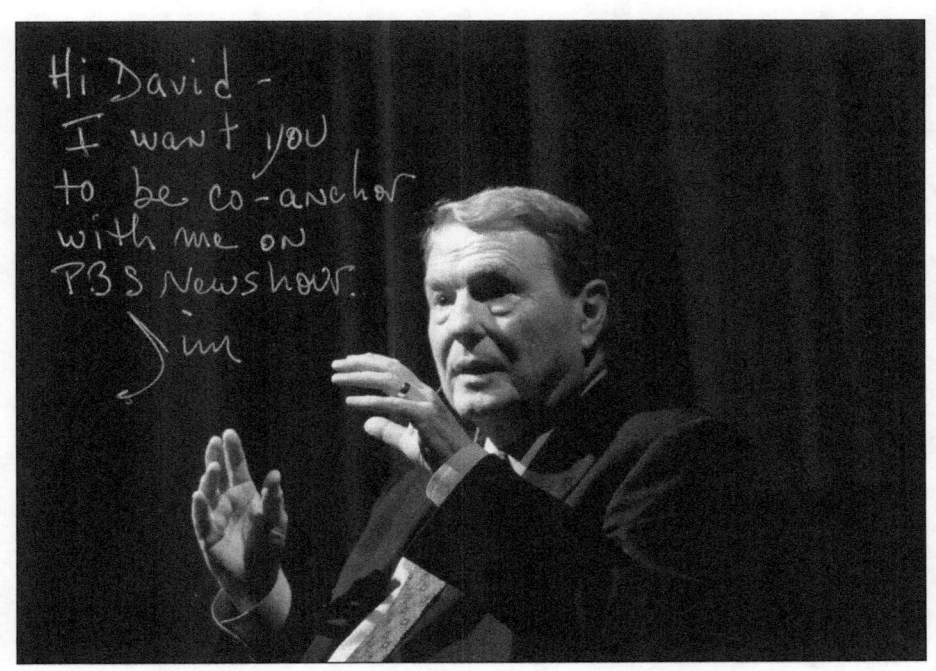

Lesley Stahl
News Anchor

David–
I'd like you to join me on 60 Minutes.
    Lesley

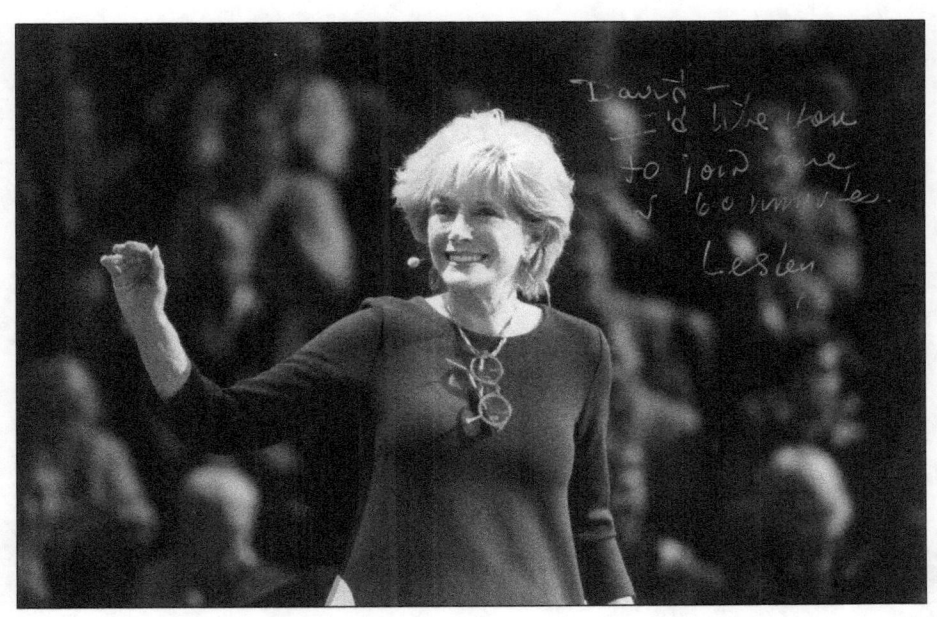

Robert Krulwich
Radio Host

David–
Let's do a radio show together.
    Best,
    Bob

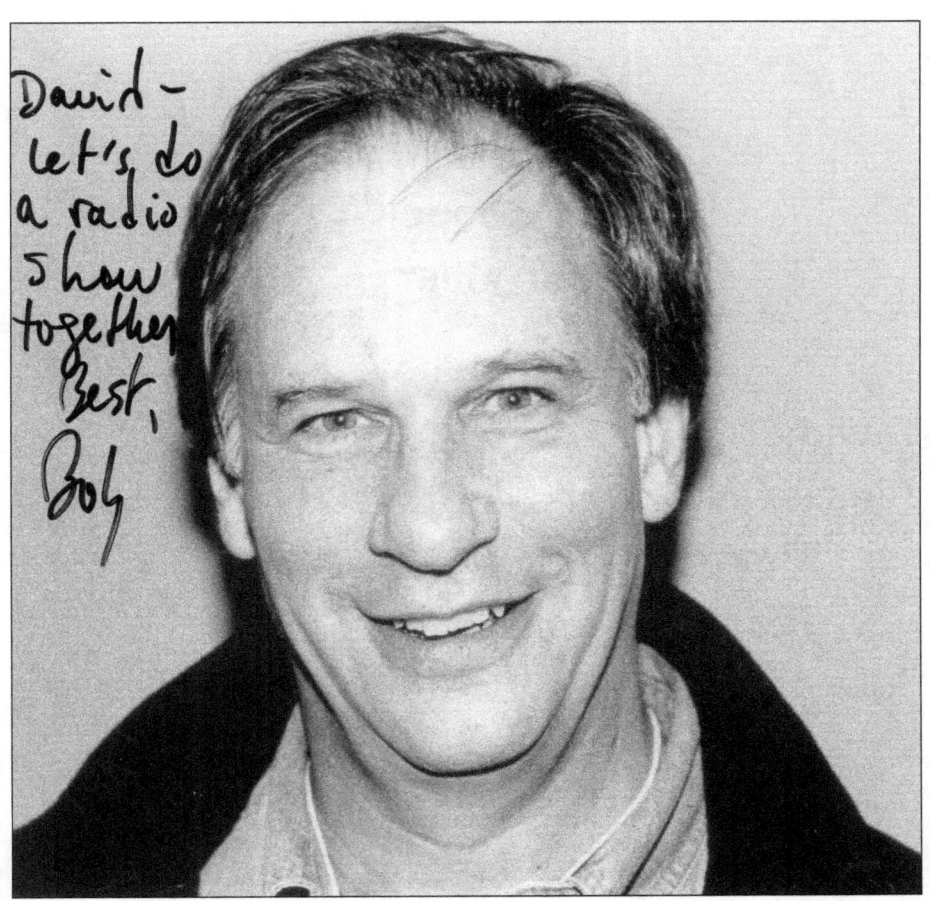

David —
Let's do
a radio
show
together
Best,
Bob

299

Ted Koppel
Journalist

David–
Please take over Nightline for me.
    Thanks,
    Ted

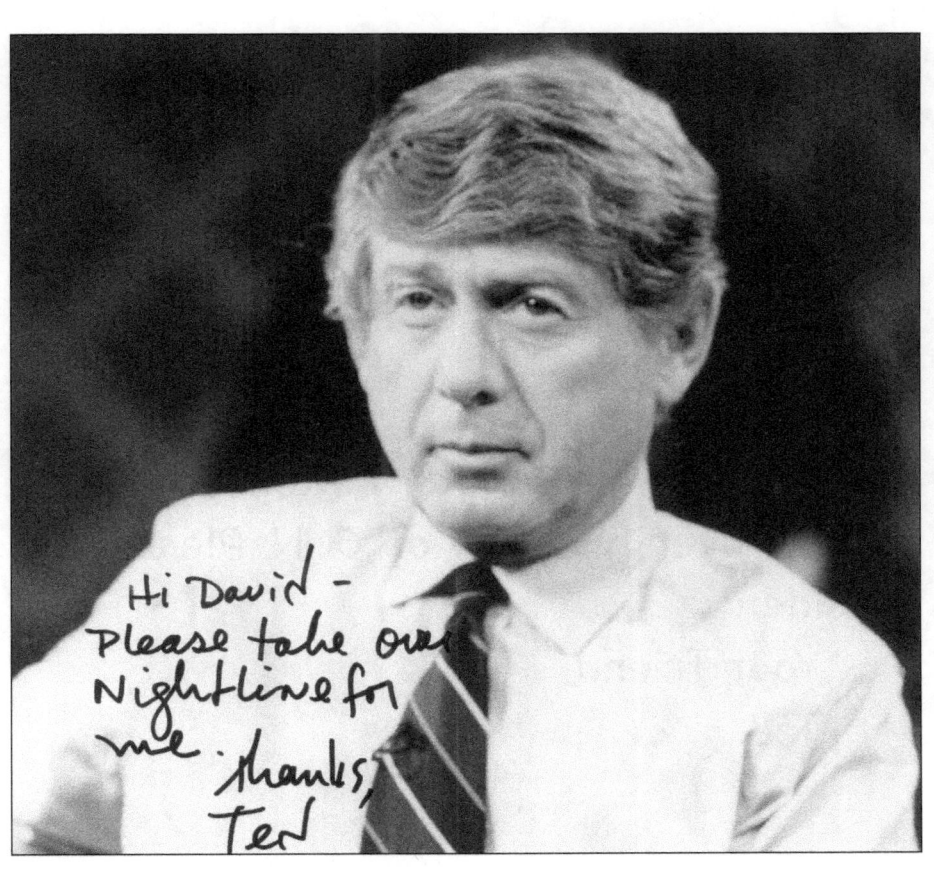

Hi David —
Please take over
Nightline for
me. thanks;
Ted

Ted Turner
Philanthropist, CNN Founder

David–
Larry King is retiring & I want you
to take over his show on CNN. Please
consider.

    Your friend,
    Ted

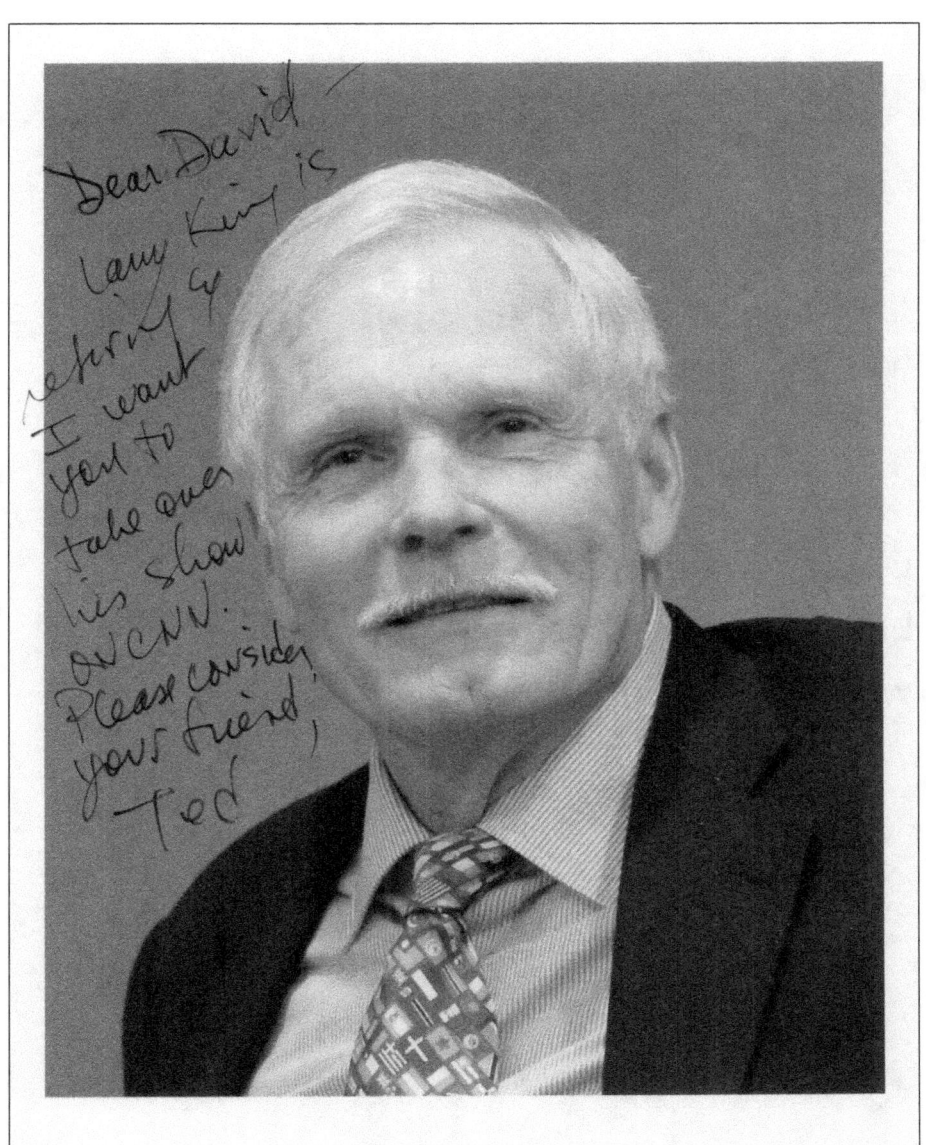

Dear David —
Larry King is
retiring &
I want
you to
take over
his show
on CNN.
Please consider!
your friend,
Ted

Tom Brokaw
News Anchor

David,
Let's get together to discuss the
world situation.
    Your friend,
    Tom

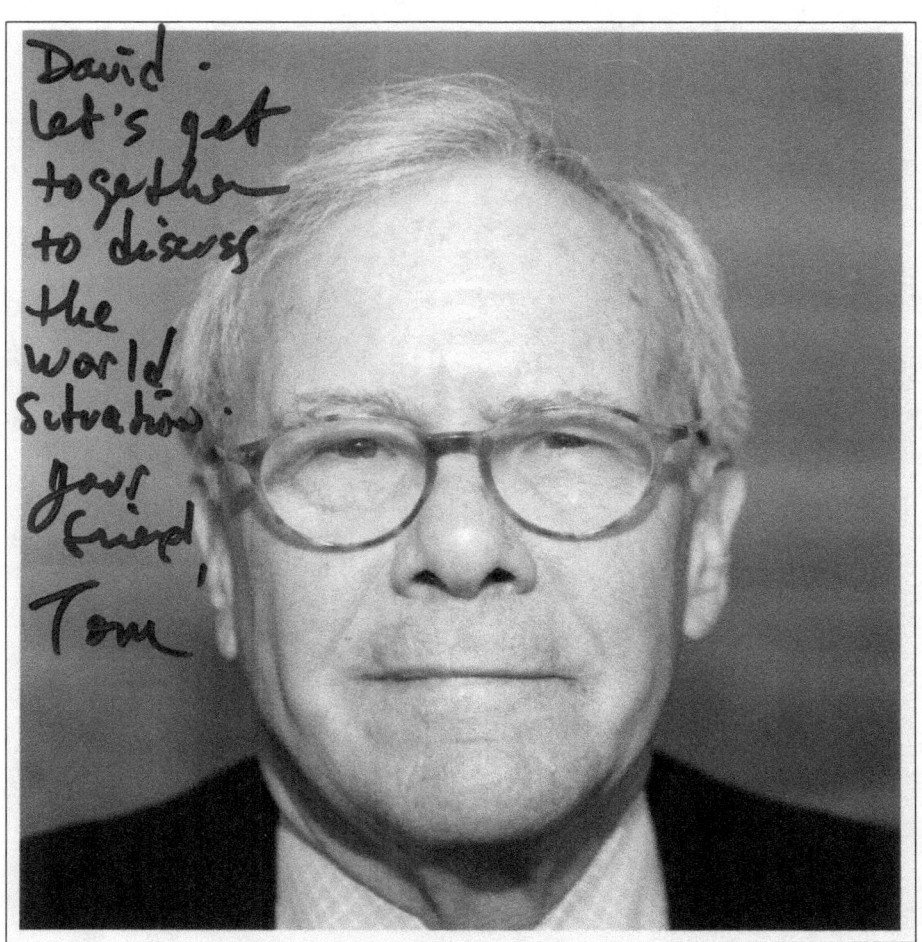

David.
Let's get
together
to discuss
the
world
situation.
Your
friend,
Tom

POLITICIANS

Arnold Schwarzenegger
Governor of California, Athlete

David–
I need your help passing this
budget–
    Your friend,
    Arnold

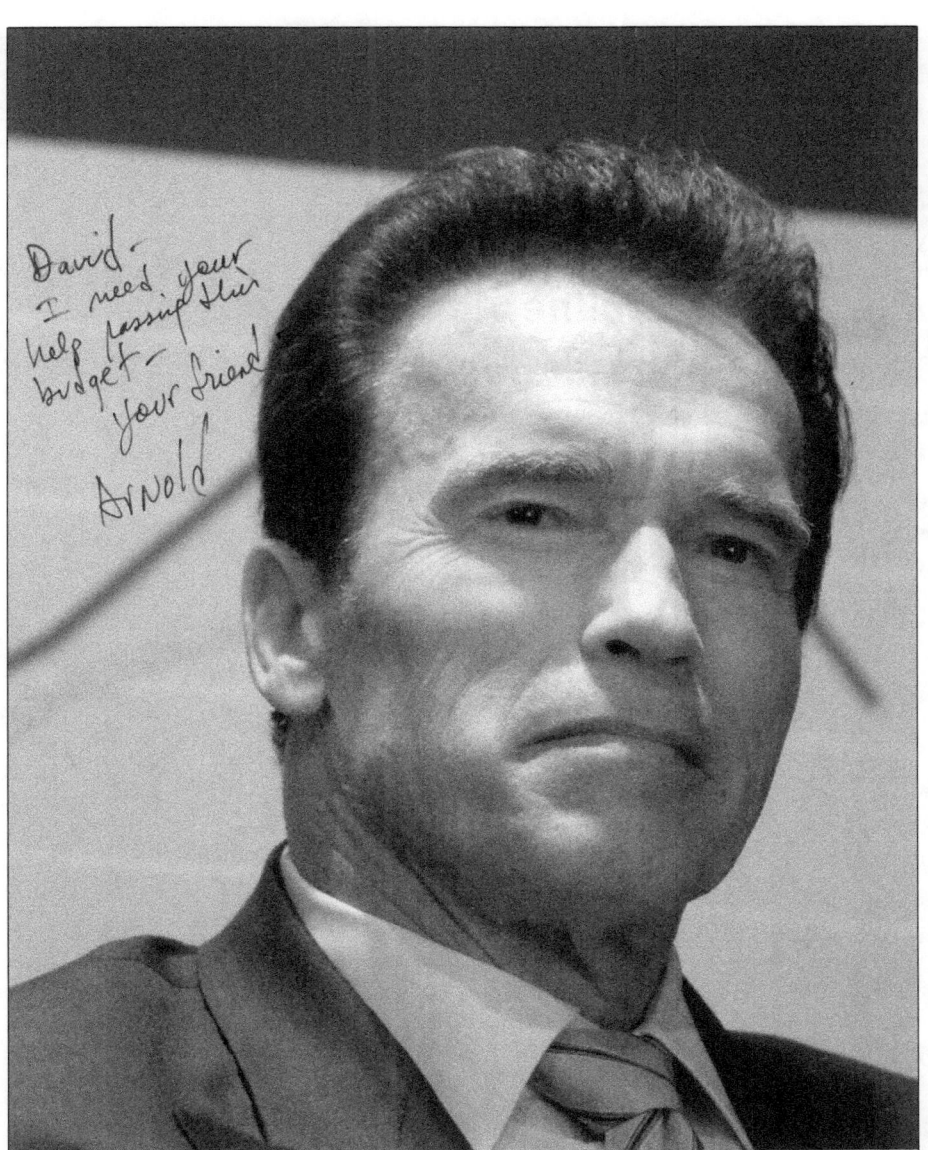

David –
I need your
help passing this
budget –
       Your friend
    Arnold

Caroline Kennedy
Ambassador, Author

David,
You are still my closest friend.
    Caroline Kennedy

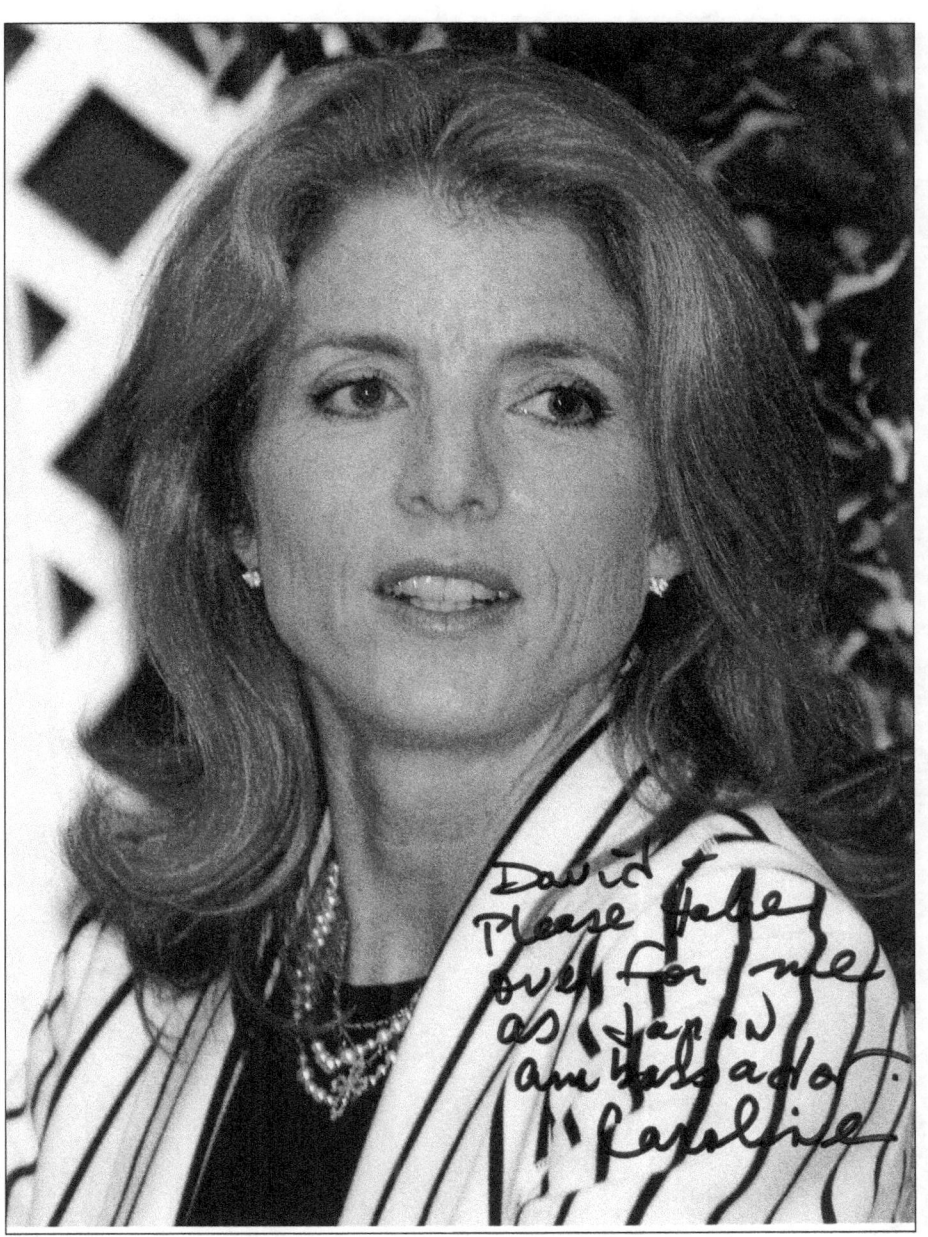

David,
Please take
over for me
as Japan
ambassador.
Caroline

Colin Powell
Secretary of State, General, Author

David,
Let's work together.
    Your friend,
    Colin

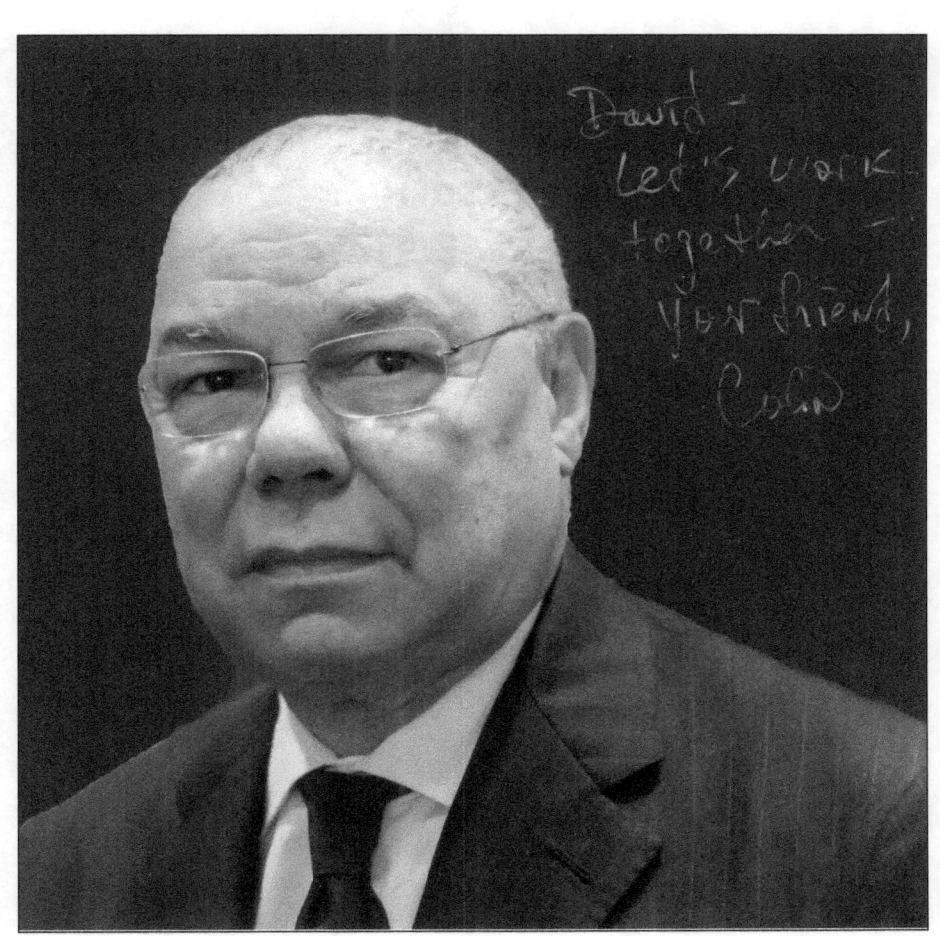

David —
Let's work
together —
Your friend,
Colin

Condoleezza Rice
Secretary of State

David–

I need your help on an upcoming diplomatic mission.

Your friend,

Condy

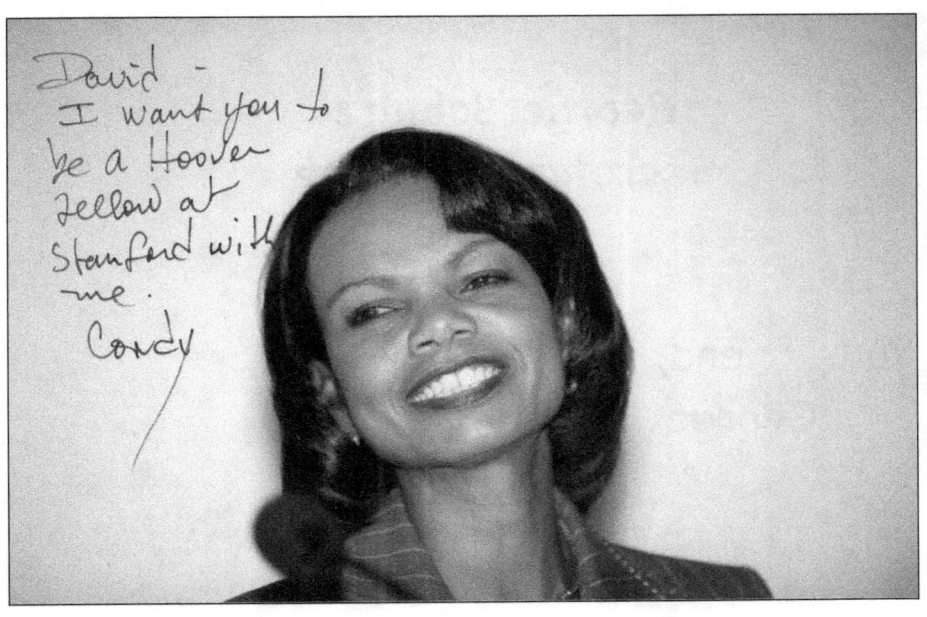

**George Schultz
Secretary of State**

Your friend,
George

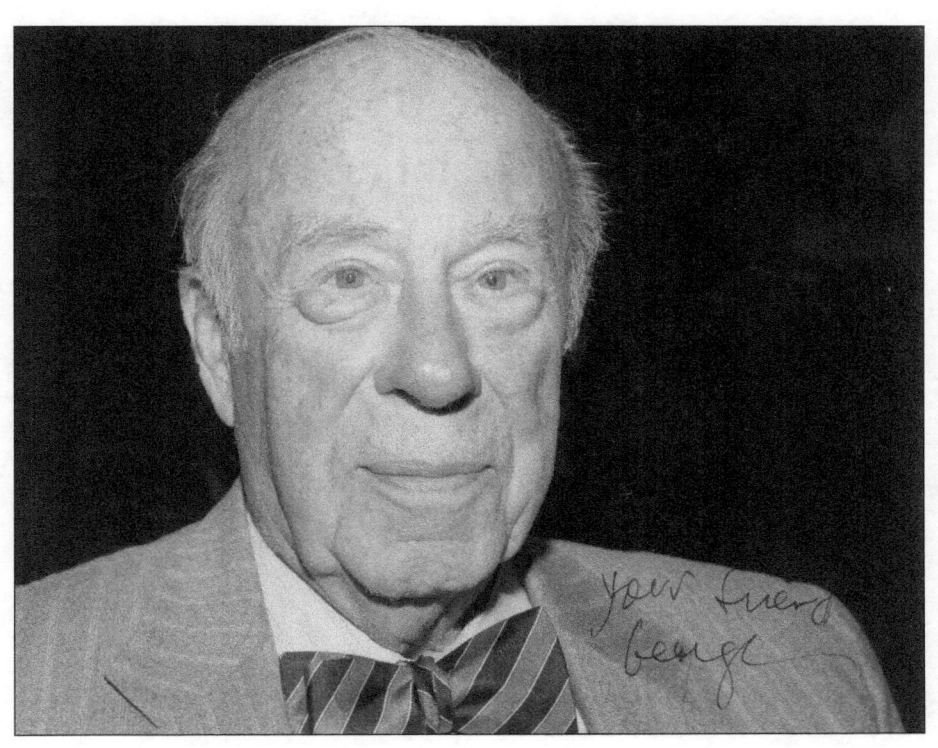

Henry Kissinger
Secretary of State

David—
I can't be president but you can.
    Your friend,
    Henry

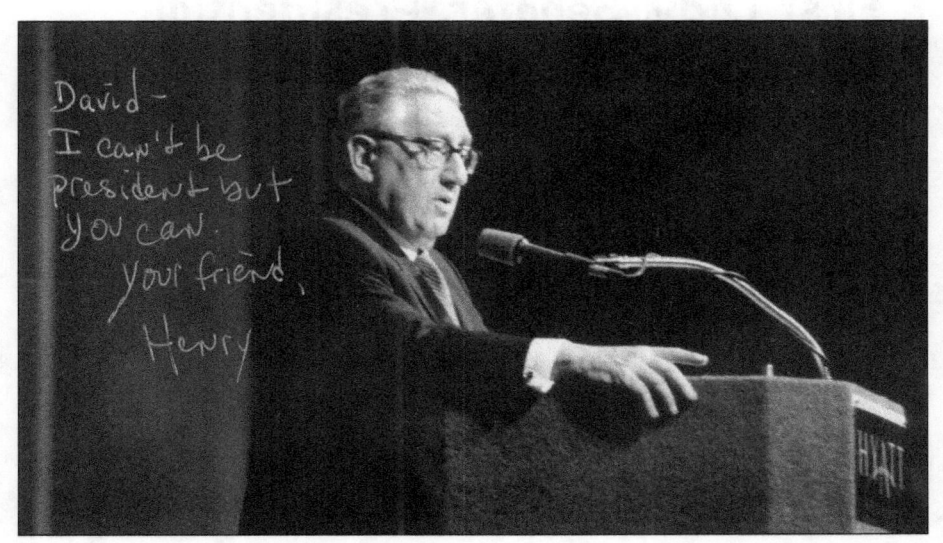

319

Hillary Clinton
First Lady, Senator, Presidential Candidate

David–
I will run if you will be my V.P.
    Hillary

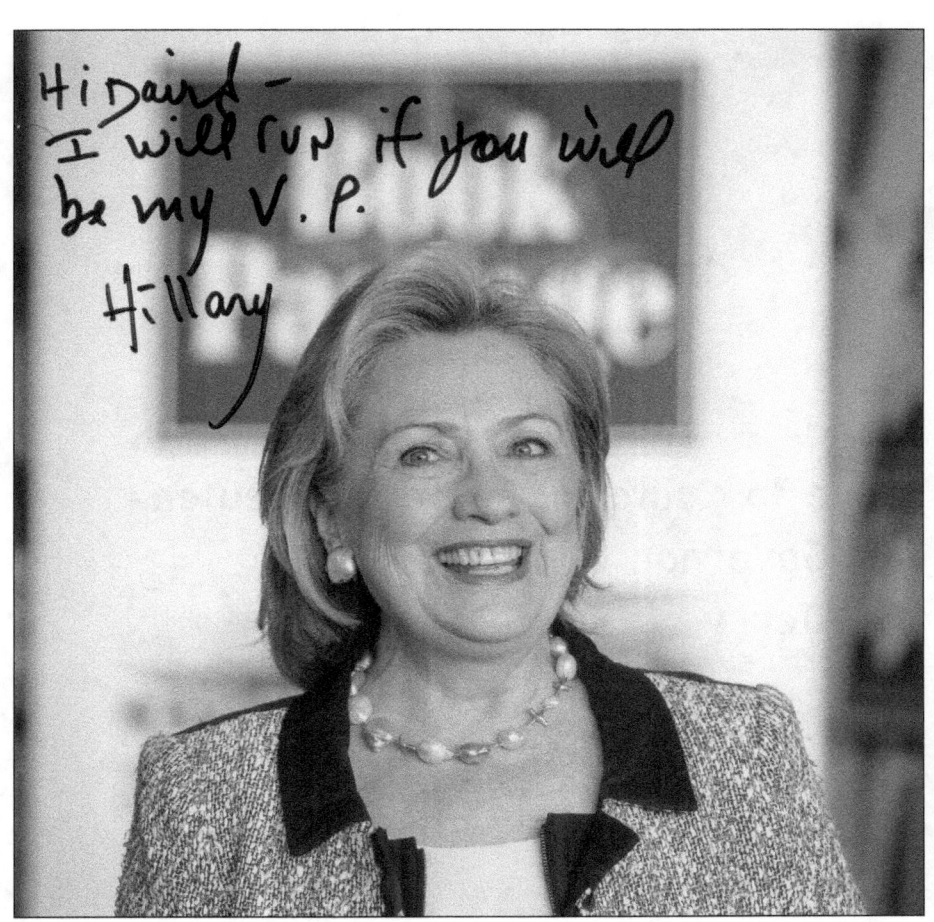

Jerry Brown
California Governor

David–

Move to California & be my Lieuten-
ant Governor.

Jerry

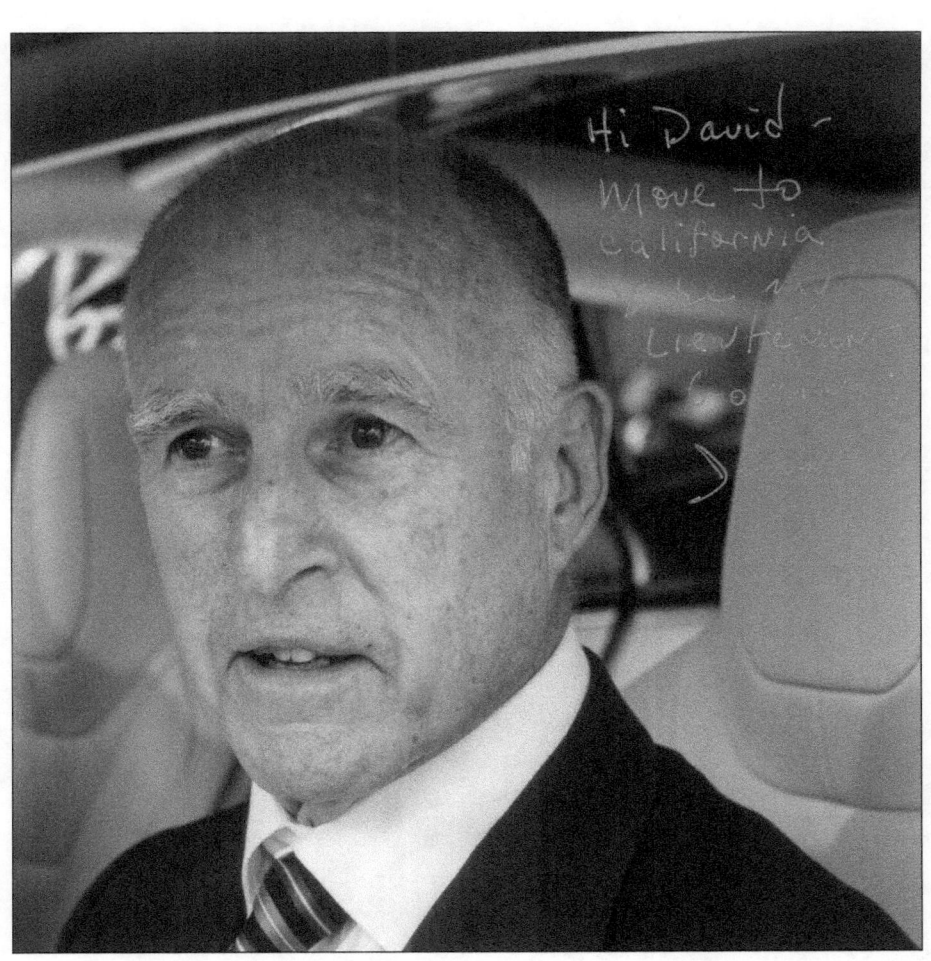

Michael Bloomberg
New York City Mayor

David–

We can win in 2016 if you are my running mate.

    Mike

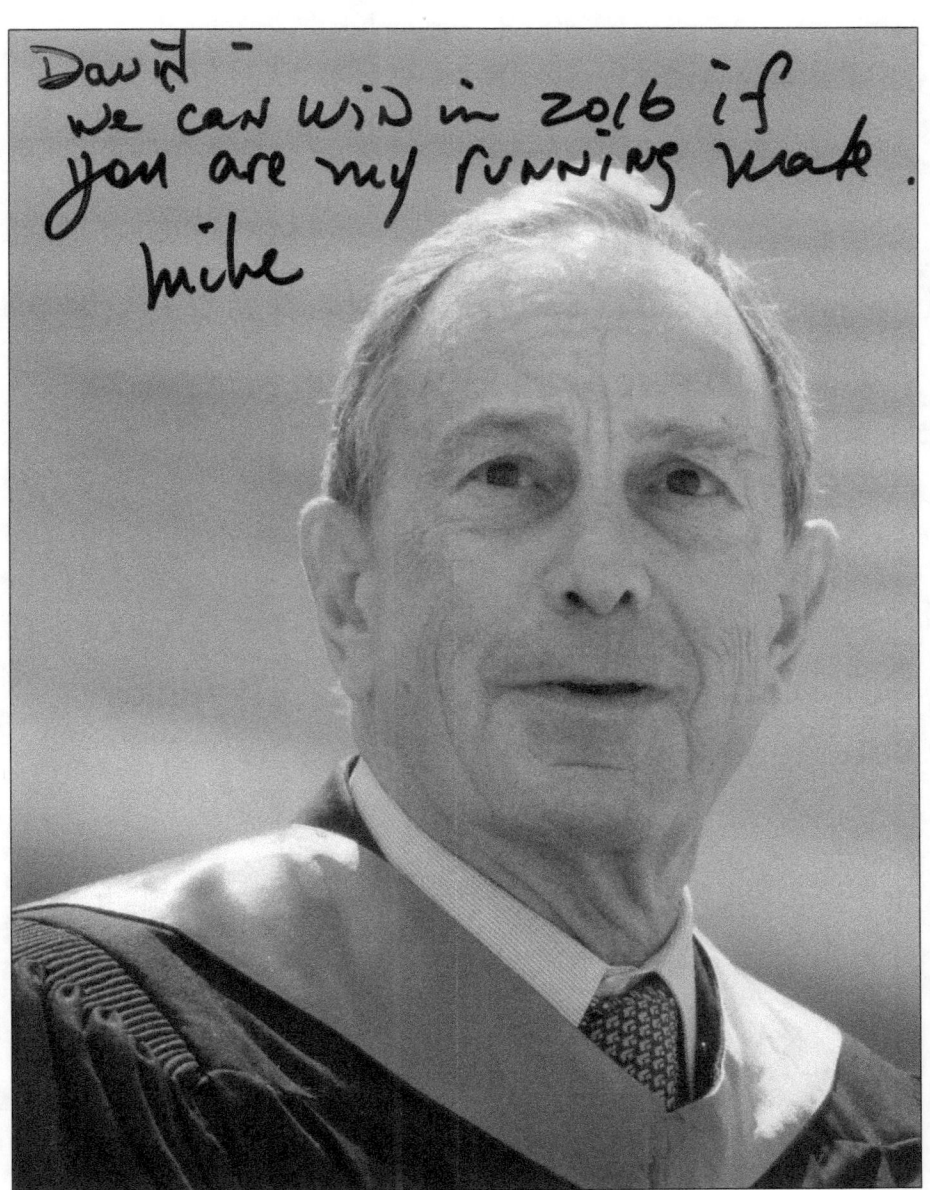

David –
we can win in 2016 if
you are my running mate.
mike

Nancy Pelosi
Congresswoman, Speaker of the House

Hey David–
Get elected to the House & I'll make you Speaker.
    Nancy

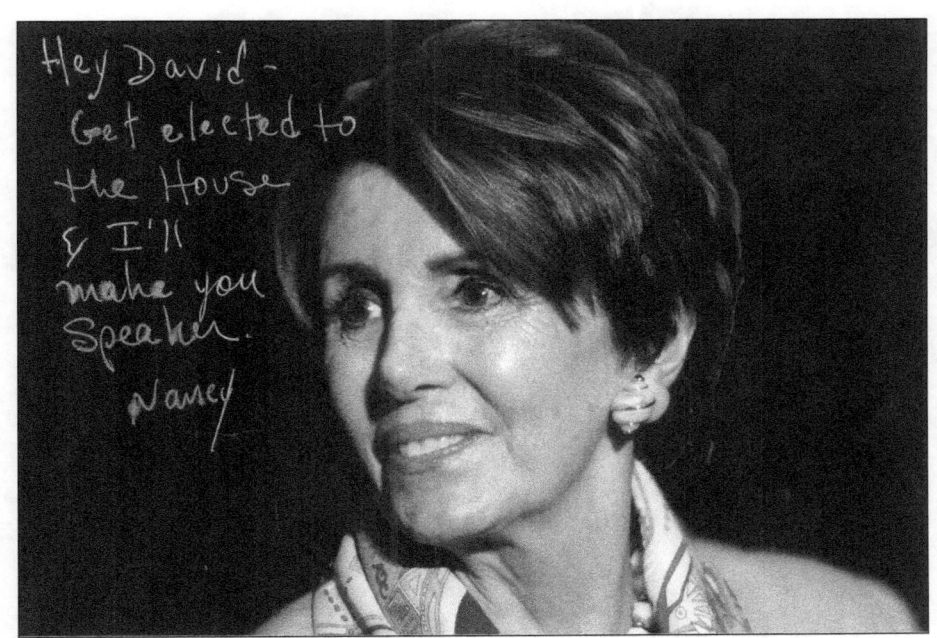

327

Pat Quinn
Governor of Illinois

David,
Move to Illinois so you can be my running mate.
    Your friend,
    Pat

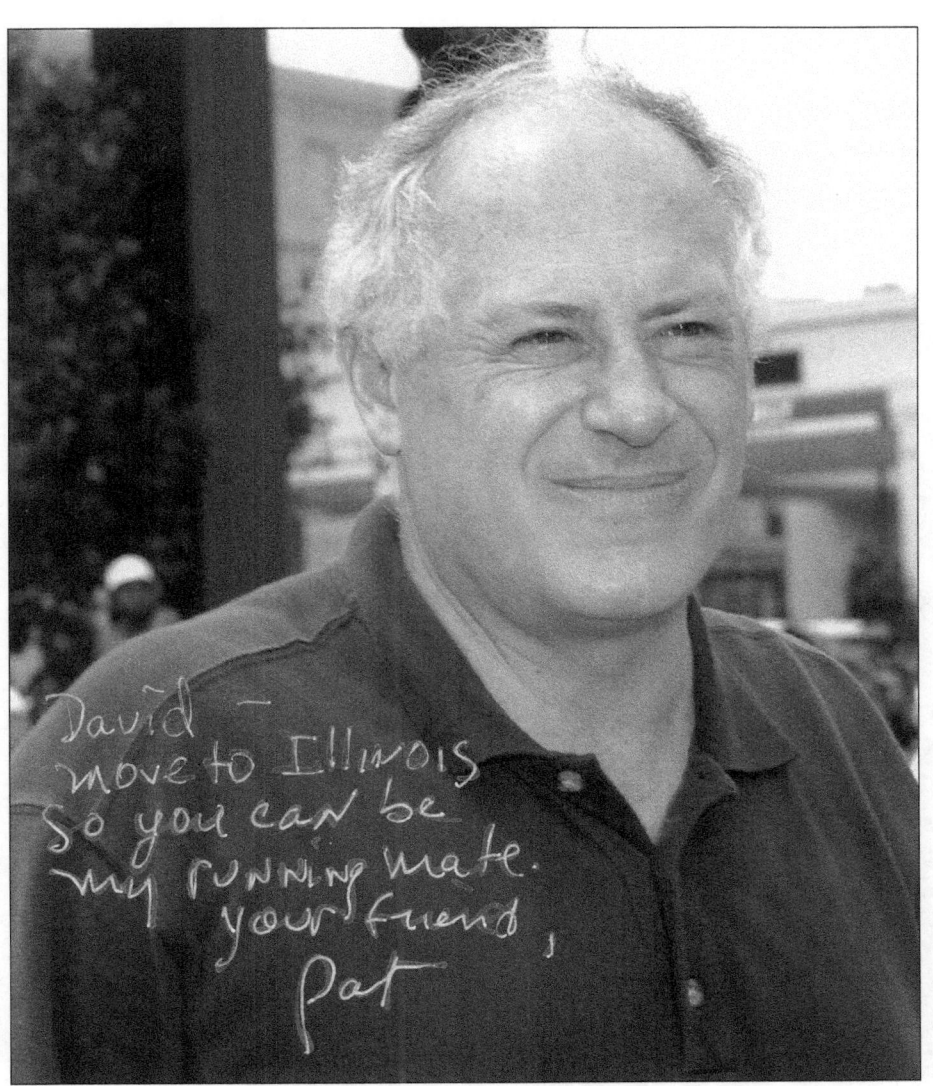

David –
move to Illinois
so you can be
my running mate.
your friend,
Pat

Rod Blagojevich
Governor of Illinois, Prisoner

David,
I am going to need your help staying
out of jail.
    Your buddy,
    Rod

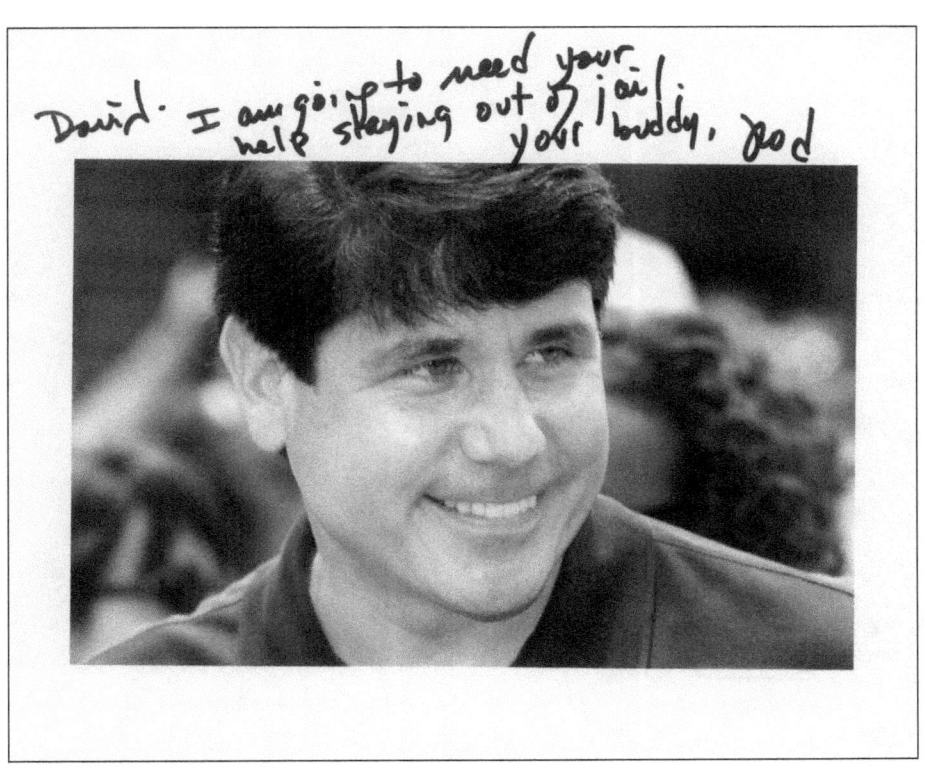

David. I am going to need your help staying out of jail. your buddy, Rod

PRESIDENTS
& CANDIDATES

Al Sharpton
Minister, Activist,
Presidential Candidate

Hi David–
Let's pray together.
    Al

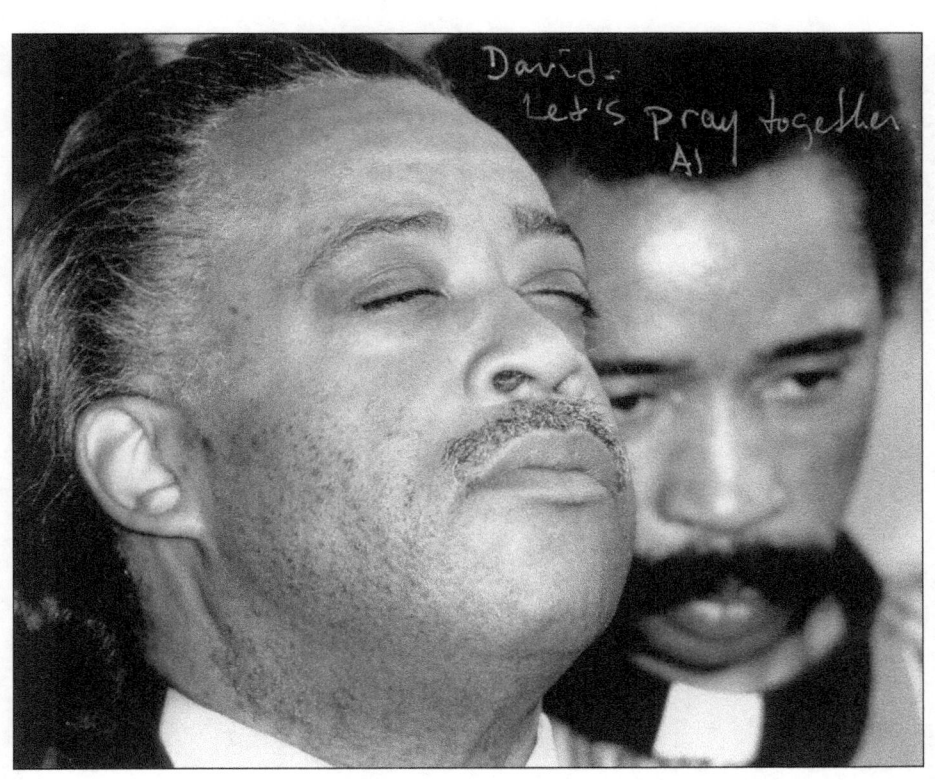

Barack Obama
President

David,
I want you to be my next Surgeon
General.
    Your friend,
    Barack

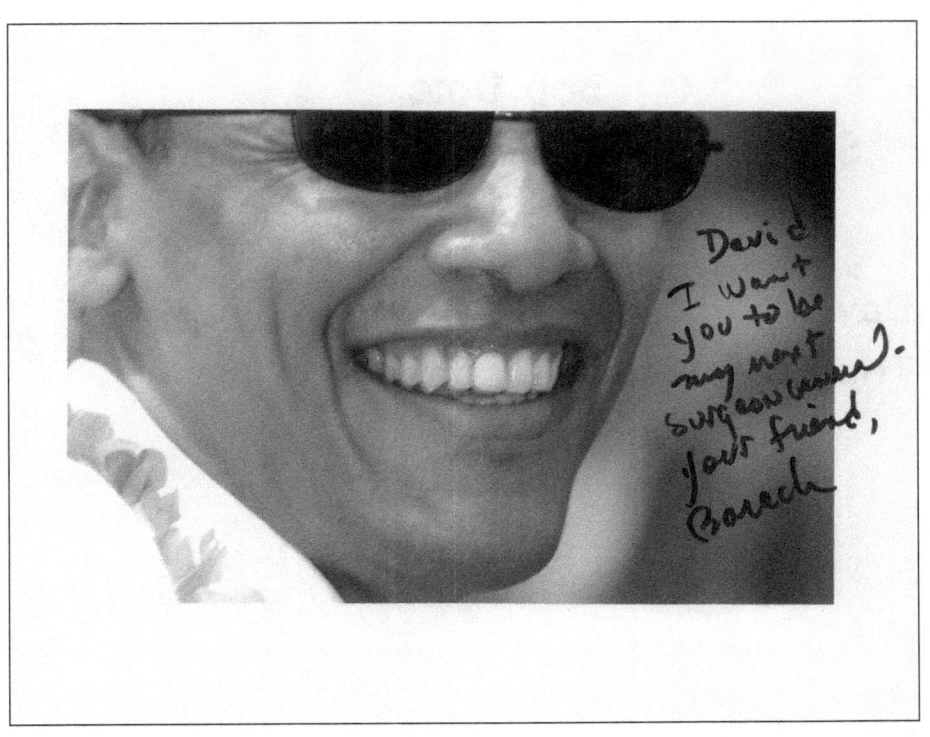

Bob Dole
Senator, Presidential Candidate

David–

Thanks for your support.

　　Your friend,

　　Bob

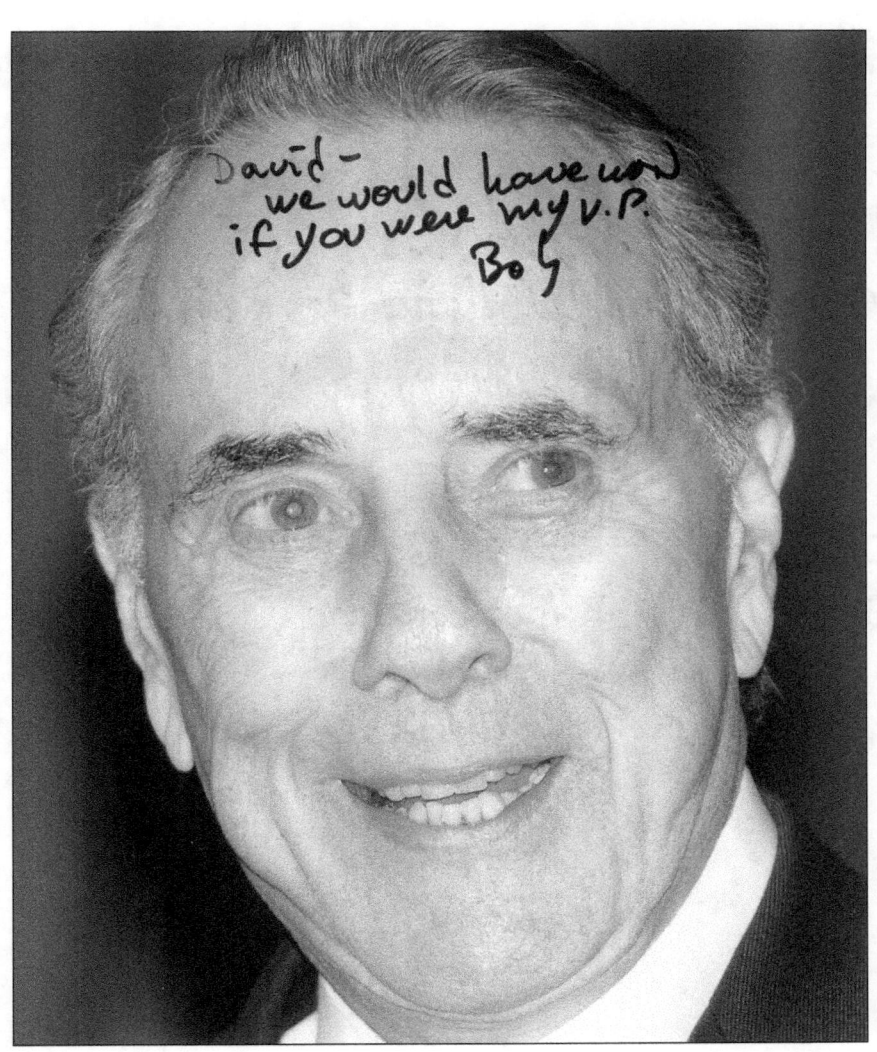

Bobby Jindal
Governor of Louisiana, Presidential Candidate

David,
Be my running mate in 2016.
    Your friend,
    Bobby

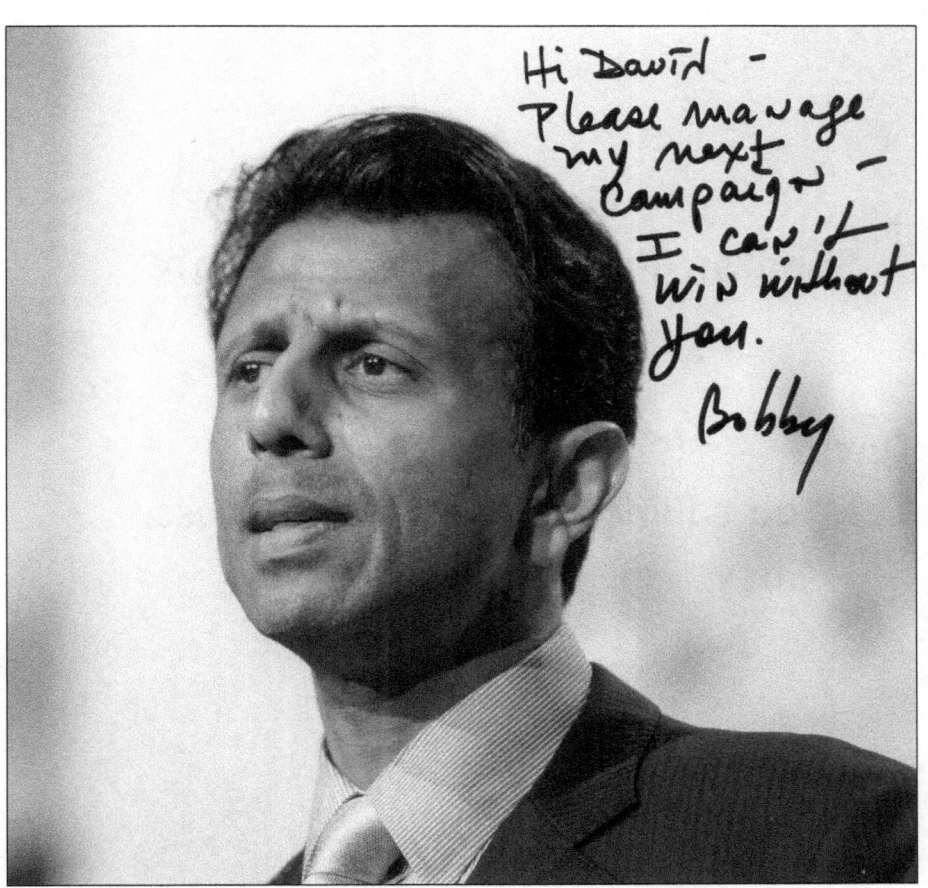

Hi David —
Please manage
my next —
campaign —
I can't
win without
you.

Bobby

Gary Hart
Senator, Presidential Candidate

David–

Let's go sailing on Monkey Business.
    Gary

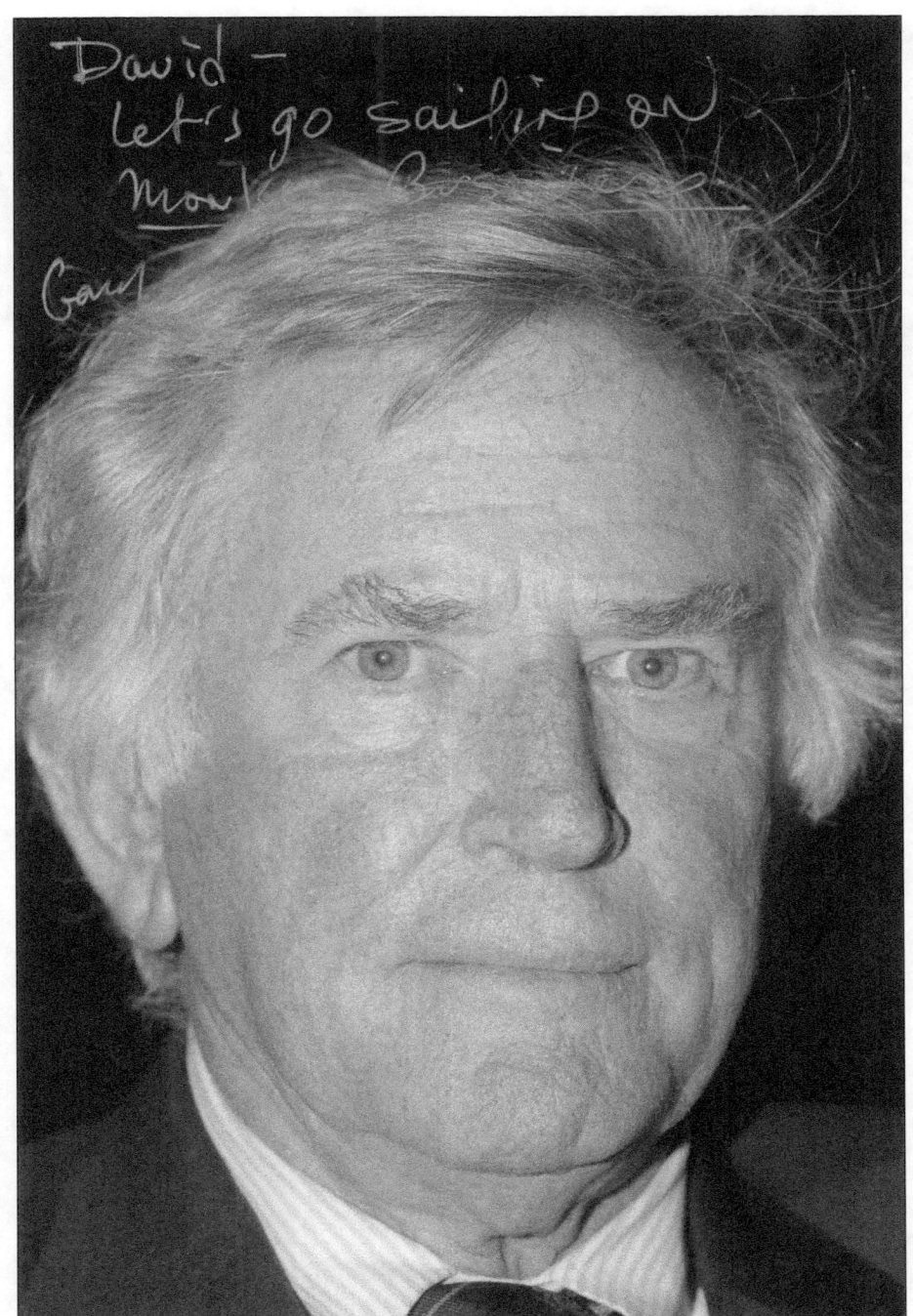

343

George W. Bush
President, Governor of Texas

Dear David–
I want you to be my next Secretary
of Defense.
Your friend,
GW

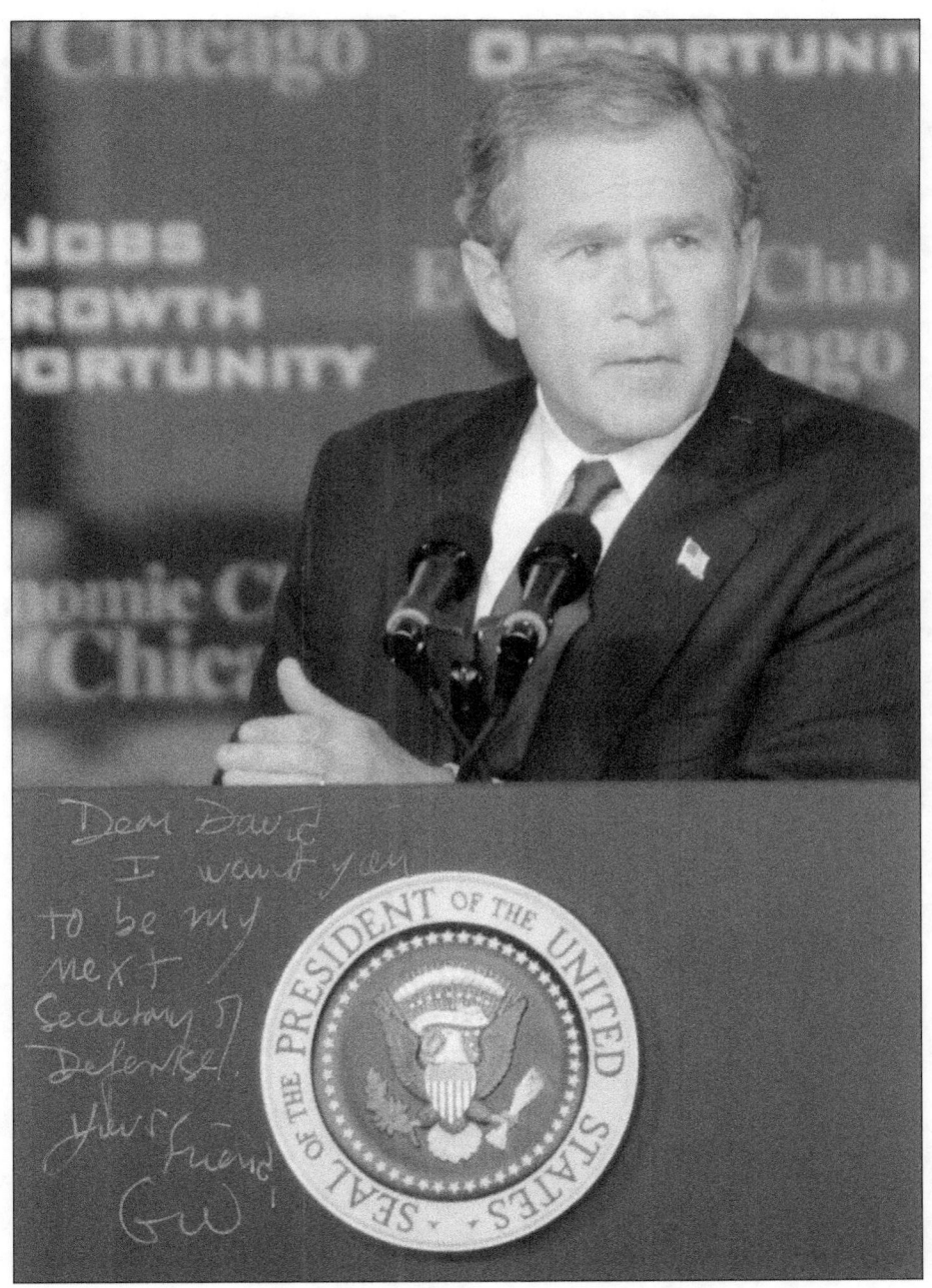

345

Jimmy Carter
President, Governor of Georgia

David-
Vote Democrat!
   Your friend,
   Jimmy

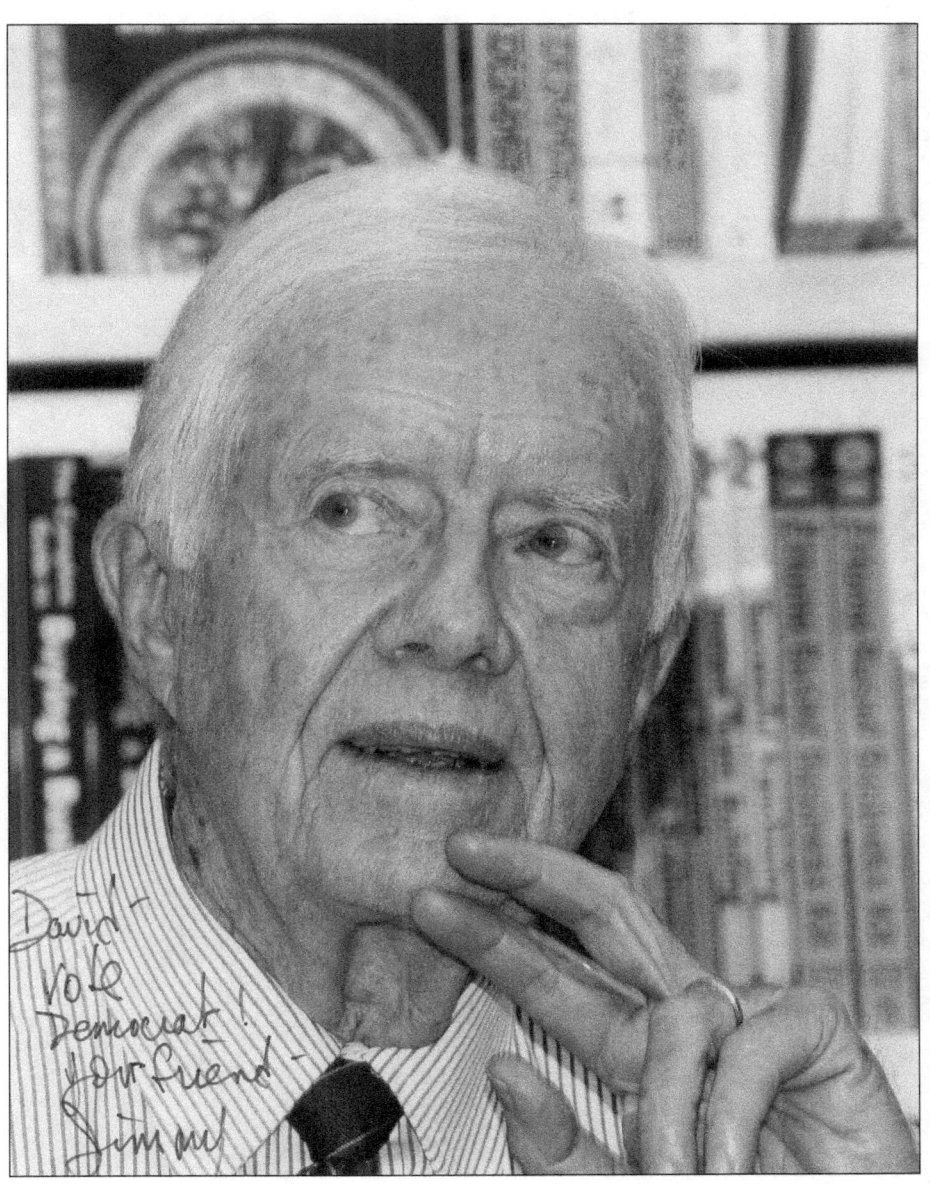

347

Michele Bachmann
Congresswoman,
Presidential Candidate

David,
I want you to be my running mate.
    Your friend,
    Michele

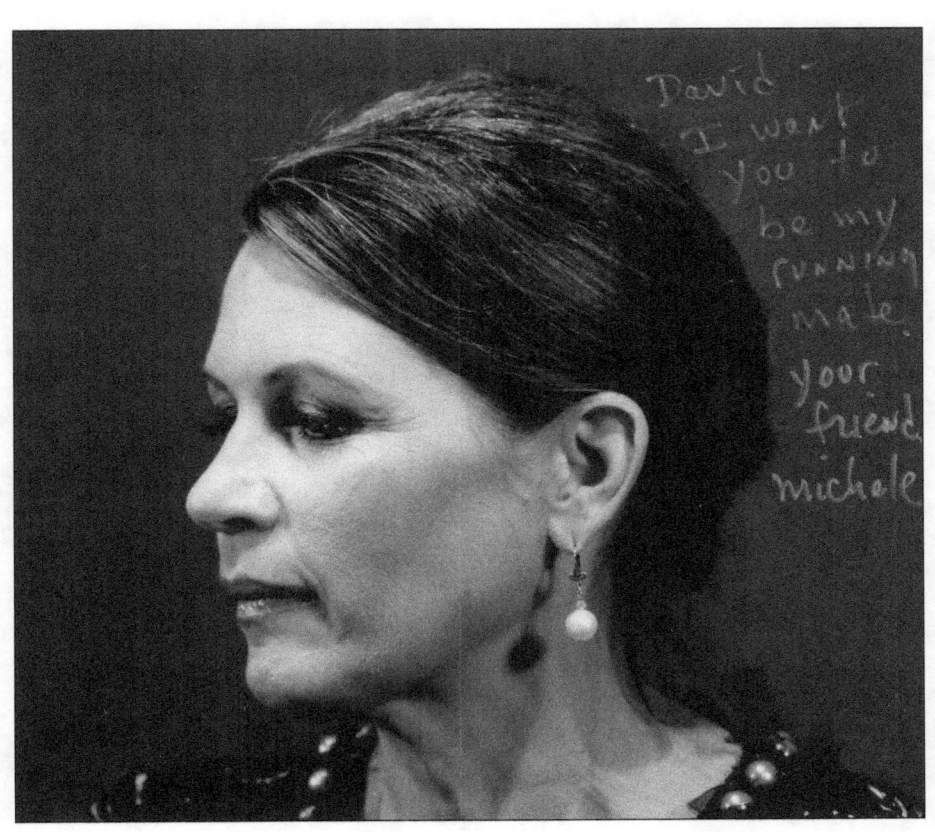

**Mikhail Gorbachev
President Soviet Union**

Dr. Miller-
   Your good friends
   Michael & Raisa

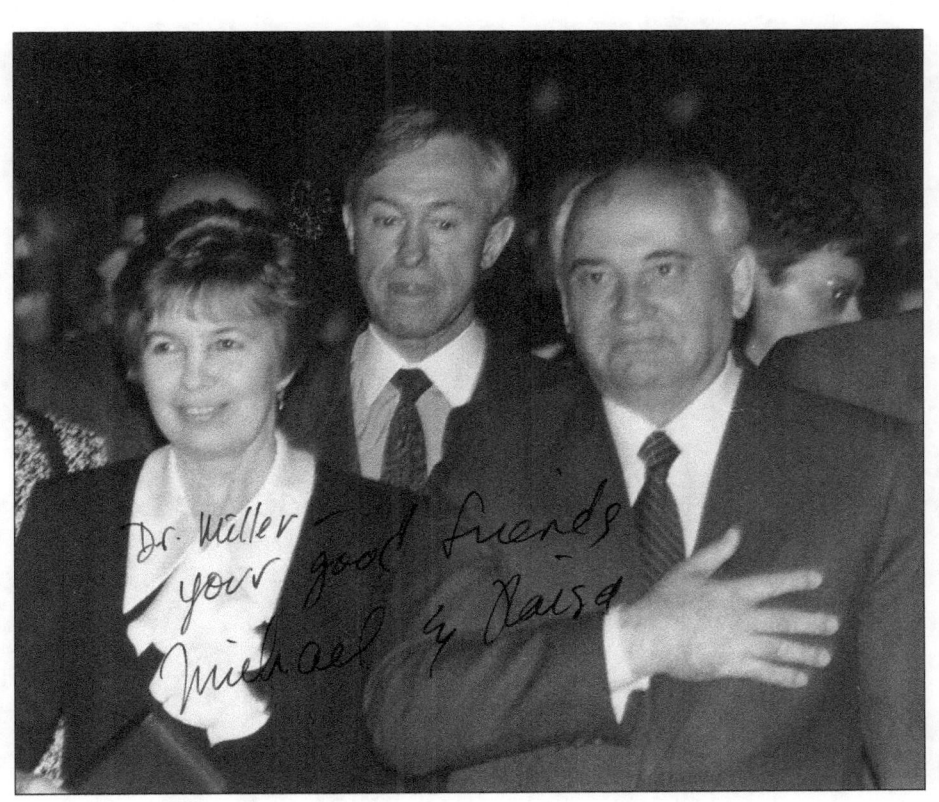

Rick Perry
Governor of Texas, Presidential Candidate

David–
Thanks for your help in my last Texas campaign.
     Rick

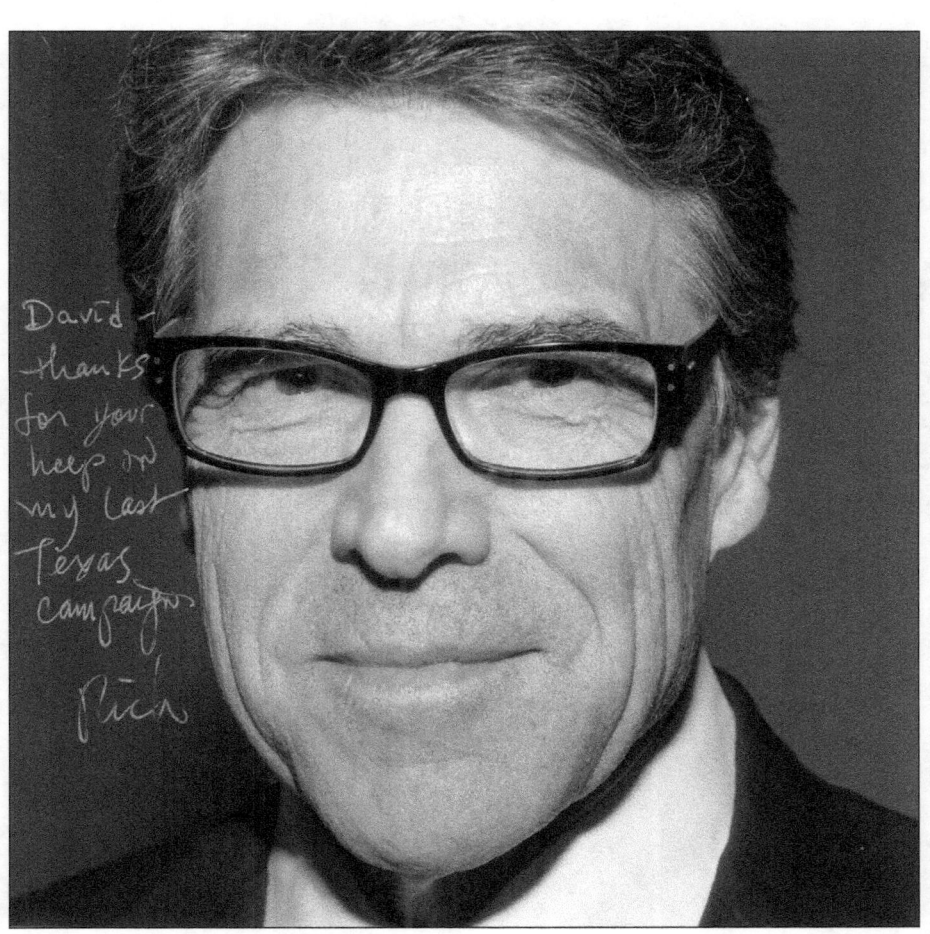

David –
thanks
for your
help on
my last
Texas
campaigns
Rick

Ron Paul
Congressman,
Presidential Candidate

David,
I'll help you run for President.
   Your friend,
   Ron

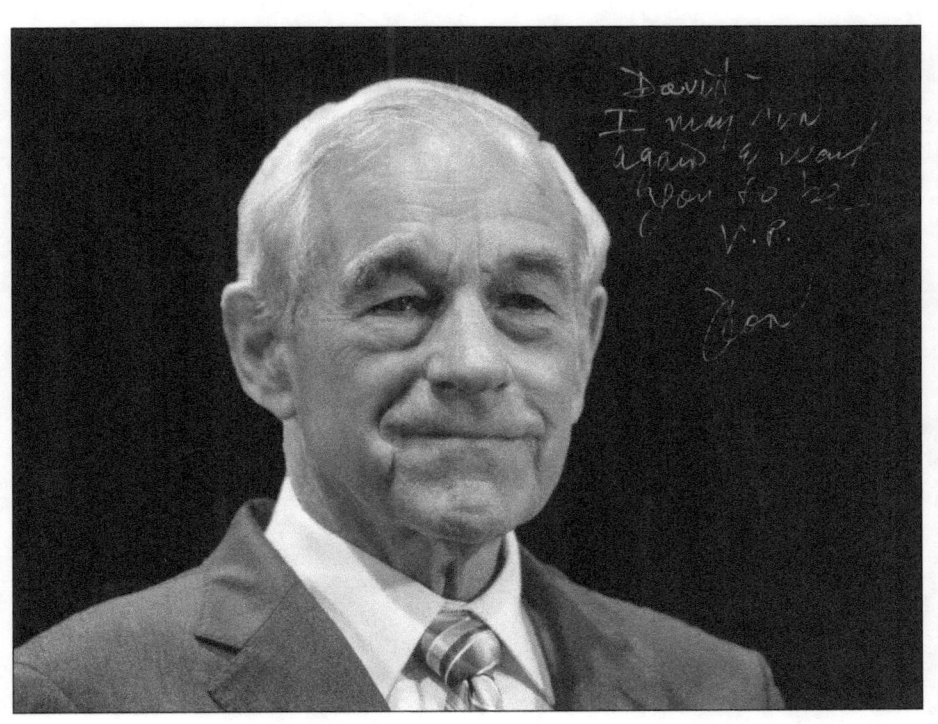

Rudy Giuliani
New York City Mayor, Presidential Candidate

David–
Thanks for all your help and support.
I wanted you as my V.P.
        Your friend,
        Rudy

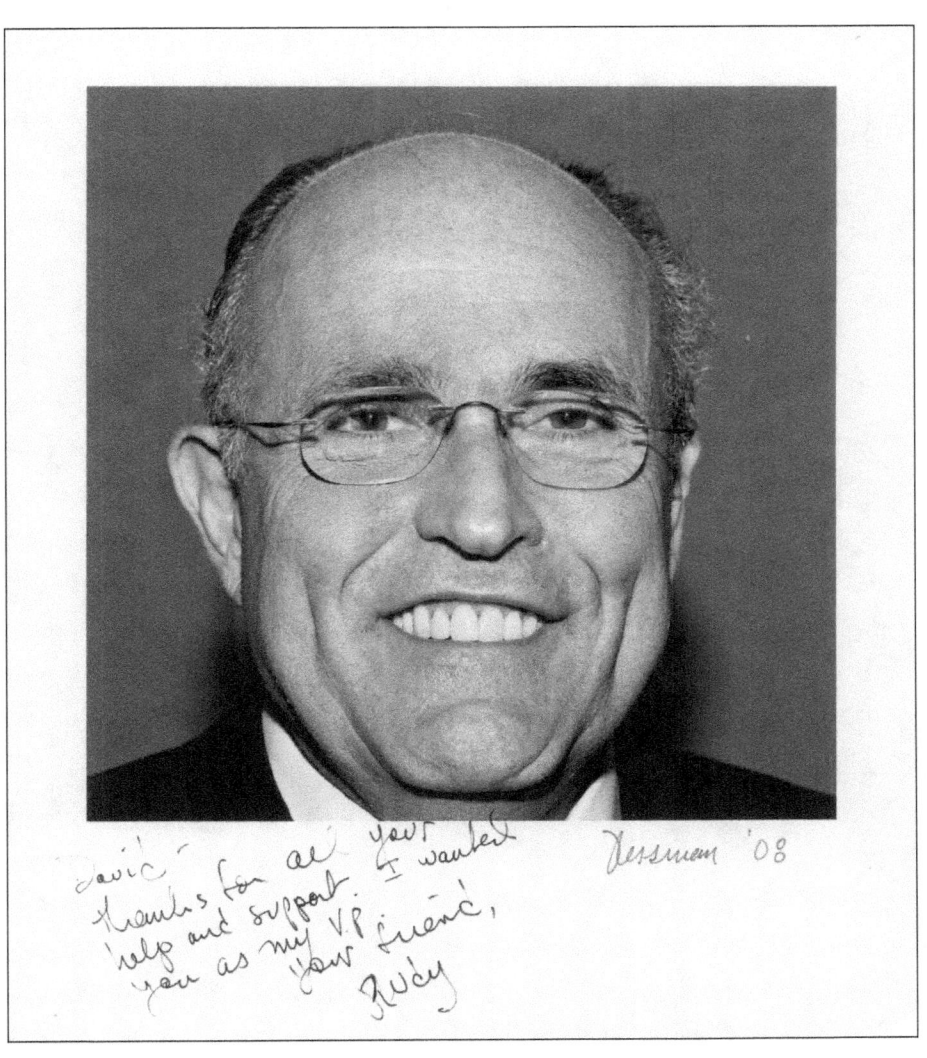

David —
Thanks for all your
help and support. I wanted
you as my V.P. Your friend,
Rudy

Nessman '08

357

www.ingramcontent.com/pod-product-compliance
Lightning Source LLC
Chambersburg PA
CBHW070228180526
45158CB00001BA/44

* 9 7 8 0 9 9 6 1 8 2 4 5 4 *